The Indefinite Article

Anxiety and the Essence of Artificial Intelligence

Michael Roth

Printed in the United States of America

First Printing, 2020

Paperback ISBN: 978-1-7343428-1-9
Hardcover ISBN: 979-8-4843847-7-8
Library of Congress Control Number: 2020935401

Lensgrinder, Ltd.
Kirkland, WA 98033

Questions, comments, concerns? mtroth@lensgrinder.com

Studies in Phenomenology & Social Philosophy

Lensgrinder, Ltd

Kirkland, WA

Dedicated to

William Vaughan

in friendship and admiration

Contents

Acknowledgements

The interests of the "theorist" and the "telemeter" are often aligned. Both *Telemetry Phenomenology Commonwealth* and *The Indefinite Article* elaborate this ad nauseum. The difference is that the telemeter understands what they are doing. As a telemeter you cannot be in bad faith about living in the bowels of the beast, and -in times of pandemic when everyone needs the data so they can "see" what is going on- the telemeter persists in building the invisible infrastructure that facilitates our social isolation as a form of *Mitsein.* This is both my tenure and my confinement.

Parts of *The Indefinite Article* have developed over decades and the memory of influences may have become clouded by the years. I would like to try to acknowledge those who participated: Meaghan Morris and Annie Pritchard both read and commented on the Writing with Metal chapter. David Jacobson provided feedback for Carnival and Resistance as did an audience at the Miami University of Ohio Philosophy Department. Laura Haber and Walter Feinberg were crucial to the editing I did for Producing Enlightened Subjects although Wally's help always came to me through Laura's vision for her original version of that piece. Bill Vaughan provided guidance and insight in understanding the role that On Becoming (what one is), Anxiety and Death, Non-Fictional Fabrications, Antagonisms and Foundations, and Privacy might have in the longer project and its relationship to *Telemetry Phenomenology Commonwealth.* An audience at a reading for the Philosophy Department Colloquia Series at the University of Michigan-Dearborn helped me digest and address the issues and problems in early drafts of Five Vignettes. For Between the Origin and the Movement, I must acknowledge the editors at International Studies in Philosophy who cultivated the review for inclusion in their journal (Volume 33, Issue 2, 2001). And finally, it would be impossible to overstate the influence and help that Georgia C. provided throughout the process of writing and editing this work. She is my inspiration in all things.

The Indefinite Article

If it should turn out to be true that knowledge (in the modern sense of know-how) and thought have parted company for good, then we would indeed become the helpless slaves, not so much of our machines as of our know-how, thoughtless creatures at the mercy of every gadget which is technically possible, no matter how murderous it is.
—Hannah Arendt, *The Human Condition*

Introduction

> What counts now is the mutual insight of two personalities
> who recognize each other as such; who in effect can say to
> each other 'I guarantee you the development of your
> personality and you guarantee me the development of mine.'
> That is the basis of all real community thinking, and such a
> community can only start with friends...[1]

Organization claims and controls the social sphere through telemetry. This surveillance and the disciplinary action it supports is how populations are maintained and modified, understood and analyzed. The methods of such organizations are not attributable to any single human being, rather the organization must appropriate human beings and their products for the sake of advancing its aims and pursuing its agendas. Governments and corporations as well as social institutions like "public education" and "the family" need people to carry out the processes and procedures that give them life and actualize them. They need human beings to be the subjects of their action: governments are meant to govern people; corporations provide services for people. There is more to it than that. They have employees and workers; they have consultants and stakeholders. Organizations do not do anything on their own in some ethereal world of non-human action. Rather, they employ human means to carry out their operations and actions, to pursue their ends and maintain their structure. The organs are hierarchical, and process based. Tutorials are produced, wikis maintained, training sessions offered, interviews and focus groups conducted, all for the sake of molding human agency into organizational requirements and fitting it into organizational memory and mission.

These organizations are artificial in that if you view them historically, they are themselves fabricated over time. Their origins may lie in collections and associations of individual human beings or they may lie in the action of other organizations. State and federal governments in combination with human beings who declare themselves officers, work together to form associations through the filing of articles of incorporation, the establishment of an accounting practice, and the opening of bank

---

[1] Young-Bruehl, Elisabeth. *Hannah Arendt: For Love of the World.* New Haven: Yale University Press. 2004. P. 433. The author is rendering a description of key aspects of Heinrich Blücher's oral philosophy.

accounts. Bodies of revolutionary agents organize to overthrow one government and replace it with another, committees write legislation and then hand it over to executive agencies for enforcement. People write and read FAQs, they go and work in information kiosks, they learn how things are done and they follow the steps to get the necessary result: acquiring a registration for their boat, renewing their driver's license, applying for food stamps, and so on. The processes and procedures display rational structure and suggest a form of intelligence. To the extent, however, that the organizations are fabricated, we say that the intelligence they display is artificial.

This may be a disappointing spin on a term that so powerfully captures the collective imagination, but it is imperative to grasp this notion in such pedestrian fashion. Artificial intelligence, in its essence, is not something that lies off in the distance of some imagined human future or part of some leading-edge set of technologies currently under development. Under the approach that I am offering here, artificial intelligence is at the core of human existence and has been for millennia. It is in this sense that I will regularly use the notion of "person" to describe any actor or agent who exhibits intelligence, artificial or natural. An octopus, a beaver, or a human being might be examples of natural intelligence, natural persons who carry out meaningful acts that produce and reproduce life and an environment for themselves. Governments, corporations, and institutions might be examples of artificial intelligence, which likewise act accordingly to produce and reproduce their "lives" and their surroundings or environmental situation. The distinction may be arbitrary, but it bears some intuitive currency in ordinary relationships.

Human beings walk into stores and fill out forms to make a purchase, they use on line banking, they shop with credit cards, and they use various kinds of mini-functions on their mobile phones to communicate with each other or acquire the use of any of a vast array of personal services. The global internet offers compute and storage to enable these actions and behaviors with great efficiency and convenience. There are platform providers that dominate the compute and storage markets and enable first party and third-party service providers to easily make use of their platforms for the sake of integrating their product into the web of functional capabilities available to the population for purchase with a small monthly fee. The walk-in customer at the department store, using cash to buy what is on the floor, old school, is participating in this system to the extent that the store is a third-party consumer of one of these platforms. The cloud is everywhere, and all facets of social commerce, organization, and government have their place in it. The governments of the world use cloud compute and storage, some maintain private sovereign clouds to secure highly sensitive data and behavior that, on the one hand, needs to partake of the available global services and, on the other hand, needs absolute secrecy from any agents that do not need to know.

Everyone knows this. And everyone also knows that computer software is what drives it. They may also know that computer software is often organized by methods and functions making up components and applications and that these are the operational basis of all the activity taking place on the global internet: send message, commit transaction, scroll, or like. People also generally understand that software is not always reliable and that contextual conditions can cause issues in usage. What may be unknown to some, however, is that software as it is currently engineered, tracks its own execution for the sake of maintaining availability and purpose. The base data flow that describes the proper and improper functioning of the components is called telemetry. To say that telemetry is how organizations claim and control the social sphere is to suggest that the data flows that are used to surveille the systems at work for their performance and reliability are also used to direct and understand the behavior of those applications. Since the applications are there for the sake of interactions with human beings who employ them in their various practices, understanding the behavior of the applications amounts to understanding the behavior of the human beings who use them. In the domain of telemetry, the user ceases to exist as a human being, but becomes a functional piece of the system as it is monitored and maintained.

There is a software problem to be solved in sending a message. The message must be described by a data structure, the data structure must be transmitted over a channel, the channel must be secure, the delivery guaranteed, etc. Another "problem" in this equation is that the message must be sent. To the extent that there is a message sent, the user can be constructed as a piece of the software system: the message sender. And to the extent that the system which can send messages has an interest in making sure that messages are sent, the problem space of the system will include getting users to send messages. The telemetry morphs from making sure message sending takes place with high reliability and low latency to including a concern for the volume of messages moving through the channel at any given time. Why has the number dipped? Monitors and alerts are set off if the hourly or daily number drops below the expected volume. There must be something wrong, someone or something should investigate.

A telemetry event is a side effect. The operation is a click or a submit, a get or anything at all that might be performed in a digital context. The operation may be extremely fine-grained, or it may be coarse-grained with many component parts. The event emitted by the operation is not the intent of the operation, it is a biproduct to indicate the execution outcome, the amount of time the operation took to execute, the dimensional data in state at the time the event was emitted, as well as either the material or formal result of the operation. Emission is for the sake of collection where analysis will be performed against the data from a variety of operational instances brought together in common storage. The upshot of analysis can be a set of correlations or related factors that can be expected given a specific input condition. This outcome can be fed back into the system that originated the event and can be used by the operational code to adjust the future operations performed. This amounts to a mode of measurement that is integral to the operations being measured and where the feedback amounts to an integration of the measurement with the future performance of the actions measured. Here, the integration is for the sake of optimizing the operation and therefore "improving" the measure, where that amounts to pushing it closer to a goal value or Service Level Agreement (SLA).

Human beings tasked, for example, with getting the measured value close to some goal value may not have full context on what it is that they are doing. They know some number is 3.7 and that it needs to be 4.0. They may know that the director of their group has set this objective and that they will be financially rewarded if it is achieved. They may have some sense of what the number means in terms of their own operations, but it may be unclear how that transfers into greater integration between different groups or more revenue for a dependent service or any of millions of other relationships and associations that may lie at the root of the organization's reasoning as to why that number has to inch upward. Division of labor not only indicates that the functions of the organization or society are divided up among its members, but that the meaning of the functions themselves may be distributed as well.[2]

It is philosophically problematic to think that the people, like the group director, who are tasked with the meaning or integration of meanings, are somehow the true agents of the operations. This director does not know the detailed workings of those within their group who are striving to get that number higher. They may know the reasons or meaning of it, but their knowledge is not exhaustive. Details of the operations are distributed throughout the organization. It makes sense to say that the organization knows everything, but no one person does. The knowledge is spread out across the different participants, and to complicate matters, some of it may exist only in code or in processes that are enforced by software, but which

---

[2] Vico's *verum-factum*, as it turns out, has been intensified and superseded here. "Man" does not know history and the civil world because "man" does not make history and the civil world, rather the organizations are what do the making and so they are the ones who know. Cf. Arendt's discussion in *The Human Condition*. 1958. Chicago, IL: University of Chicago Press, pp. 297-298.

are poorly documented (i.e., the detailed description of how some reporting system arrives at the number 3.7).

It is common to think of processes and mechanisms available for human use as augmentations of the user's capabilities. In a dispute with an insurance company regarding payment on a claim, for example, it is possible to leverage state government organizations and procedures to force the insurance company to persist in their investigation and take various matters of fact into account when making their decision to cover a claim. An individual in such a position might also search internet sources for precedent in how to proceed with their situation. From the point of view of the experiencing individual engaged in such activities, these processes and mechanisms appear as helpful augmentations of their person assisting them in carrying out a plan or project. Much more difficult, however, is the effort at seeing the entire fiasco of phone calls and electronic mails as a mechanism or process that augments the functioning of one or more organizations, such as the insurance company itself and the government body that regulates it. It is not so common to perceive, or conceive, in the human being an augmentation of the processes and mechanisms at work in constructing an environment of significant relations and things. The insurance company may cut costs by employing a smaller number of adjustors and investigators with higher workloads and then rely on government and customer intervention to assist them in case triage. They close the case quickly and move on. That percentage of cases that are reopened because of government intervention on behalf of complaining customers will reflect only a portion of existing cases. Thus, the company employs public resources and unpaid labor for the sake of reducing its workload.

No specific human agent in the process may have full insight into all the workings of this complex association of processes and mechanisms, but the organizational structure provides a rational set of operations that introduces intelligence. And this intelligence is real with real effects and real inputs. The point of view of the various human "inputs" will display a boundedness to that person's place in the world and will reflect a "homey" interpretation of events: this is my job, this is my issue with the insurance company, this is the process I have to follow, this is the device I need to use, this is the statute I need to respect, and so on.

To coordinate these behaviors, organizations rely on metrics. The case worker is likely being evaluated based on the number of cases processed per week or day, average time to close the case, dollar amount payouts on the cases they work, and so on. And their managers are evaluating their performance based on these metrics, using them to compare their work with that of their colleagues. Models can be built off the correlation of various of these factors and the revenue achieved by the organization such that, although no one knows the reasons or meaning for the correlations, they still see "proof" that higher case counts closed per day correlates with increased revenue. And no one person may "know" that this is because the rapid closure of cases offloads triage labor to state organizations. In such a case, if there were to be a congressional investigation into the practices, no one employee of the insurance company would be able to produce damning evidence of wrongdoing. Neither the implementers of the processes and procedures nor the agents and investigators themselves will have a sense of an intent to do harm and all will be able to testify honestly to that end. Only a full evaluation of the social relationships between agents within the company, within the state organization, and among the customer advocates, would provide the basis for such an interpretation.[3] And by interpretation, I mean something that could be challenged and argued over by observers with vastly different points of view and predispositions toward different conclusions about its veracity. The absence of a singular or set of human agents clearly engaged in wrongdoing might make it impossible for any set of individuals to agree on the causes and effects.

This circumstance is secured by the dual nature of telemetry to both reveal and conceal. It is common to characterize telemetry metrics as being the eyes of the organization insofar as the telemetry is used to produce metrics measuring operational success along various axes. By attaching telemetry to a process, we "turn the lights on" and make the process itself visible. This visibility enables the correlation of the behaviors captured in the telemetry with other data that is captured in other systems against commonly defined dimensions such as the date and the location of an operation. While making such behaviors, processes, and correlations visible, the telemetry will also conceal any agency that might be involved in the procuring of such results. Dumb correlation does not seek to uncover causes and motives, it only associates attributes or features with each other enabling predictions in terms of one set of features based on the changes and variation discovered in another set. In the end, both revelation and concealment are achieved when the telemetry clearly predicts that getting the number from 3.7 to 4.0 will have a 10-million-dollar impact on revenue, whereas getting it any higher will have diminishing returns or returns

---

[3] Such a view on organizations draws somewhat from Schutz, who draws from Weber, in *The Phenomenology of the Social World*. Translated by George Walsh and Frederick Lehnert. 1967. Evanston, IL: Northwestern University Press. For example, "From the sociological point of view, therefore, the term "state" is merely an abbreviation for a highly complex network of interdependent personal ideal types." P. 199.

disproportionate to the required effort. No qualia necessary, the subject can be constituted without it, and no other ingredients are required.[4]

This revealing and concealing nature of telemetry and the way in which it is used to supplement the powers and potential of organizations is what constitutes the essence of artificial intelligence. The pattern at work is tripartite and is immediately recognizable to all practitioners of new AI technology: emit, analyze, feedback. The emission of the event is bound to the act, the analysis is the deliberate construction of dimensional features and correlations, and the feedback is what powers the prediction of future associations and correlations based on what has been "observed" thus far, where observation connotes the collaborative and deliberative interaction of emission and analysis. A large distributed system that employs such a pattern may embody a lifecycle such that days or months pass between analysis and feedback or emission and analysis. A smaller system, like a robot traversing terrain to carry an item from point A to point B, embodies a significantly more compact shape and lifecycle, needing to execute the pattern in full within a few milliseconds. The pattern at work is the same and it is telemetry bound as the essence of all artificial intelligence.

This should suggest that the essence of artificial intelligence is nothing artificial. Rather, this patterned framework is a reproduction of a projected emergent pattern collaboratively developed over millennia by many civilizations and analyzed by many representative philosophers and thinkers. The nature of "computation" or "intelligence" as acting upon observations that have been processed and analyzed in correlation with other observations of like kind is not supposed to be artificial. Aristotle, Locke, or Kant all considered their contributions to the formulation of a pattern of human rational action to be contributions to science based on observation of human history and action. "Rational being" situates the human within "nature" as the animal that it is. The pattern is believed to be natural and emergent or reductive in occurrence, what makes it artificial is

---

[4] As an aside, this illustrates the voice of the current fabrication, this indefinite article, as that of the telemetric subject itself. My apologies if it makes the reading experience unhuman, but it is meant to be a moment in the synthetic demonstration itself: this very same revealing concealing movement of the telemetric as it describes itself at work. No experience necessary. "If, without knowing his own voice, he should not find any public, but speaks solely for some record kept by no one, then I suppose we have to admit that he is a true manufacturer of the standardized prose: an autonomous sound in a great empty hall. It is all rather frightening, as in a Kafka novel, and it ought to be: we have been talking about the edge of reason." From C. Wright Mills, 1959. *The Sociological Imagination.* New York, NY: Oxford University Press, p 221.

the implementation of organization, process, and mechanism based on that pattern.

Some readers may have detected references to Heidegger in the discussion so far. The revealing/concealing nature of telemetry recalls Heidegger on truth as *aletheia* or unconcealedness. The suggestion that the essence of artificial intelligence is nothing artificial may recall Heidegger's remarks on the essence of technology as *poiesis* which itself is nothing technological. These points of contact are superficial, however, and there is a more notable connection here, based on remarks he made in the last sections of *Being and Time* where he tries to offset a public notion of time against clocks as measuring devices with a true temporality disclosive of Being.

> When this question is answered [n.b. the question concerning the meaning of Being], there must arise a more primordial understanding of the fact that the *measurement of time*—and this means also the explicit making-public of time as an object of concern—is grounded *in the temporality* of Dasein, and indeed in a quite definite temporalizing of that temporality.[5]

What interests me in this passage is the relationship between publicness and measurement on the one hand and its foundation in something that is not at all public on the other. Measurement would seem to be functioning as a bridge. Temporality has its locus in a phenomenological existential quality of experience and temporalizing activity is the basis of any such experience. The creation of the clock as a device for measuring time has its potential in this factical quality of existence (*Dasein*). The temporalizing nature of experience makes it possible to date events and to situate them relative to each other. Because of this, refinements are possible to augment this "datability." Heidegger's primary focus is the clock as such a mechanistic refinement, but he also trains his eye on the processes and procedures accompanying this publicly agreed upon mechanism. He struggles with this throughout those last sections as he discusses the day and the sun and the use of sundials as phases along the way of developing the current mechanical means for segmenting and organizing time sequences.

The emergence of an aboriginal or primordial quality such as temporalizing, existing in such a way as to realize a past that projects a possible future in present momentum, is bridged by a measuring device

---

[5] Martin Heidegger. *Being and Time*. Translated by John MacQuarrie and Edward Robinson. New York: Harper Perennial Modern Thought. 1962. P. 468.

responsible for publicizing this quality. This provides a powerful heuristic for understanding how telemetry comes to have the role that it does have and how that role is of existential significance in human experience. If the pattern of "computation" or "intelligence" or "understanding" as I have relayed it in its tripartite form is given that primordial position, telemetry functions as the measuring mechanism that bridges the gap between its phenomenological place and its public place of reckoning in common spheres of activity carried out by all kinds of agents with various material constitutions. This would be the case regardless of whether that primordial facet is spun via the work of Aristotle, Locke, Kant, or Heidegger. The existential analysis of "computation" or "understanding" is important to the matter but the upshot remains the same regardless of which flavor of philosophical system one rests upon. Measuring intelligence, publicly availing oneself of computational constructs to fabricate artificial means of realizing those relationships, holds regardless of the spin one puts on that existential analytic.

What I am being careful to convey to you is that these patterns that I am excavating from Heidegger's work in this introduction are not themselves bound to that work. Rather, I hold that these are phenomenological claims that can be evaluated independently of any careful or scholarly reading of any philosopher's corpus. The basis in the structure of experience as the experience of a physiologically bound entity integrates with a public rendering and the bridge between the two is measurement, where measurement constitutes the application of a standard to the underlying experience for the sake of enabling public communication.

The subtitle of this book refers not only to the "essence of artificial intelligence" but to "anxiety" as well. Here, anxiety inundates a social actor with an individuating state of mind, a point of view that turns them away from their social involvements in a state constituting their singularity. There is method in this association. Namely, the essence of artificial intelligence as it has been spelled out, reveals in its primordial basis a highly personal form of phenomenological experience of an individuated being. Although I hold that in the common sense given to the word "privacy" in contemporary parlance, there is none, I am willing to denote this primordial condition as that of an "ontological privacy" insofar as that indicates the introduction of a problem rather than its tidy conclusion. I, and many others, are anxious about "ontological privacy" although I, at least, do not see its protection in the GDPR.[6] I am not sure there are any

---

[6] General Data Protection Regulation. Regulation (EU) 2016/679 of the European Parliament and of the Council of 27 April 2016 on the protection

organizations or institutions that can provide a protection for this kind of privacy. This is not to say that privacy, conceptualized as a property right where there is data or emissions of any kind that somehow belong to me and which I have a right to control, is not important or worth discussing. My point is that whatever value there is to such privacy, it must rest on top of this ontological concern that amounts to the existence of those persons experiencing it and engaged in a social context that elaborates and cultivates its everyday qualities among the rest of human kind and the organizations and institutions that we have fabricated in the construction of our environment.

Such an anxious isolation must be spatio-temporal in nature and attached or articulated as the characteristics of the being in question. The temporalizing agency and action of any such "person" elaborates or emerges as an association or an entering into relationships. Such rudimentary orientations and involvements express an attunement and yet may themselves be subjected to further associations or relationships expressed reflexively. It is possible to discuss both the power of the temporalizing actions to emit meaningfulness in such associations and the power of reflexively associating with an emission that itself associates. This is an important difference because it provides the source of both the act and the measurement of the act where the latter employs previously obtained associations developed over time and in common across many instances as a set of mannerisms capturing various qualities of those same measured emissions. Organizations develop and persist as containers of processes that enable these reflexive relationships and offer them, through training and cultivation, to agents fumbling with the early emissions that take place whenever the body acts. The emission may suffer such reflexive input gradually or radically and may be imitated or practiced when refining and developing the nature of the emission relative to the physical characteristics of the entity. Crawling, picking things up, making sounds, are all emissions of activity with environment-provided reflexes based on observed and learned optimizations obtained from models in the environment: parents, siblings, playmates, teachers, etc. It is no wonder that anxiety surfaces as a persistent state of mind in beings living under such conditions.

Anxiety, viewed in this fashion, never leaves one alone, rather it is the basis for integration and socialization, it is the acquisition of measurements for the sake of refinement of actions that will integrate and adjust one's behaviors to norms and standards enabling more thorough integration into

---

of natural persons with regard to the processing of personal data and on the free movement of such data, and repealing Directive 95/46/EC. http://data.europa.eu/eli/reg/2016/679/oj

established practices and procedures. Organization is the construct or fabrication that provides a process based container for such procedures and the emission, deliberation, and feedback loop is how the individual expresses themselves, deliberates on outcomes in relationship to observed and reflexively understood outcomes in parallel instances, and feeds the results of that deliberation back into the process of further emission via trained expressions. Such agents become constrained by acquired organizational procedures and in so doing acquire personality in accordance with the various organizational processes with which they have integrated and to the extent that this integration has occurred. The unique trajectory of each agent supplies enormous variation within the given organizations and institutions appropriate to their era or geographical location. Human being embodies a variable cross section of organizations based on spatial and temporal action sequences and we have traditionally thought of this as their individuality and its concomitant biases.

The individual is cultivated, therefore, as a confluence of attributes and facets. The agent acquires dimensionality through organizationally targeted agency that shapes and orders their muscle qualities and coordination, their thought processes and responses, as well as every expectation and recollection that they orient themselves by in their continued agency. The ends they develop and pursue, the emotions they experience and present, the sensibilities they value and share, all are reflectively applied to the emissions process through this emergence of a primordially private attunement through a network of measurements and into a public domain of organizational and institutional practices and procedures. It may be that historical conditions provide socially acceptable preferences for the organizations responsible or appropriate for various acquisitions; and it may be that there are radical adjustments to these roles due to changes in the social fabric or the environmental context where persons are found. For example, characteristics once driven by an institution of family traditions may be "privatized" such that an economic body such as a corporation takes control over the institution and organization of those same practices. Where once, a child learned various behaviors from a brother or sister, mother or father, new conditions may arise such that these associations are developed in the process of consuming video-based entertainment products orchestrated by the Walt Disney Corporation.

Philosophically, this will become a critical issue when trying to understand how a thinker is in the position to see what they see or proclaim what they have proclaimed. How does Hegel know that there is a historical dialectic and that it proceeds in the fashion he specified? How come Kant did not know it? The *Phenomenology of Spirit* may have, as one of its essential preconditions, the battle of Jena. Anyone who did not live through that battle could not have written that book. The specific associations and the confluence of organization and institutional relations are not incidental to the products and fabrications of the persons who have lived through them, they are implicit in those associations. The value of the philosopher lies in the combination of their capacity to articulate that confluence and the power of the confluence itself. Hegel read Goethe at a specific time, he conversed with Hölderlin, he learned from Schelling and Fichte. These are not accidental characteristics, but intricately bound dimensional attributes and features of Hegel's personhood. Not only are the organizations and institutions of the world forms of artificial intelligence, but there is a sense in which every person is such a fabricated or cultivated outcome.

The blowhard philosopher who proclaims himself one of the world historical geniuses because he has written some tome that now stands beside the great books of the ages takes a tacit acquiescence in the metaphysics of subjectivity by proclaiming his own genius. Rather, the philosopher worth reading, and properly situated within the domain of the post-metaphysical self, is most likely an historically significant confluence of organizations. A person cultivated through the confluence of hermeneutical phenomenology, telemetry-based systems design, and participation on a leadership team for a large corporation may be in a position to comprehend the confluence so long as that person's capacity to articulate and exposit those relationships and associations meets with a socially communicable and inspirational genre. That last requirement need not be specific to the contemporary epoch within which the philosopher is rendering the position. The position itself, like Spinoza's for example, may need a century or more to find its proper audience or may come a century too late, as in the case of Frege. These matters are never determined once and for all but are open to constant appropriation and association by the ongoing organizational processes and procedures as they change and are changed, develop and are developed.

There is a common discourse on the conflict that can occur between the common life of an influential thinker and the work they have produced. Heidegger is a good example. How can we continue to read and be influenced by his work when it is becoming increasingly clear that his "dabbling" in National Socialism was not an anomalous occurrence but a crucial set of involvements that may have left a trace throughout his life's work? If we take Heidegger to be something other than the subject of the Heideggerian philosophy, itself a comet providing an aboriginal insight into the ontological attunements of human being, then this concern changes in nature. Rather, Heidegger becomes an opportunity to understand further the confluence between these variable associations. What are the characteristics of National Socialism? How do they all fit together? How was Heidegger related to them? What drew him into the dynamic, whereas someone like Jaspers was not so drawn? In what way do the details of that allure and those associations find their way into his musings about authenticity and inauthenticity, for example, and their relationship to the existential structure of those entities which fall victim to such modes of Being? In what sense does his notion of facticity materialize a state of exception? To the extent that these are instructive or informative questions, to the extent that they teach us something about human existence and human social organizations and the way that processes and procedures are retained and communicated, the study of Heidegger and the Heidegger affair is endlessly captivating and important. This can be true in the case where a brilliant novelist is also a rabid anti-Semite or where a great Film Director is a rapist.

No doubt such libertinism may be jolting to some readers, but it is an imperative of this approach that the ethical and the moral surface as organizationally and institutionally bound processes and procedures. I make no assumptions of this or that ethical position or this or that moral stance, rather the investigations herein form the beginning of an inquiry into what are the reliable milestones of these domains and what we can rely upon in deliberations. Most of what is called "the good" or "the just" is bound to some historically delimited set of organizations and institutions and the most sincere avowal of a value amounts to a phenomenological emission based on feedback from deliberations that are the result of associations and relationships obtained throughout one's development. One way to put this is that the ontological status of the ethical is deeply troubling insofar as it is unclear what we are doing when we engage in ethical discussions and deliberations. Are these forensic operations, are they deliberative, do they take historical precedent as their source or are they based on some rational autonomy yielded by the light of nature? Can one merely decide to be a Utilitarian or Contractarian? Or is one's education and upbringing determinate in making one position more deeply ingrained in people with specific experiences and histories?

A corporation that provides a compute and storage platform for use in the implementing of democratized AI (which amounts to a platform that provides the power of big data analytics to smaller companies that do not have the resources to do so on their own, allowing them to take part in all the mischief through a monthly service fee) may have a set of doctrines they make known when it comes to "ethics" or the value of "privacy"; and that corporation may have an interest in ensuring that the social dialogue around ethical computing and the respect for privacy follows suit with a set of principles that prove the corporation should proceed as is when producing a specific flavor of compliance platform for safeguarding information. In short, their findings are likely to be highly self-serving and it will be in their interests to promote a dialogue based on the terms they have set down for the debate. Many interlocutors will not be fooled, but it is possible to be fooled in a vast spectrum of different ways. That is, it may be possible to reject the corporation's claims to its own purity but accept the terms and conditions of the debate. For example, we may proclaim that Microsoft or Amazon fail to honor the true property rights of individual customers when handling their data in documented ways, but we may agree that ultimately the way they have characterized the dilemma, as being a matter of how one's personal data is handled, is what the domain of "privacy" is all about.

Under such conditions we may fail to raise any concern about the basic attunements at work in personal associations with organizational and institutional processes that are meant to provide a procedural augmentation to human operations and practice. We ignore our social anxiety and our "ontological privacy." We may overlook the measurements that are taking place and the way in which those measurements are producing a public mechanism for shaping and ordering behaviors relative to the various domains of human life. Focusing completely on the data and not the process whereby it is collected, analyzed, and fed back into future digital operations, may lead to a condition where individuals are oblivious to the impact corporate organizations are having on social institutions through their shaping and reshaping of our emissions to match with the analysis and feedback optimizing what their systems are producing; and they may remain oblivious to their active role in the process. Here the corporation may have "privatized" child rearing and education, it may have taken over the entertainment of all the people of the earth, and in so doing may be promoting its own vision of the world (its own power of association and process-oriented organization) over any approach that might be better suited to the supposed or hypothetical notion of a human well-being or general utility. And what is worse, we might like it.

At least one thing that is wrong with much of the contemporary wide-scale political discussion on matters of surveillance and the control of behavior is that focus is on the individual agents and not so much on the organizations at work in / as / through them. Just as desire makes the rational agent susceptible to violations of moral imperatives, social integration of personality is what makes persons susceptible to coercion and colonization by organizational practices. The experience of desiring it and liking it may be the organization at work. Visibility into these phenomena require that it be possible to cultivate a critical attitude that experiences the organization's operative presence in the conditions of critical analysis. Working for a large corporation, for example, might yield direct experience of this to a person with the right confluence of other critical qualities. A lead engineer for the Data for Machine Learning Services group may transform right in front of their colleagues into a guy who wants to go grab a bite to eat. Phenomenological complexity reaches crescendo when he talks about the project they are working on while eating his lunch. A corporate organization eating its lunch thereby becomes the emissions producer of the analytical contents of a critical approach aiming at changing the emission conditions.

Experience with such corporations would show how little they really want to have anything to do with storing personally identifiable information (PII) describing their specific subjects. The telemetry-based client-side pre-aggregate not only improves scalability by distributing compute and reducing storage requirements, it factors out PII by dimensional slices that provide enough information for models but do not carry any of the liability that comes with PII. Post GDPR, PII is poison and no organization of scale with legal intentions would want to have anything to do with it since the real value can be found in the correlated data in its aggregate form where that schema has reasonably and broadly selected features. The corporation does not want to know everything about you in the abstract, they want to be able to situate your action into proper aggregate associations that describe your attributes and correlate whatever is known about you in a current context containing profile information in your possession with whatever is known about the population at large. This is how that provider can predict your actions. Once they can predict your actions, they will know how to respond and counteract what you do with additional operations that increase the likelihood that you will do what the host wants you to do. The purpose of telemetry is not necessarily to create a complete 1:1 digital model of your existence, rather, through aggregate associations, the interest is in predicting your behavior based on a reasonable set of relevant associations that can be assigned to the current action context that the two of you, customer and provider, are in the middle of performing. To satisfy this, the data never needs to leave your device.

What follows is a brief attempt to lay out a more complete rendering of this vision of the world and the way in which human persons exist within it. I call the approach phenomenological because it is not meant to persuade the reader of a set of truths. Rather, this work is itself a fabrication that results from the set of associations that constitute an historically determinate existence. This is the way that the set of associations has cultivated the investigator's understanding of the world, made the world and their role in it an issue for them, and the dynamic that has been yielded by their specific expository characteristics as determined no doubt by a set of educational capabilities and genetic predispositions (extreme myopia, for example, and the need to see whatever exists through a lens). It is rendered publicly, based on measurements and observations relative to the attunements and emissions of the last half century, just in case it is of interest or significance to a reading audience.

The context of the work is to construct a sketch of emissions as sociological imagination, the ontologically private facet of human being and its construction as biologically integrated beings existentially conjoined in social relations.[7] The early chapters on Writing with Metal, Carnival and Resistance, and Producing Enlightened Subjects should provide some of the philosophical background for how this relationship and set of associations is understood in the light of several significant philosophical contributions of the last century, most notably Deleuze and Guattari's *A Thousand Plateaus*, Mikhail Bakhtin's *Problems of Dostoevsky's Poetics*, Foucault's *Discipline and Punish*, and Horkheimer and Adorno's *The Dialectic of Enlightenment*. These function as traditional emissions to set the stage.

In the middle chapters, the advent of measuring as a bridge between these attunements and public organizations and institutions will be the topic of analysis and deliberation: the measurement being measured. On Becoming (what one is), Anxiety and Death, and Five Vignettes Exclusively Concerned with Genre are meant to provide a sense of how beings oriented temporally, as expressed in the first part, are prone to specific types of reflexive orientation. We are the kinds of creatures that question, that take up positions relative to themselves, that are involved and oriented toward understanding the world and, therefore, execute self-understanding in relationship to the world where one is coming to be. You will find that I often do not know whether my remarks are limited to the nature of human being, or to any conscious being or any rational person or agent that is undertaking a set of associations for the sake of disclosing a set of world conditions or significance. The nature of fabrication is such that any associating that emits, undergoes analysis, and then feeds back into further emissions is embarked on association and action of an artificially intelligent quality. Human beings are augmented, organizations established, institutions embodied, and this is how human beings store their history in living mechanisms that ensure that the embodied understanding persists for future generations through continually cultivated social orders. This

---

[7] If there was ever any doubt as to the veracity of this biological integration and social constitution, the worldwide pandemic of 2020 should at least make its hypothetical consideration reasonable, if not indubitable. And this need not relate to how much of a threat the virus poses, it may refer to the intensity of the response and the instigation of it through latent anxiety based on that very boundary of individuated concern over and against social relations (cf. the mechanics of separation described in Freud's *Inhibitions, Symptoms and Anxiety* or Lacan's *Anxiety*). This boundary which binds is invoked *in* the partiality of the agent *as* it flees in the face of itself *through* a desevering of its relationship *with* the world, inserting bias and desire into the heart of its involvements, into its spatio-temporality.

seems to hold for any agent capable of meeting the procedural qualities of the description and so I see no reason not to suggest that "intelligence" itself is an artificial fabrication that inhabits orders and organizations whether they be organisms or procedures, conscious beings, "robots," or distributed networks of collaborating nodes of varying physical constitution, and so on.

The payoff for such middle way analyses and deliberations are the articles of the final third of the project: Non-Fictional Fabrications, Antagonisms and Foundations, and Privacy. The orientation in these chapters is to gain some level of insight and perspective on the meaningful outcome or feedback associated with the analysis. That is, what is the ethical outcome, where do we stand, and how should we proceed, given this turn of events and the state in which we find ourselves? These questions are tempered by the possibility that "we" are not the ones asking them and that ethics is the way organization renders values in / as / through human experience. The concern is for where the locus of action comes from and whether an understanding of conditions of possibility can ever properly translate into an action plan. What forces are at work holding things back and holding them in place, preventing what must happen from happening or what could happen from happening more often? Whatever you think is the most pressing matter of the day, the telemetric must be understood in order to clear the way for addressing that concern. A sociological methodology void of hidden evaluative presuppositions or orientations must be developed to identify and excavate the forces at work in human civilization, directing collective aims with only partial awareness by participants. But can it be? Is it possible? An undesirable but existent state not only demands change but indicates its own possibility as historical fact. Questioning concerning new states must account for that possibility and accommodate mitigations without repeating the pattern from the status quo.[8]

On the darkest days, the result might be that human beings are swarm-like and driven only by the historically dominant pattern of power currently occupying organizations and institutions most commonly cultivating human qualities throughout the world. It may be that there is no way to construct ex nihilo a rational organization that deliberately changes the direction of any one civilization or set of civilizations. Or it may be that understanding rendered public does not have the capacity to orient masses of people

---

[8] In other words, if personality has been colonized it must be the case that personality is such that it can be colonized. Changes to that condition risk repeating the dynamic of colonization. Frederick the Great may have been a reasonable king, but he was still a king.

toward different social orders and institutional procedures. In any case, the proposal is that there is no clear sense of the universally identifiable measures that serve the process of determining which of these outcomes predominates given a set of observations or analyses. We have seen this again and again when real world political movements employ theoretical doctrines and then try to produce associative analyses describing the relationship between the one and the other. How can one compare the contents of *Capital* or *Capitalism and Freedom*, to name just a few competing theories, to the actual civilization of this or that nation at this or that point in history? When evaluating a country positioned in the world at a specific time and in a specific set of relationships with others past and present, how can one characterize its organizations relative to a qualitative sociological theory outlined in a book?

Such a blueprint theory of earth's history is not sustainable as it no doubt leads to chicken and egg type reasoning while asserting a mystified subject to alleviate the confusion. The books or analyses are themselves contributions to the various institutions and associations that form, they trigger educational moments, and they facilitate conversations that lead to orientations and groupings. The ongoing emissions of earthly existence constantly perpetuate renewed need of analysis and feedback. The procedures degrade and undergo transformation in response to environmental conditions reflecting degradation and change. Books contribute, public discourses, new devices and mechanisms for obtaining measurement, slogans and memes, all kinds of associations are at work in cultivating assemblies of existence and characteristics of dimensional attribution. My contribution is merely one more along these same lines, suggesting that the telemetric measuring mechanism that predominates under contemporary historical circumstances has a grip on the analytical deliberations that feedback and coopt emissions in accordance with that set of rules operative in those same conditions of analysis and emission cultivated by the telemetry. Legislative bodies should not only educate themselves in the matters of compliance and protection of personal information, but they should take as their constantly guiding clue the state of associations that are predominant within any domain, the interests that are reflected in those associations, the ways in which measuring in those domains can impact the formation of future associations and involvements, and the way that being able to predict (or self-fulfill in prophesizing) the outcome of such behavior redirection will serve the interests of some conditions and associations more so than the interests of others.

Corporations in the United States have been recently recognized as having the rights of persons.[9] Yet contemporary civilization has not caught up with the meaning of this recognition. Corporations, initially, are the outcrop of a right to associate, they are meant to reflect the procedural association of multiple persons and yet, by being granted personhood, this association itself becomes the fabrication of something more than mere association. It becomes the embodiment of organization in the collective set of associations of multiple human beings. As such, the corporation takes on the capacity to form and prevent associations of its own through its action. It takes note of who it interacts with, what they do during those interactions in minute detail, and how those minutiae relate to details of other associations carried out by the corporation in its various interactions with other agents and persons. If a political organization declares that there is a right to freely associate and if that is decreed to lie at the origin of the corporation's fabrication, then it is imperative to understand the impact any act by such a person might have on the rights of others to freely associate. The right to property is the basis of the regulations against theft or malfeasance in the appropriation of property from another. Likewise, the associations protected in the formation of the corporation must be constrained relative to their impact on the associations of those others with whom the corporation regularly engages. Again, this means that a regulator should not be exclusively concerned with protecting my privacy as though they were looking out for my property in the body of personally identifiable data describing who I am, but they must also protect infringements upon my associations, my manner of learning the world as well as orienting and involving myself in it as an intelligent being in the midst of its own temporally based cultivation.

A proper philosophical dispute about whether corporations are people is the point. The corporate ontology is at issue and requires that the organizations that have instituted the conditions become the target of existential analysis, that their emissions be measured, and that the feedback from that analysis be instituted for effect on future emissions. In short, the "ethics of facts" described later, where every "is" hides an "ought," suggests that the interesting questions are not just philosophical but historical and structural. It also suggests that the "issue" is not hypothetical and rendered complete by this or that person's opinion on the matter, regardless of how well they have supported their opinion with arguments. The fact of the matter lies in the actual procedures and policies that predominate among

---

[9] Citizens United vs Federal Election Commission. 558 U.S. 310. 2010. The informal recognition, however, goes back to the 13th Amendment. Cf. Hartman's *Unequal Protection: How Corporations Became 'People'—And How You Can Fight Back.*

existing organizations and the current environment within which people are involved with those organizations. It is not up to me whether a corporation is a person and it does not matter whether they *should* be people. My argument is that they are judicially asserted to be such, and this has a set of conditioning impacts on various organizations and action conditions in the world. If that is acknowledged, I hold that the constraints needed to ensure "ontological privacy's" protection under the conditions at work in the essence of artificial intelligence, will be more clearly revealed in the way various like-minded civilizations need to orient themselves toward the associations that emerge as emissions, analysis, and feedback. In so doing, a repurposing of the telemetric follows insofar as it functions as the measurement bridge between personal phenomenological attunement or anxious questioning and the public domain or commonwealth thus providing the mechanism that occupies the body. Organizational telemetry that reveals the behavior and personality of corporations demonstrates the way they can be engineered to integrate with social ends. It remains in what is human among us to understand what those are meant to be.

Writing with Metal

Metallurgy in Deleuze and Guattari's "Nomadology"

Why write about this? Does the writing multiply the effect, demonstrate the phenomenon? Is it me who writes or some telemetric organization to which I am subject? Is there a difference and how am I to understand it? Is this the "Nothing of Revelation" of which they speak, the very "shadow text" itself? At the least, it may be the threat of it: I cannot say who is watching and what they see.[1]

What follows is not about metallurgy and the life of the smith or artisan. It is about one of the practices [of writing] in Deleuze and Guattari's work *A Thousand Plateaus*.[2] To orient ourselves for the project ahead, the project on an indefinite article -a flow to be followed, we will opportunistically attempt to fabricate an illustration of proletarian prose buried beneath the surfaces of their work. Among writers, writing often exemplifies a revalued praxis (Nietzsche, Blanchot, Derrida); and this is the case not only for Deleuze and Guattari in their connecting aspects of "minor literature" or "expressive machines" and the common practices of nomads peopling the plateaus of their work, but it must also be the case *here* in what is, of course, a piece of writing. The question opens: is it possible to write reflexively about writing as praxis without becoming alienated from the writing process? And what organizations are at work in this alienation? Or still more forcefully: is all such reflection a division of labor within the work that alienates the writing from the written? And does this organizational division of labor become especially flagrant in the context of a discussion of Deleuze and Guattari since the view of writing we seek to describe can only be elaborated by the authoritative voice of a managing owner in the moment of criticism? This, it turns out, is *the* question of theory.

At the beginning, the aim of this chapter will be to mine resources out of the raw materials to be found in the subterranean caverns of *A Thousand Plateaus* and then use those resources to produce a renewed practice [of

---

[1] Riffing on Scholem and Benjamin, Zuboff and Agamben. Try as I may to be a serious scholar, my efforts always begin, and perhaps end, with a riff.

[2] Deleuze, Gilles and Guattari, Felix. *A Thousand Plateaus: Capitalism and Schizophrenia*. Translated by Brian Massumi. 1987. Minneapolis: University of Minnesota Press.

writing]. The section on the "itinerant" artisan/metallurgists[3] with their rough hands and sturdy shoes will be the material of our excavation; writers gazing at the mechanosphere of the planet earth while practicing their craft will be material for our product; and, finally, writers as potential commodifiers looking for a market will be the object at work in our distribution. In this last part, the essay will risk becoming an impossible example of itself, containing itself in a visible moment of ideological manipulation: a thesis [sic] that in its moment of meta-reflection would begin to act as a mirror held up opposite the mirror of the analysis, an infinity that smooths space in the course of striating it.[4]

Excavation

In addition to a close reading of Proposition 8 of the treatise on nomadology, let the context here be an organizational interest in the pattern of "excavation" itself and let the notions of nomad and state serve the purpose of delineating a contrary dynamic between a flow—or the persistent disruption of an order, on the one hand, and a stasis—or the rational establishment of an order, on the other. The use of mundane categories of action can then provide illustrations for evaluating the offset of organizational interactions. More to the long-term point, it can show the way in which a technology can straddle organizational typologies and enable confluence between otherwise disparate structures. In *A Thousand Plateaus*, the metallurgist serves this purpose as does the telemeter in our

---

[3] Deleuze and Guattari, *A Thousand Plateaus*, pp. 404-415. The section that we are focusing on here is called "Proposition VIII. Metallurgy in itself constitutes a flow necessarily confluent with nomadism."

[4] There are two components of this sentence requiring emphasis: 1) the component of exemplarity insofar as it places this partial piece within a context inscribed by many other partial pieces. It is not a declaration of self-consciousness in the form of self-presence of this phenomena of writing to itself in this essay, but an insertion of this partial piece into other writings that also inscribe the field of writing with a reevaluation (i.e. Nietzsche, Blanchot, and Derrida); and 2) the component of the infinity of the mirrors reflecting each other. Of course, the mirror is one of the focal images of metaphysically based epistemology and to see any piece of writing as a mirror of the world is to view it within the domain of a metaphysics oriented around transcendent agents. This image of a mirror finding nothing to reflect but another mirror displaces the image in the act of discovery.

larger context.[5] From the perspective of both the state and the nomad, the metallurgist is something of a lens grinder whose musculature and dexterity is regulated by the processes and procedures imposed by the tools of the trade.

The metallurgist enters *A Thousand Plateaus* when the problem arises, "[h]ow do the nomads invent or find their weapons?"[6] The proposition that circumscribes the following section is that "[m]etallurgy in itself constitutes a flow necessarily confluent with nomadism."[7] Deleuze and Guattari are concerned with practices and processes, procedures delineating separate areas of life and experience. The distinctions are made in accordance with an internal design of each of the various realms. This internal design ought not suggest a rigid structuralism since the various realms (or assemblages) are not clearly demarcated or held in strict relation to a locus of some logical norm. The use of the word 'flow' suggests that this boundlessness always carries within its motion the potential to overflow into the design or economy of another flow. No doubt exuberance is at work in all flowing procedures. Bear this in mind as we learn of the nomads beginning their journeys, since they will be taking place right alongside the metallurgists performing their crafts and the state its territorial rule.

> The law of the State is not the law of All or Nothing (State societies or counter-State societies) but that of interior and exterior. The State is sovereignty. But sovereignty only reigns over what is capable of internalizing, of appropriating locally. Not only is there no universal State, but the outside of States cannot be reduced to "foreign policy", that is, to a set of relations among States. The outside appears simultaneously in two directions: huge worldwide machines branched out over the entire ecumenon at a given moment, which enjoy a large measure of autonomy in relation to the States (for example, commercial organization of the "multinational" type, or industrial complexes, or even religious formations like Christianity, Islam, certain prophetic or messianic movements, etc.); but also the local mechanisms of bands, margins, minorities, which continue to affirm the rights of segmentary societies in opposition to the organs of State power. ... What becomes clear is that

[5] For more background on this, see *Telemetry Phenomenology Commonwealth: Corporate Surveillance and the Colonization of Personality*. 2019. Kirkland: Lensgrinder, Ltd.

[6] Deleuze and Guattari, *A Thousand Plateaus*, p. 403.

[7] Deleuze and Guattari, *A Thousand Plateaus*, p. 404.

> bands, no less than worldwide organizations, imply a form
> irreducible to the State and that this form of exteriority
> necessarily presents itself as a diffuse and polymorphous war
> machine. It is a nomos very different from the "law".[8]

The state designates a region that exists mediately over and against an exterior region, a trans-frontier world where the designs and rules of the state's territory do not apply. This "deterritorialized" outside is the region of the war machine, of the nomad. There are numerous sorts of nomadic organizations ranging from multi-national corporations to religious sects and including grass roots political movements opposed to the machinery of the state through localized regions of conflict. The state, for Deleuze and Guattari, is not a universally dominant apparatus or group of apparatuses; its areas of influence are limited and, as we shall see more thoroughly in what follows, it is in the interests of the state to grant autonomy to these movements in order to enter into an alliance that will extend state power. The "nomos" of the nomad exterior to the state is therefore the design of the war machine's flow opposed to the judiciary design of the state's "law"; this opposition may be, but need not be, one of hostility.

This twofold exclusive opposition of the state and the war machine is not maintained for very long. As stated above, the nomad springs into being simultaneously with the metallurgist, they are confluent. The metallurgist is neither internal to the law of the state, nor on the outside with the *nomos* of the war machine. Yet the metallurgists are not nomads just because they are external to the state, nor are they citizens of the *polis* just because they are not carried away by the *nomos*. They are a separate, third element that alters the relations of the first two and flows based on its very own design. The third term dispels any possibility of maintaining a simple relation between nomad and state based. Its introduction requires a movement beyond simple theorizing by writers trying to make sense of relations in terms of their *relata*. The entry of the metallurgist along with the nomad thus commands a deeper investigation into the design of the various flows: this is perfectly consistent with the authors' frequently asserted "empiricist" position.

This resulting triad is by no means clearly delimited. For example: the nomads as a military war machine are notorious throughout history for their weapons and their use of them against the state as well as in the service of it. In the case of the saber, for example, the nomadic Scythians are widely accepted as the transmitters of this piece of technology to several sedentary organizations (i.e. the Persians' State). The fashioning of this weapon

---

[8] Deleuze and Guattari, *A Thousand Plateaus*, p. 360.

required "a sedentary milieu"[9] and so, it was thought, had to be located within the Chinese empire and not the work of the nomads themselves: at least this production was located among the metallurgists who lived within the Chinese state. Contrary to popular archaeological opinions, this fashioning of the saber by the metallurgists of China had to be done with some degree of autonomy from the Chinese state. It is true that they were not nomads, but it is equally true that their separation from the state was complete enough to prevent anyone from calling them citizens or pointing to behaviors governed by rules originating from its laws and in conflict with the metallurgical processes being followed. It is most probable that the craftsmen willingly gave their products to the nomads allowing them to use them for their purposes as far and wide as their journeys would take them. To demonstrate the necessity of this triadic relation, Deleuze and Guattari find it necessary to investigate the "technological line or continuum" that is metallurgy. For only in understanding how the technologies of metal's flow progress will the necessary independence of the metallurgist from the *nomos* and the *polis* be demonstrated.

Two categories are used in conjunction to define such a lineage or "machinic phylum" and they are best understood through the example of the saber: 1) operations or "singularities" of a certain technological advancement like being able to melt iron at high temperatures and successive decarbonations or removing of carbon compounds from the metal for the sake of purifying it. A line of technological progress can be seen in productive operations that undergo changes through history as they become perfected. Although the procedures can undergo radical transformation, they still hold together in a single line. 2) "affective qualities or traits of expression" (material traits of the product when completed) such as hardness, sharpness, and the gloss of the metal as well as any kind of design or tracing that results from the internal qualities of the steel cast in such a fashion. These affective qualities[10] are tied intimately to the operations that enable them (#1 above) and it is these affects that enable the operation to hold together in a single line of technological progress.

---

[9] Deleuze and Guattari, *A Thousand Plateaus*, p. 405.

[10] To make this point a little clearer, the reader might recall the frequently suggested meaning of "affects" taken from Spinoza. For Spinoza, the affective qualities of an entity are essential to the being of that entity. In the case of the body, the question as to the affections of the body is identical to the question what can a body do? When we are asking after the affective qualities of a line of technological development, we are asking after a development in the performance of a certain procedure such as slicing or cutting in the case of the dagger/sword and piercing in the case of the knife/saber.

What makes widely different procedures into linear developments is that they are both used to get the same affective quality or performance out of a machine or a thing. When these two attributes converge in different weapons, the weapons are said to be members of the same phylum; if there is a divergence in the attributes, then we speak of differing phyla. The example the authors give is that of the saber-knife as opposed to the sword-dagger. Although these weapons are similar, they are not convergent in their differing constitutive operations or expressive traits. Both the knife and the saber are mass produced dye-cast products resulting from pouring molten iron into a mold, whereas the dagger and sword are hammered out on a smith's anvil, one at a time after intense heating of the iron. Aside from these variations in operations, the two phyla also have different affects: although similar, the cut of the sword differs from the pierce of the saber, the saber is much softer than the sword and far lighter, they look different, reflect light differently, and wound differently.[11]

These various phyla are united in a single phylum (the science of Metallurgy) within which metal is engaged in continuous variations brought along by various operations and affects. Instances of these variations are called assemblages. In the saber, which arises out of the developments of metallurgy, we see the latest achievements of casting procedures and cutting techniques. There are multiple lines tracing their way through metallurgy converging and diverging in various assemblages as implementations of the science. For instance, there are lines that connect different assemblages like the saber and the knife as well as lines that connect the same assemblage - for instance, any progress made in making sabers. One could easily trace the history of sabers, the history of a casting technique and the various weapons made with it, or the history of metallurgy proper. Likewise, do these lines interact in various manners: machinic phyla influence the fashioning of assemblages while assemblages can influence the line of the general phylum (i.e. what can be done with molds will influence the kinds

---

[11] Simondon's *On the Mode of Existence of Technical Objects* (2017. Translated by Cecile Malaspina and John Rogove. Minneapolis, MN: Univocal.) is an extraordinary example of a work that unpacks the essence of the technical through the exploration of phyla. The objects are reduced to pure function and then there is an elaborate analysis of the forms that the function has taken over many years of evolution and development. This may recall the first section of *Telemetry Phenomenology Commonwealth* where we consider telemetry as an analog act performed by efficiency experts. Insofar as telemetry originates as an emission of measured events, we may also consider it as a phase in the history of writing where the store gathering the data together for analysis and feedback amounts to an advance in genre. Kafka's lineage, in what follows, constitutes the phylum of the writing machine and the advent of the telemetric.

of weapons made and the kinds of weapons made will influence the progress of metallurgy -the aim and use of it).

But it is jumping the gun somewhat to call the unifying phylum a metallurgy since the material of the phylum is not metal but the amorphous matter of an historical flow. In a sense, to call it metal is already to delegate the matter to a machinic phylum of some kind. Rather, it is suggested by the authors, that we call this matter a "fuzzy aggregate." The material is amorphous until the artisan, say a blacksmith, instantiates or embodies it into the weapon. This is not to say that the matter is completely moldable, it is not. This matter hovers between a natural state of some underlying essence and an artificial state resulting from the artisan's effort and fabrication. Its fuzzy aggregation is in-between essences -metal is a matter-movement with qualities, yet there is room in the metal for the shaping or building of additional qualities by the artisan who is adding an artifice to a natural element that will best achieve a useful combination of the two. In other words, you can do a lot of things with flowing molten metal, but you cannot do anything you like with it. The flow of metal carries within it a fuzzy boundary beyond which it has no potential.

This procedure of the artisan, who acts while respecting this fuzzy boundary, is called "following." It means that they must follow the lines or traits of the metal in some fashion. Similarly, they must "follow" the lines and traits of the procedures they are currently able to perform. Also the artisans must "follow" the material in the sense that they must find it where it lies: in the woods, in the ground, or in the air. Artisans must be prospectors in their following so that they can invent as they will or build as they must. If they are forced to work from another's plan, they are not artisans, but workers. The artisan is defined ultimately by this following and this prospecting (which is a kind of following) insofar as they are performers of *procedures aimed at the flow of matter as it flows and as it can be made to flow.* "The artisan is *the itinerant, the ambulant.* To follow the flow of matter is to itinerate, to ambulate. It is intuition in action."[12] The flow of matter is a deterritorialized flow the pursuit of which is equally deterritorialized (external to the law of the state). This following that is without a territory of its own, is all made for the sake of a territorialization or reification unique to the artisan or metallurgist. Such an itinerant nature is clearly different from the nature of the nomad: following is the itinerant action that seeks out the nomadic flow of matter (in a manner of speaking, the matter -metal- *is* nomadic and so following it is itinerant).

It is not accidental that the itinerant artisans follow metal as their material of choice. There is a "primary relation between itinerance and

---

[12] Deleuze and Guattari, *A Thousand Plateaus*, p. 409.

metallurgy."[13] Deleuze and Guattari wax poetic in praise of metal and metallurgy:

> In short, what metal and metallurgy bring to light is a life
> proper to matter, a vital state of matter as such, a material
> vitalism that doubtless exists everywhere but is ordinarily
> hidden or covered, rendered unrecognizable, dissociated by
> the hylomorphic model. Metallurgy is the consciousness or
> thought of matter- flow, and metal the correlate of this
> consciousness. As expressed in panmetallism, metal is
> coextensive to the whole of matter, and the whole of matter
> to metallurgy.[14]

What does this amount to? It is metal's fluid qualities that excite the authors; but more than metal's fluid nature, its becoming-hard. Metal as a category is like the abstraction 'matter' because metal, when heated, becomes the amorphous flow that matter always is. And a great many things can be done with metal in pouring molds, but nothing can be poured that transcends the possibilities of metal, that is, metal must be followed. The thinking that works with metal, that shapes it and invents with it, is a thought given over to the principle of matter itself.[15]

The matter flow of the artisans is in the subsoil, metal exists underground, and so they must follow as subterraneans -as members of "secret societies, guilds, journeyman's associations."[16] And it is underground, in the earth amid forests and near mountains far from the towns, that the artisan comes into contact with the nomad. They must rely on the nomads for their access to the raw materials they need, since the woods and the mountains are their roaming grounds. Although artisans have anvils in the town and require the assistance of farmers for their sustenance, the focus of their craft is in the mines outside the town. The mine belongs to the nomad and is the main source of matter's flow. Of course, this does not

---

[13] Deleuze and Guattari, *A Thousand Plateaus*, p. 410.

[14] Deleuze and Guattari, *A Thousand Plateaus*, p. 411.

[15] The logic of production in the realm of metallurgy suggests the movement of substance in Spinoza's *Ethics*. Metal is the amorphous substance seeking attributes in determinate entities. To this extent, metal becomes the matter ontology is made of and not merely a regional issue of practices and purposes (but this is no doubt to overly philosophize the work of Deleuze and Guattari -although this leads to interesting conclusions when we make the move toward writing in the next section).

[16] Deleuze and Guattari, *A Thousand Plateaus*, p. 412.

mean that miners are nomads, only that those who control the mines are. The artisan's underground craft lies between the state and the nomads.

The way of life lies between the two: artisans live as one would live in a cave. They stay in one place only for the sake of the materials that they can gain from that place and will move on as soon as things get scarce. They do not territorialize the earth when making a home (they do not build houses); neither do they maintain a pace that pauses only as a way of continuing their travels (they do not pitch tents). Artisans bore holes into the earth or at least follow the flow of bored holes in such a way as to always be living among them. One who lives in caves must always be interested in holey spaces; and the artisan, as someone who lives in a space defined by such holes, is equally defined by those holes that they have found as they follow matter. Although they may not dig the holes, they certainly are responsible for their existence since the cave as a dwelling place is more than just a hole in a rock. The cave lies between the house and the nomad's tent.

The way of labor lies between the two:

> The metallurgist belonging to an empire, the worker, presupposes a metallurgist-prospector, however far away; and the prospector ties in with a merchant, who brings the metal to the first metallurgist. In addition, the metal is worked on by each segment, and the ingot-form is common to them all: we must imagine less separate segments than a chain of mobile workshops constituting, from hole to hole, a line of variation, a gallery. Thus the metallurgists' relation to the nomads and the sedentaries also passes through the relations they have with other metallurgists.[17]

Artisans relate to each other in the same way that artisans relate to nomads and sedentaries. The holes of the artisan, their cave dwellings, are connected by a line that resembles the one stemming from each workshop into the mine and into the city. The products of the other artisans are worth studying for their productive value just as the mining results of the nomads and the working habits of the sedentaries are worth studying for possible contributions to future work. The artisan conforms to a design of pure exteriority. Their relation to the state, to the war machine, and to other metallurgists, is always one from an exterior locale within the boundaries of an interior locale. Artisans are always experimenting with the work of others from a position beyond it, they are both inside and outside these works. And because the artisans' work follows the flow of matter, it is an experimentation with their own practices: as the experimenters

---

[17] Deleuze and Guattari, *A Thousand Plateaus*, p. 415.

extraordinaire, artisans are external to themselves.

The way of space lies between the two: the holey space of the artisan is related equally to the smooth space of the nomads' constant flow and the striated space of the state's sedentariness. The relation to the nomad is one of connection whereas the relation to the sedentary is one of conjugation:

> On the side of the nomadic assemblages and war machines, it is a kind of rhizome, with its gaps, detours, subterranean passages, stems, openings, traits, holes, etc. On the other side, the sedentary assemblages and State apparatuses effect a capture of the phylum, put the traits of expression into a form or a code, make the holes resonate together, plug the lines of flight, subordinate the technological operation to the work model, impose upon the connections a whole regime of arborescent conjunctions.[18]

A holey space deepens into a burrow, a cave becomes a mine -it might be said that the back of the cave is the plane where the artisan meets the nomad. At the front of the cave, the hole opens into the air in a way that resembles the spaces between lines in a grid; the hole is the in-between of a piece of graph paper's striations. The metallurgist resides between the state and its codes of operations and the nomadic design of unbounded movement. These artisans are those who dwell within range of two very different ways of movement. The design of the state is an ideological mapping out of the ways and means of daily life. All practices within the state take place within narrowly defined codes of behavior (family, school, etc.). On the other hand, practices within the nomadic war machine are infinitely malleable, always changing and transforming in the name of the maintenance of the flow and the continuation of movement without interruption. Global capitalism, for instance, is willing to constantly transform its standards and practices to maintain its development. Furthermore, non-international nomadic movements in opposition to the state also follow this same design of constant movement to maintain their distance from the state apparatuses.[19]

---

[18] Deleuze and Guattari, *A Thousand Plateaus*, p. 415.

[19] There is a difference between local nomadic movements and international movements, but there is a likeness of design between the two according to Deleuze and Guattari. A local movement may no doubt be opposed to an international nomadic movement, but this opposition would be badly served in ignorance of the common patterns and points of contact. I am left wondering whether any nomadic organization could ever have become global without some form of state alliance; and this might be a way the local vs.

The relations that place the artisan between the nomad and the sedentary may have been exhausted by the preceding description, but metallurgy's autonomy can only be fully supported by the earlier presentation of the technological lineage that is exclusive to the metallurgists/artisans and separates them necessarily from the other nodes of the triad. The artisans cannot be fully allied with the state as they must follow the flow of matter, and they cannot be fully allied with the nomad as they require their own territoriality for their production and their machines of production (the anvil and the hearth). The lineages of technology or machinic phyla that are the essence of their praxis give them the required leverage to retain this independent role. The state does not dominate or oppress the artisans to gain the full technological benefits of the artisan's craft; the nomads do not rage in war machinic fashion against the artisan, for the nomads are also in need of the artisan's weapons. In both cases, the involved are willing to tolerate and actively support the artisan's invention so as to gain the tools for work (in the case of the state) and the weapons for war (in the case of the nomad).[20] At this point, the importance of exuberance as a trait of all flowing becomes clear. Exuberance and the experimental relation of the artisan to the others indicates an overflow of relations between the two extremes. We must recall that the codes of the state and directives (*nomos*) of the nomads may overflow into the experimental practices of the metallurgist and into each other.

This concludes the excavational aspect of our close reading. Suffice it to say that here I have tried to follow the flow of matter proceeding through Deleuze and Guattari's text so as to harvest from it raw materials for an assemblage that will bring together operations and traits currently available in the lineage of writing and theorizing. Now I would like to go on to the productive segment in which the assemblage will be constructed as either tool or weapon, depending on whether the state or the war machine incorporate it.

---

global opposition becomes more firmly drawn.

[20] As we turn to the discussion of writing, it might be worth pointing out that the figure of the artisan might also represent the mental laborer in Marx's historical materialism: the intellectual. The intellectual may be employed by the state and receive grants from the war machine, all in the name of a productive capacity that will benefit either of the organizations. This could also describe the intellectual laborer aligned with corporate research and development.

Production

The major claim in this mapping procedure, this production of ideas beyond the flow of the work of Deleuze and Guattari, is that writing constitutes a flow confluent with the nomad, metallurgy, and the sedentary. Often, writing is associated with the state apparatus; while its products might be appropriated as weapons by a war machine for its use, the state more regularly uses these results as tools in its own business (the law, political propaganda, commentary, etc.). This position is analogous to that of *A Thousand Plateaus* regarding metallurgy as a fashioning of weapons that, although associated with the state, is not joined to it. Writing is not a nomadic practice although I shall demonstrate that the nomad plays a part in the writer's work and appropriates it for use as a weapon. The technological lineage will reveal this independence since, as in the case of metallurgy, assemblages invented out of variations in a technical history must be autonomous to ensure high quality in developments that will be advantageous to all concerned. Since a technological lineage is ultimately a kind of flow, isolating it from the flow of the sedentary *is* establishing it as independent; and an independent technology is only a small step from complete autonomy because the state and the war machine, if they wish to make use of that technology in their own ways (either as weapons or as tools), will have to stand back and support these engineers of the writing-flow.

Writing is not the technological lineage that is the object of this search, rather it is the phylum that unites these various lines of technics. That is what I mean when I say that writing functions like metallurgy in an independent flow, that writers are like artisans in their crafting. What is it then that functions as a technological lineage in writing, a technique in writing? A technological lineage is an abstract universal that progresses in the form of various embodiments of the operation or the affective quality. It would be something like iambic pentameter, irony, narration, or rhetoric: vastly different lineages that are nothing beyond their specific examples and yet find their specification in numerous instances spanning time and space. Each of these operations have various affects attached to them: enchantment, wonder, persuasion, etc. These embodiments, constellations of operations and affects, are also called assemblages. The written assemblages are the sign, the word, the sentence, the paragraph, etc.; in other words, the statement or written utterance in every form from the most atomic to whatever complexity the imagination can invent. These assemblages are so open-ended because they are a cutting into the matter-flow of writing: the line. It is the line that provides the continuous flow of material conveying operations and affects in a way ripe for scissiparity by the artist or artisan, ripe for territorialization in composition. It should be clear that these technological lineages exert a considerable influence on the kinds of assemblages that are segmented from the matter-flow of the line, whereas the assemblages themselves will influence the future progression of the technological lineages.

The fuzzy aggregation of writing should be obvious. It is defined somewhat by the material it uses, the line itself, and yet the boundaries of the line are as anexact as human experience. The number of written languages, and the infinite possibilities of further instances, is as wide as possibility itself; and yet each instance is merely a clarifying of the fuzzy domain that pre-exists the invention of a language or technique. No doubt the ease with which the fuzzy aggregation of writing is apprehended results from the nature of the line. The line, like matter, like metal, is ripe for molding. Much like Derrida has shown, pan-graphism or grammatology is excellent in its descriptive power of praxis and events; it might be said that the line is description itself, is the production of the described. And this use of writing need not stay within the boundaries of the "literal" since drawings and music are ways of making the line dance: this choreography of the line is precisely the use given here to "writing." The line has immense possibilities, just as metal and matter, and parallels them as a minor scientific physics of the fluid, of becoming.

We can look to the line as the model of deterritorialization, it exhibits the perfect qualities of a constant flow, of an always in the middle, of a creation *of* the middle at a place along its flow. And yet the artist, unlike the nomad, does not make the line into an ultimate praxis. Rather the artist takes on a relation to the line that seeks to territorialize it, to cut into its progression and invent from it an assemblage. It is this picture of the artist's work that makes the artist, like the artisan, an itinerant or ambulant as opposed to a nomad. The artist is, like the artisan, not a migrant as there is no effort at forming a circuitousness of the path: the artist, unlike the migrant, does not want to return to old ground that has been healed from the effects of past use. Instead, artists continue along the line in an ever-differing fashion of "following" the line.

This itinerancy, this territorializing along the deterritorialized line, is a following of the matter-flow of the line, going to the place where it is and cutting into it as it allows itself to be sliced. Artists often give thanks to a muse in the openings of their work; if not a muse, they may describe an experience in diaries, letters, and autobiographies that they felt their words descend from elsewhere as though they were anything but productions of the artist's mind. Religious and political sermons are examples: the suffering of a people, of the faith that one feels, often puts one in a position to be affected by the line's progression in artistic fashioning. Any rational description of this incredible aesthetic affection is set aside here. Rather, this phenomenon is dubbed "following" for the simple reason that it *seems* that way, it *seems* that the artists are following a line beyond their own cognitive scheme, or productive realm. Again, this, like the artisan's invention, is not a passive or passionate feeling; instead it is an affection of the body. A great deal of power is required for artists to lend themselves so readily to the affectations given by the line -and the use of Spinozan terminology is no accident here. The artist is asking after the powers of a body and so is looking into the ability to be affected as it conjoins with the ability to affect. Affection, for Spinoza, was an awareness or understanding of causes and effects leading to a current state of affairs and, through this understanding, would come a knowledge of what further activity would best remain in line with the preceding chain. In this sense, individual activity is no more than a swinging door between being affected and affecting. The swinging door of the artist is a cutting into the line that invents new assemblages, a cutting that "follows" the line.

That writing constitutes a following that is both inventive and governed by tradition, causes tension in various contemporary positions, two of which will be mentioned here: 1) that writing is short term memory. It is anything but that in that the traditions of affection are so deeply ingrained in the writer's mind that they come as though they had been forgotten. That the artist uses sentences or narrative is sometimes overlooked as technical tradition by armchair theoreticians of art. The deep structure of art and the remembering of it in the act of invention, in the swinging of the door upon its hinges, ought to be recognized as crucial to the practice of artistry as described by "following." 2) Also, in a similar fashion, it should be recognized that, in art, it is not the case that anything goes, that all brands of invention are permitted. For the grain of the line's flow has a rhythm and will grow monstrous in certain embodiments just as it will grow beautiful in others. The act of the artist is equally susceptible to being realized as beautiful or as ugly (not sublime) and so there do appear to be "rules" of invention; although those rules are deeply malleable and open to various implementations and interpretations.

In further reflections of similar matters, the most inventive artist is aware of affective historical lineages, technologies of the line and the flow of the line itself, and uses these in the invention or production of assemblages. Despite the fact, as Deleuze and Guattari point out, that Kafka was hostile to any submission to a master, it is obvious that he followed the line in various of its flows. He wrote stories and used methods of narration. He warned of the danger of control and surveillance and the impact disciplinary structures might have on the lives of human beings living among them. His genius was evident in the way he discovered function underlying large-scale apparatuses and could pull together patterns and connected histories to draw out trends. He may have been the first to see the telemetric at work as a phylum in human institutions. The possibilities took place within an arena of sense, in a direction, and as an itinerant cutting into the matter-flow of the line driven by his independent vision.

The absence of masters in Kafka's work implicates all artists working through the functional history of their domain and following the various lineages. It may be granted that the artist has a relationship to another artist as a student relates to a teacher or master, but —as Nietzsche emphasizes— a student repays a master poorly if the student remains a student. "Why do you not wish to pluck at my wreath?" Zarathustra asks at the end of Book One. What I mean here is that the master-student relation is no more than an accident of chronology and the human constitution, it is a merely formal facet of the lineage. That it was Schopenhauer who Nietzsche recognized as an educator is purely contingent on Schopenhauer's having been born half a century or so before him. Nietzsche renounced Schopenhauer in the same moment that he elevated him as his educator, for the untimely meditation dedicated to the master does more to overcome the master's pessimism than any argument or critical inquiry could have.

This masterless life of the artist, this refusal to form a rung in a hierarchy (which should not be confused with a failure to learn from one's predecessors or follow their line) seems comparable to an underground existence. The artist does not form a branch on a tree representing the history of art; rather the artist is a further twist or turn in a rhizomatic labyrinth that is for them always already there, full grown and mature. It is just as possible for Epicurus to have been Nietzsche's educator as it was for Schopenhauer to have been. And the points of contact need not be linear, the historical network is a graph with multiple edges connecting the nodes. And the traversal of the edge may be a partial impact of granular affective qualities. Nietzsche's reverence for Schopenhauer does not require that he embrace Buddhism, since the lineage does not progress in that fashion. This absence of a need for following lines back to their roots is a further example of the rhizomatic character of writing: that is, the underground quality of the artist. This underground feature, this secret feature, does not carry with it a membership card or any privileges like the guilds or journeyman's societies of the artisan. It is a society that is so secret that the artists themselves are never certain that they are members. And although they can hope and dream, their admission is only secured by future artists who read them and recognize them as compatriots (this relationship results in an obvious infinite regress that certainly contributes to the artist's anguish). The externality of artists as writers is evident not only in their relation to the state and the war machine but to other writers and to themselves over time.

This relationship of artists to each other, this relationship characterized at least partially by anguish (and certainly by joy as well since there are those

immense moments of kinship that strike the artist at the most unpredictable
of hours), parallels the relationship of the artist to the sedentary state
apparatus and the nomadic war machine. The artist must live among the
sedentary: although some aspect of writing may be done while on the move,
another aspect of it requires a chair or at least standing still. Such living in
the midst is not accompanied by recognition: the sedentary citizens of the
state are as separate from the artist as the whole of the preceding artists (this
is the Bachelor machine described in the last few pages of the Kafka
book[21]). The nomads stand opposed to the artist, for although they may
walk together along the line, eventually the artist must pause in an act of
territorialization foreign to the nomad. It is the nomad who the artist re-
invents in the assemblages (or possibly the sedentary citizens), but this
invention only serves to further the gap between them as the moments of
their likeness dissipate in the separation that is required for this act of
invention both in that it is territorialization foreign to the nomad and a
territorialization that acts upon the deterritorialized other without rigidity
making it alien to the citizen.

One might go so far as to say that the artist's workshop must be among
the sedentary for only there are they offered the solitude and calm they
require, whereas the material for their artistry is derived entirely from the
nomads. This is clear from any of several assemblages that deal with
characters as nomads. One might wonder if there ever was a book or an
essay or a poem the contents of which were not nomadic. Notice that
writers in writings by writers are never writing in these writings, but rather
are always in between writings, travelling along the flow, following it
(Raskolnikov, Dedalus, etc.). Notice further that it does not mean that
certain writings are not appropriated by the state apparatus and the
sedentary folks that populate them for their own use as tools (i.e.
propaganda or entertainment), and marginal readings or deconstruction
are ways of looking at an assemblage in a manner restoring the nomadic
quality that the sedentary have otherwise expelled from the work.[22]

It is precisely because of the mutability of most assemblages that the
state enables the writer to keep writing. Because the assemblages are just as

---

[21] Deleuze, Gilles and Guattari, Felix. *Kafka: Toward a Minor Literature.*
Translated by Dana Polan. 1986. Minneapolis: University of Minnesota Press.

[22] Reading might be confluent with writing in such matters. We will return
to this in the third section below. Reading and writing, merged as a pair, show
the confluence of telemetry gathered for analysis and feedback. The telemetric
is a form of machine reading and writing for the sake of learning: writing and
the emission phylum of events, reading and the collection phylum of analysis,
and then education as the application phylum of feedback. We should bear
this in mind as we discuss distribution in the next section.

easily incorporated into the lives of the sedentary as into the lives of the nomads, the state has reason enough to allow the artist to propagate. States have endowments and universities and other public places for the artist to gain a niche that will enable survival (and flourishing). Because the assemblage can be easily plugged into the state's flow in a way that makes it into a tool for the state's projects, it can go on in an independent fashion. Despite, or rather because of, the qualities Plato enumerated in the *Republic* (Books three and ten) and the *Ion*, the state will allow the artist to persist. That is, because writing is a possible way of misleading and fooling the people, because it may function in a platonic system of truth and ideas as a simulacrum, it is precisely what the state needs to further its power (i.e. propaganda, circus, legislation, codes of conduct, etc.).

The nomad offers raw materials to the writer. Whether it be the line itself as a nomadic flow or the activities of counter cultures and the bizarre, it is still all fodder for the artist's imagination and expository deployment. Artists follow flows by walking, and they walk the streets at all hours of the day and night. And in the urban milieu and the *nomos* of the countryside, one is equally likely to catch sight of the dispossessed and wandering nomad. And if the person is not nomadic, say a farmer, still the territorialization of the person or event (a farm for instance) will become a deterritorialization -a ripping from rigidly designated previous boundaries- and a replacement of that event or person with a new territoriality that is not a reterritorialization; that is, not an imitation or reproduction of the real thing: rather a production of the sedentary as artistically flowing, as a line. When artists look at a sedentary farmer, they are seeing nomads. Artists see nomads everywhere and it is in that sense that they relate to the nomad, while the nomad, the deterritorializing war machine, can further their travelling with the weapons fabricated from this invention. The nomad enjoys the artist's products because the artist makes everything, including the sedentary that does not appear as such, into a vision of the nomadic. The citizen enjoys the products because they stimulate the desire for motion and self-adulation. The artist translates an otherwise useless sedentary world into terms the nomads and citizens can understand and so puts it to use as a weapon or tool in their work, banded travels, or guerilla warfare. Insofar as the war machine can also be the worldwide culture and media industry, it too enjoys the contributions of the artists who demonstrate the marketability of the most sedentary way of life. Insofar as the state encompasses a population, it may use these products to keep its citizens in their seats.

Given the preceding remarks, it may be concluded that the artist is independent from both nomads and citizens; and that there is good reason for it as well as for letting them remain that way. The holey space of the artisan -the itinerancy or territorialization along the flow of the line- has an external relation to both the smooth space of the nomad (it bores its holes -assemblages- right into it) and the sedentary citizen (it is between the state's striations that the artist lives while boring in such fashion). It is this in-between space of artists that makes them into cave dwellers: their abodes are stationary, like their flexible territorialization in the form of assemblages, and yet they are not permanent abodes like houses. Instead, they occupy the place for writing only long enough for that instance of invention. When the territory is newly defined, they pick up and move - walking alongside the nomads- until they come to a new place for their work, another cave providing shelter, since they have carried nothing with them (again this resembles the bachelor machine of the K factor).[23]

The writer as itinerant follower of the line in its polymorphic flow has been produced out of the raw materials taken from Deleuze and Guattari's work. It is now essential to enter the marketplace with the product (assemblage) of this act of writing. We must recall the opening paragraphs of this essay in doing so since this entry into distribution must take place reflectively or else it will cease to be itinerant and become absorbed in the fabric of the nomadic or sedentary ways of life. If artists enter the marketplace uncritically, they will have no choice but to sell their products to the highest bidders who will use them as either weapons or tools.

Distribution

The itinerant has issued a product that is to be assimilated into a larger constellation. Properly speaking these products can *be* neither tools nor weapons on their own, in themselves. They must be taken up into a predominating field of reference where their relations with other assemblages will give to them their tool-like or weapon-like associations. To have made a tool or a weapon is *already*, therefore, to have distributed it; *already* to have built distribution into its assemblage:

> Thus one cannot speak of weapons or tools before defining
> the constituent assemblages they presuppose and enter into.
> This is what we meant when we said that weapons and tools
> are not merely distinguished from one another in an
> extrinsic manner, and yet they have no distinctive intrinsic
> characteristics. They have internal (and not intrinsic)

---

[23] Deleuze and Guattari, *Kafka: Toward a Minor Literature.*

characteristics relating to the respective assemblages with
which they are associated.[24]

The tool and the weapon, like the artisan/metallurgist/writer/artist, carries
the exterior relations of its context around within it, constituting it as it is:
this just is what we mean when we call it an assemblage.[25] Distribution,
therefore, is an essential moment of any essay on the artisan(-ist) and an
essential moment of all artisanry(-istry).

More is revealed in this character of the tool/weapon than a procedural
point for this project. The interior exteriority of the tool and weapon as
well as the artisan/metallurgist suggests something further about the person
of the writer. We already discussed the extent to which the writer is not a
party to the mainstream currents of the war machine and the state, now we
can point out that this interior exteriority of the writer resonates in the
echoes of Deleuze and Guattari's "minor literature." The role of the miner
is the holey movement of the excavator -of a digging that makes the inside
into an outside, that procures a labyrinth. Among others, this labyrinth may
take on the name of "Kafka." In the miner's digging, we have discovered the
minor's writing: a minor literature.

Minor writing (and it is no doubt interesting that the question as to
whether there is any other kind is thinkable) is a writing from the outside,
a writing that implicitly carries its entry into the mainstream markets as a
stranger -as an alien force in the process of production. "A minor literature
doesn't come from a minor language; it is rather that which a minority
constructs within a major language."[26] Kafka is a Czech Jew writing in
German and this supplies him with an uncanny capacity to deterritorialize
or disrupt the reified codes of the national language of Germany. The

---

[24] Deleuze and Guattari, *A Thousand Plateaus*, p. 398.

[25] With this instance of "assemblage", the term erases clarity. The larger
context (the constellation) as well as the "tool" both fall within the auspices of
assemblages. This blurring of the line, this line put in motion at top speed, is
the line of flight that shakes all borders (striations) between entities and sets the
world forth as a relational context -territorialized in analytical acts of abstraction
or "intuition." The authors' mention of Husserl suggests the problem dealt with
in the third of the *Logical Investigations* where the relations of parts and wholes
are considered. Husserl claims a holistic view of the transcendental "world" and
sees every content or object within that world as, to some extent, a part of it.
Yet, he also sees each object as a whole of its own further analyzable into parts.
Assemblage in Deleuze and Guattari seems to be operating in a similar fashion
-a sort of theoretical phylum.

[26] Deleuze and Guattari, *Kafka*, p. 16.

uncanniness of Kafka's production, however, is a consequence of its residence within this same German language. This lends an extraordinary equivocality to Kafka's works: on the one hand, Kafka comes to reside within German as an outsider and thus transforms the German language with his disruptive prose. On the other hand, German appropriates Kafka and makes of him a German writer.

This equivocation of minor writing places it amid an essentially political tension: the tension of insurgency and counterinsurgency, revolution and reaction, resistance and coercion. Because the writer's production is an interior exteriority whereby the minor dwells (digs) within the major as an outsider (*entfremdet*) excavating uncanny (*unheimlich*) materials, there is always an impossible tension between the distribution of the product either in the service of the state or against it. Although it has been determined in advance that the writer will create something distributable, it is indeterminate whether this distribution will be revolutionary or reactionary. The distributor may always threaten to coopt the product.

This product that will *either* disrupt *or* entrench gains, in its distribution, an essentially collective value. It will *either* transform the constellation of the collective *or* it will help to maintain it. The product will have global, world historical, impact through its role as either changing the relations of the existing constellations or in assisting them to thwart other forces that are striving to transform it. Such a writing belongs, in one way or another, to "the people." It is always the writing of "the people": where this could mean both that the people are the "who" that writes and the "what" that is written (i.e. the subject of enunciation and the subject of the statement).

> The three characteristics of minor literature are the deterritorialization of language, the connection of the individual to a political immediacy, and the collective assemblage of enunciation. We might as well say that minor no longer designates specific literatures but the revolutionary conditions for every literature...[27]

Deleuze and Guattari view their notion of minor literature as revolutionary and this is what distinguishes it from so called major literature which fills the role of reaction against all minor affronts. This results from their understanding the minor writer as nomadic. This essay has not attempted to ex-posit Deleuze and Guattari's positions, but rather to opportunistically excavate them in a moment of production and distribution. In doing so, we have developed a view of the minor that is realized by digging in the mines as a writer/metallurgist following the line. This enables us to reveal an issue

---

[27] Deleuze and Guattari, *Kafka*, p. 18.

that eludes Deleuze and Guattari: the equivocation of writing as the interior exteriority of both the state *and* the war machine.

The state and the war machine in conjunction form an apparatus or constellation that covers the polar spectrum of the inside and the outside, the either/or of an onto-theo-logic (cf. the quote above from TP 360). The smooth exterior movement of the nomad allies itself with the striated interior codes of the sedentary so as to formulate a global organization spreading into all the far corners of the earth and taking up residence there.[28] This alliance of the state with the war machine suggests a new flexible structure of power whereby traditional methods of resistance may be more readily co-opted into conformity with the status quo. If we consider revolution to be nomadic, and therefore akin to the war machine in structure, we already produce a flow that can easily merge with the movement of the contemporary powers that be. For some, this may be desirable, but if it is it can hardly be called revolutionary.[29] To the extent that Deleuze and Guattari view the minor writer as a revolutionary, they must give up the belief that such a writer should be nomadic.

But how can such a writer attack the state? The writer's product has within it the characteristics of a tool or a weapon, but the product is not employed by the writer in the constellation that it carries within it as part of its affective quality. Rather, the war machine and the state form these constellations. The war machine may be a revolutionary organization such

---

[28] Guattari in his *Molecular Revolutions* argues that Capitalism cannot gain total control over the world economy. His argument is based on Gödel's incompleteness theorem which states that any axiomatic system will of necessity generate propositions the truth value of which will be undecidable. Unfortunately, Capitalism as a nomadic war machine cannot be understood as axiomatic since this is a coding of a system that is specific to state organizations. The terrifying result of this is the failure of his argument against Capitalism and the implication that a neo-fascist state in collaboration with a global imperial war machine may spread infinitely everywhere adding all "propositions" to the system by the brute force of axiomatization.

[29] This indicates that it is indeed problematic to merely assume that a data driven theory or analysis could be produced to address any problem of coercive territorialization let alone imperialist colonizing as deterritorialization. The theorizing itself may be a ruse or trojan horse that brings the outside agent inside the problematic space, mapping it, and rendering it remotely visible in telemetric fashioning. This is at least partially because the phyla of surveillance and discipline have not been properly integrated into human history. For example, their relationship to the god that sees everything, the notion of a moral education, and the role of conscience in character formation, along with many others.

as Deleuze and Guattari's favorite example, George Jackson, who writes "I may be running, but I'm looking for a gun as I go."[30] But the war machine may also be a capitalist organization or a media-communications organization that has reactionary characteristics. Deleuze and Guattari would say that the writer produces weapons for such revolutionary movements, but we have already seen the problem this fails to address. Forces both nomadic and sedentary are allied in the "total mobilization" of economic and military warfare; and such actions are frequently carried out in the name of National Security. The fact that the work of a writer may be both reactionary and nomadic (i.e. through the cultivation of a theory of subjects proving that they are controlled by processes of analysis) indicates that the minority of the miner-writer must take place in a locale beyond both the sedentary *and* the nomadic where there are no flows to follow. The so-called "revolutionary" movement of the nomad has been closed off by the global war machines: George Jackson's legacy has no doubt been crushed by the covert tactics of COINTELPRO.[31] Writers of revolutionary stature can no longer depend on some independent nomadic movement to carry the torch of their ideas. Revolution must now be understood as an itinerant writing, but from what material can it draw?

For minor writing to be revolutionary it must disrupt. The power of disruption is the interior exteriority of the products of writing, this interior exteriority is disruption itself, the disruption of an imminent structure by something transcendent to it and vice versa. To this extent, the nature of writing is always potentially revolutionary. It is no doubt this potential, this internal characteristic of revolution, that leads Deleuze and Guattari to understand writing as nomadic. It is also this very same structure that opens writing up to coercive appropriation. Writing may always be both the subject of enunciation and the subject of the statement. In the latter, writing is representative, it is the representation of objects. The statement is the logical structure of predication whereby all subjects copulate (through the copula and what we will later look at under the guise of delegated telemetrics) with their objects and their accidents. Any writing taken as representation is transformed by the constellation that receives it in that form. No doubt this can happen in the manner of tools as well as weapons.

All writing, even what has been emitted in events by the subject of enunciation for the sake of analyzing the subject of the statement, can be

---

[30] Quoted by Deleuze and Guattari, in *A Thousand Plateaus*, p. 204 from Jackson's *Soledad Brother.*

[31] Counter-Intelligence Program of the FBI initiated during the Nixon administration to break up Black nationalist movements and assassinate its leaders.

read as representation. When it is, it stands firm as the mirroring of objects over and against perceiving subjects. Television commercials and the instruction manuals for machinery equally strain to bring about a desired relation to the objects of the world by consumers and members of the labor force alike. Here the revolutionary potential of the minor writing is made to spin its wheels in place while upholding the status quo for both the nomad and the sedentary worker. Writing may emit in the manner of theory produced at state owned and operated institutions of higher learning where intellectuals serve the status quo. And this will no doubt operate co-extensively with a devout revolutionary potential. Academics may view themselves as revolutionaries producing in like manner while oblivious to the extent to which the distributive component of their production coerces the work into a collaborative category of reaction: a free market of ideas where revolution is bought and sold within the commercial zones of the state. This is especially true when the academic strives to exploit social media for the sake of achieving the status of "public intellectual." The work itself is weaponized or made useful for the sake of attracting attention from an audience, making the academic into the very line that is to be followed.

This condition suggests the remark at the outset regarding *the* question of theory. The danger is that the state or the war machine will appropriate the productions of state or corporate sanctioned minor writers (and other "intellectuals") to promote the combined movement of the two, and this not necessarily with the consent of the writer. Althusser's claim regarding the extent to which a revolutionizing of the intellectual must occur before the intellectual will cease to be a bourgeois comes to mind. In other words, there is a sort of "theory" that more readily lends itself to the malleable coercive forces of the state and war machine, a writing that more readily lends itself to the representation of objects and their analysis.

Juxtaposed to this writing, there would be a writing incapable of such cooption and which corresponds to the minor writing of the subject of enunciation: a writing that, because it writes, cannot be objectified in a mirroring representation. In such writing, the mirror of nature that is the traditional image of the mind, is mirrored in return and thus disrupted as a representing machine. Here, the itinerant writing's motion infects everything that was once meaningful and blurs its images through a perpetual shaking and trembling.[32] This would be a non-representative

---

[32] Shaking and trembling are not nomadic, they are not smooth but "function in fits and in starts". The jostling of the constant shaking of the mirror that grounds all representation stands midway between the smooth movement of the nomad and the coded, striated movement of the sedentary worker. Shaking is essentially itinerant movement.

writing that, when taken up by the logic of internal/external neo-fascist imperialism, would resist falling into the role of tool or weapon and deconstruct these same constellations where they have been appropriated. We are visualizing and hoping to demonstrate tools and weapons that are not objects, that carry within them their own faultiness as objects and as such destroy the projects of those who attempt to employ them.

It may be easy to be deceived here. It is not enough to merely write *about* shaking and trembling, rather writing must tremble and shake. Writing itself (and that means theory, practice, or any itinerant procedures that regulate action via technique or as technology) must tremble and shake so much that it can no longer *be itself.* It is when theorists write *about* trembling and shaking that they are most likely producing artifacts for coercive powers in the alternative mainstream flows of the state and the corporate war machine. To outstrip the "about," to perform an about face from representation and measurement at a distance, is to revolutionize theory and seeing along with it, it is to grind a new set of lenses. Confluent with this, it is to revolutionize practice: this is the significance of all itinerant writing. It is a writing that renounces all nomadic wandering without moorings along with the stationary decay of the sedentary. This renunciation is for the sake of a new form of action, a new characterization of the act residual to the forms of the technological regulation that determines what a body can do, that shapes its doing, and orients its behavior and possibilities. Such a writing performs the back and forth movement of a double gesture -the movement of the interior exteriority- which both disrupts the status quo and builds an itinerant replacement in the ashes of its remains as its residual.

It remains to be seen whether the revolutionary potential of minor writing can be actualized at scale in civilizations where reading and writing are becoming something of a lost art no longer suggesting a common pattern provider for action.[33]

---

[33] No doubt these last paragraphs only serve as the first awkward steps along the projected way of this itinerant minor writing. In addition to the current work, further steps might be taken through an examination of the "logic" this itinerant way provides and the constellation that such a logic suggests. This is part of the aim of *The Poetics of Resistance: Heidegger's Line.* 1996. Evanston: Northwestern University Press. *Telemetry Phenomenology Commonwealth* paints a darker picture by claiming at the outset that the association of reader and writer embodies exactly that intimate association which is the object of attack by telemetric social logic. The back and forth of this hope and cynicism inhabits everything that follows.

Carnival and Resistance

> He is often at his most provocative in the tiny fragment, in
> his jottings for future projects not yet worked out or beyond
> hope of publication; on the other hand, his longer worked-
> out pieces seem loosely structured, even luxuriously
> inefficient. Available evidence suggests that Bakhtin did not
> conceive even his published books as concise, self-sufficient
> theoretical statements. He thought, read, wrote down what
> he thought, and moved on; he was not in the habit of
> reworking his prose, because the important ideas always
> came around again in new contexts. Manuscripts themselves
> (this is by now legendary) were left to rot in damp cellars or
> were smoked away when cigarette papers ran out.[1]

Thinking, reading, writing, moving on.... This conveys more than a
quaint story about Mikhail Bakhtin, it suggests a point of view, a manner of
communion, of being in the world. Reading this I am reminded of a
wordplay in Derrida: *tombe* -it falls, the tomb. *Tombe* means both 'to fall'
and 'a tomb, crypt, or grave'. Bakhtin's relation to his own writing suggests
this wordplay as a threshold for our discussion. Words, ideas, texts fall
from his pen and hand, falling in a way without attachment, possession, or
paternalism. They fall as though they were out of control, engaged in a
dynamic they did not initiate. And this falling away is a falling in death to
the tomb or crypt of... Of what? Of a lost authority. An authority figure
whose trajectory toward death conditions his thinking and writing. Bakhtin
emphasizes the multiplication, decentering, and death of any authority
taking place in his writing; he lauds writing as a falling into the tomb of
language and all its symbolic resonance. This word-tumbling of pen and
hand, of manuscripts discarded and smoked, is the renunciation of all
monological authority of the subject in favor of a becoming other of one's
thoughts, an insertion of the other into thought, an essentially dialogical
thinking.

This insertion of the other divides the subject, splits its authority, and
then consumes its corpse on the funeral pyre analogous to the ashes at the

---

[1] From *Problem of Dostoevsky's Poetics* by Mikhail Bakhtin, translated and
edited by Caryl Emerson. Minneapolis: The University of Minnesota Press,
1989. p. xxxi. Page numbers to this source will hereafter be included in the text
in parenthesis.

end of a cigarette. Bakhtin's self-consumption, his holocaustal self-ingestion divides him from himself and calls the authorship of *all* his work into question, reveals a consummation of his project within and by itself. Bakhtin's corpus, his life's work left over, inscribes a deep rooted (rutted) doubt into the center of the subject of the work only to disperse the burned out remains of what can barely make sense to a reader. Therefore, it is problematical to say that "Dostoevsky" is the *subject* of the book written *about* him. And not only that, it is equally a problem to speak of a book written *by* Bakhtin. The tomblike text divides itself, folds in upon itself, ad infinitum leaving no coherent and univocal line of argumentation and cognition; but instead, a polyvalent network characterized in the manner of multiple tensions and local zones of force and resistance. Bakhtin's multi-voiced or polyphonic materialization in language can be shown to already suggest, evoke, or emit a discourse on power and the subject. By following through with this investigation and the way Foucault's work on power can be employed to strengthen the connections and expositions, we may begin to catch a cryptic glimpse of the way discourse on language interweaves indefinitely with discourse on power.

Direct discourse, discourse that deals with its matter in an unmediated fashion—that speaks directly *about* what is—is essentially objectifying. It stands back from its theme and, without taking an interest in its object, brings it into an order that drives the observation process itself: the sub-ject soliloquizes. Heidegger has described this in his work on the metaphysical presuppositions of modern thought whereby the entities experienced by an observer are determined before-hand as framed with a specifiable ontological quality. Insofar as the modern thinker starts from the desire for certainty in his knowledge of the world and moves on to design a foundation and an apparatus that will yield what he seeks, the subject is laid out as the basis of all certainty dispelling doubt and the object is represented as the form an entity takes in correspondence with a knowing subject. The subject is then a kind of authority regarding the manner of being of all that exists in the world since everything is determined as an object in its relation to this knowing subject. The subject itself only makes its appearance to itself in the form of objectified thoughts, thoughts represented in direct language that speaks about them. Hence the authority of the subject is also its subjection to itself, to its ordering and organizing effort at rendering the world clear and distinct, transparent to the activity of the thinking subject. The appearing subject is separated from the transcendental subject that conditions all manifest reality and which is represented in it. The acting thinking subject migrates to a position beyond the discourse in the way that an author might be said to reside outside the work, but retains an organizing principle (arche) regarding the objects within it.[2]

To the extent then that he does not wish to see in the novels of Dostoevsky a direct discourse on the part of a transcendent author who stands behind the words of each character, Bakhtin's *Problems of Dostoevsky's Poetics* cannot be understood as *about* anything. This point is imperative since Bakhtin's project requires that Dostoevsky be allowed to speak, or rather that what Dostoevsky has said already must now be listened to and engaged with; and for this to happen, Dostoevsky cannot be reduced to an object of study since objects, strictly speaking, cannot say anything at all. Great care is needed in making this point. We are not trying to say that Bakhtin's analysis aims at letting Dostoevsky emerge as a subject within the writings of Bakhtin hence making the work a dialogue of one subject with another. This would be impossible since the very concept of the subject in modern thought is so meditational that it does not allow itself to appear *as* a subject (i.e. the empirical subject is an object of inquiry). To expose Bakhtin's alternative, we must follow the threads in his argument.

> In this book we have sought to reveal the uniqueness of Dostoevsky as an artist, an artist who brought with him new forms of artistic visualization and was therefore able to open up and glimpse new sides of the human being and his life. Our attention has been concentrated on that new artistic position which permitted him to broaden the horizon of artistic visualization, which permitted him to look at the human being from a different artistic angle of vision. (270)

The claim is that in Dostoevsky's novels, a new genre is born(e), the polyphonic. This is clearly not only a matter for literature, human being has been regenerated in polyphony:

> We consider the creation of the polyphonic novel a huge step forward not only in the development of novelistic prose, that is, of all genres developing within the orbit of the novel, but also in the development of the *artistic thinking* of humankind. (270)

The passion of Dostoevsky's work is the polyphonic world of a new epoch of human thought. The human being as a thinking person is redefined and

---

[2]Cf. Heidegger's "The Age of the World Picture" in *The Question Concerning Technology,* translated by William Lovitt. New York: Harper & Row, 1977.

reconceived. No longer the res cogitans, this artistic thinker explodes the underlying principle (subiectum) of modernism.

> It seems to us that one could speak directly of a special *polyphonic artistic thinking* extending beyond the bounds of the novel as a genre. This mode of thinking makes available those sides of a human being, and above all the *thinking human consciousness and the dialogic sphere of its existence*, which are not subject to *artistic* assimilation from *monologic positions*. (270)

Bakhtin's historicism in speaking of a new discursive epoch should not be narrowly conceived. Literary genre *and* artistic thought are historically interwoven by the mediating fibers of language or discourse. Bakhtin describes numerous possible modifications of language ranging from "direct, unmediated discourse directed exclusively toward its referential object, as an expression of the speaker's ultimate semantic authority" to various kinds of "discourse with an orientation toward someone else's discourse (double-voiced discourse)." The significance of these investigations is not fully realized so long as they are read as literary studies. Instead, Bakhtin is revealing Dostoevsky, and artistic thinking generally, as a sign signifying the opening of a new era of language. In Dostoevsky's poetics and Bakhtin's dialogue with it, a new being of language is assigned. And this no doubt carries with it a new determination of thought and human being, a determination that is no longer modern.

Bakhtin's dialogue is not exclusively between the subject 'Bakhtin' and the subject 'Dostoevsky', rather it is a Bakhtinian dialogue with the dialogical character of Dostoevsky's writing. The "Dostoevsky" addressed in "Bakhtin's" book is already something more than a subject or author.

> A plurality of independent and unmerged voices and consciousnesses, a genuine polyphony of fully valid voices is in fact the chief characteristic of Dostoevsky's novels. What unfolds in his works is not a multitude of characters and fates in a single objective world, illuminated by a single authorial consciousness; rather a plurality of consciousness, with equal rights and each with its own world, combine but are not merged in the unity of the event. (6)

A conversation with Dostoevsky is already a conversation with many persons, and—since Bakhtin is equally many persons unto himself—"there

[is] already quite a crowd."[3] Dostoevsky, like Bakhtin, is disseminated among the polyphony of his work, strewn among the many voices of his characters and moods.

> Thus the new artistic position of the author with regard to the hero in Dostoevsky's polyphonic novel is a *fully realized and thoroughly consistent dialogic position,* one that affirms the independence, internal freedom, unfinalizability, and indeterminancy of the hero. For the author the hero is not "he" and not "I" but a fully valid "thou," that is, another and autonomous "I" ("thou art"). The hero is the subject of a deeply serious, *real* dialogic mode of address, not the subject of a rhetorically *performed* or *conventionally* literary one. (63)

To the extent that Bakhtin is engaged with Dostoevsky, the proposed logic internal to the corpus of Dostoevsky's work is repeated and inscribed *between* Dostoevsky and Bakhtin.

The polyphonic novel and its dialogical discourse become the matter *and* manner of discussion in the book. Bakhtin leaves off with any linguistic inquiry into language, any study of its objective nature, and embarks on a dialogue across decades with another thinker of language, Dostoevsky. The "idea" of such a language can only arise *between* the thought of these two thinkers where *between* has a "substantive" function, signifying the middle or milieu that spans their difference. Bakhtin frequently uses the word "unmediated" to describe the nature of object language intended by a lone speaker, suggesting he may want to reserve the notion of a mediated language for the dialogical. Dialogical language as a living language between points of view or positions becomes an interpersonal milieu or zone of mediation. Whereas the unmediated describes a present relation of the subject to the object, the mediated eludes the emphasis on the differends in favor of the relation or association itself.

> The chief subject of our investigation, one could even say its chief hero, will be *double-voiced discourse,* which inevitably arises under conditions of dialogic interaction, that is, under conditions making possible an authentic life for the word. (185)

Notice the way the word 'subject' may function here. It might mean

---

[3] *A Thousand Plateaus,* by Deleuze and Guattari. Translated by B. Massumi. Minneapolis: University of Minnesota Press, 1987. p. 3.

subject matter, but the meaning of the sentence—gesturing toward the 'authentic life for the word'—also implies that the language that is our double-voiced hero is a subject, a dialogical quasi-cogito. What Bakhtin is stating is made clearer a few sentences later: "[dialogical discourse] has a twofold direction—it is directed both toward the referential object of speech, as in ordinary discourse, and toward *another's discourse*, toward *someone else's speech*." (185) A milieu no doubt mediates between the two speakers who come to meet there. It is a place of community, not a mere meeting of the minds. For Bakhtin, mediation takes on its fullest sense when the speaker's relations to the objects in her surroundings occur only through and along with the voices and points of view of other speakers. This idea should not be confused with a sense of language as strictly a kind of reporting. Bakhtin is not referring to a situation in which language is directed first to the object and then to the other; but that the gestures occur at once, in the same blink of an eye. There is no private language, and no one learns it alone.

The object no longer stands opposite a directly referring and determining subject but is taken up into the polyphony of the milieu. The object gets caught up and carried away by the vast social sphere which grants the object its definition and thinghood. The relation to and association with the object becomes a social affair where the interpersonal space of language doubles as the world of things interwoven in contexts and involvements. Objects no longer stand for a being in itself of something real and experienceable, but are taken up in the dynamic of a milieu where they gain their being from the specific place granted to them within the whole and by its arrangement. Strictly speaking, the object no longer exists but yields to the disruptive world-bearing gesturing of the thing.[4]

Dostoevsky/Bakhtin (no doubt Bakhtin is one of Fyodor Mikhailovitch's many doubles) reveal the milieu of language, a polyphonic place where the dependent integrity of each speaker rings out clearly amid all others. We will be careful to distinguish Bakhtin's from other positions. This milieu is a meeting-place, but it is not necessarily a seamless community. Bakhtin's mediation involves no *aufhebung* or supersession of opposites into a higher unity, only the otherness of the different speakers is maintained as operative within living language itself. Speech relies on a distance between the speakers, a difference of both time and space.

---

[4] Cf. Heidegger's writing on the thing in a pair of essays found in *Poetry, Language, Thought*. translated by A. Hofstadter. New York: Harper & Row, 1975: "The Thing" and "Building Dwelling Thinking". Cf. also Derrida's discussion of a passage from one of these essays at the end of "Dissemination" in *Dissemination*, translated by B. Johnson. Chicago: University of Chicago Press, 1981.

Whereas homogeneity is not possible, agreement is not necessary and when it does occur it happens as an agreement *between* speakers or may be an agreement that there is a fundamental disagreement or zone of contention inhabited and constituted by all participants who agree on their terms and conditions of disagreement.

Earlier we mentioned the quasi-cogito of dialogical language as the subject of the investigation. We called it a quasi-cogito because the presence of the other interrupts the 'I think' in its traditional form. Or maybe not. Descartes' 'I think' was a dialogical proclamation with dreams, madness, and an evil demon mediating the response. Recall that in the first meditation these are stages of a reply to possible objections on the way to hyperbolical doubt meant to support the necessity of the ensuing search for certainty. The doubt of the first meditation is essentially dialogical between the meditator and the demons evoked on the cold winter evening before the fire. Even though Descartes eventually dispels the threat of doubt by securing a certain foundation that brings all dialogue to an end, the instigation to his thinking lies within the medium of the polyphonic. The milieu of dialogical language is a quasi-cogito because it contains the voices of many different speakers from which the individuating of a singular cogito can take place. The milieu of language, the apparently public place where language happens between speakers, is also a component of our ownmost inner thoughts prior to the determination of the subject (the subjugation of thought to the representation), our own "interior" meditations.[5]

Dialogue is not always a literal face to face encounter of one speaker with another but may involve a degree of hiddenness between them, an absence that manages to make its presence felt in the interior (or written) voice of the speaker:

> Especially significant and important for our further purposes
> is the phenomenon of hidden dialogicality, a phenomenon
> quite different from hidden polemic. Imagine a dialogue of
> two persons in which the *statements of the second speaker
> are omitted*, but in such a way that the general sense is not
> at all violated. The second speaker is *present invisibly*, his
> *words are not there*, but *deep traces* left by these words have
> a determining influence on all the present and visible words

---

[5] The scare-quotes are called for by the inscription of the other into thought since the other has been traditionally conceived as exterior to it. The comprehension of the meditation as an interiority inscribed with exteriority is already a movement away from the monological subjectivity and hence the inner sanctum of the intelligible author. Cf. Derrida's *Speech and Phenomena* or Lacan's *Four Fundamental Concepts of Psycho-Analysis*.

of the first speaker. We sense that this is a *conversation, although only one person is speaking,* and it is a conversation of the most intense kind, for each present, uttered *word responds and reacts with its every fiber to the invisible speaker,* points to something outside itself, beyond its own limits, to the *unspoken words* of another person. We shall see below that in Dostoevsky this *hidden dialogue occupies a very important place* and is very profoundly and subtly developed. (197, emphases added)

The public milieu is dialogical and polyphonic. A multitude of speakers come together there. Yet, we discover that the thoughts of each speaker are likewise dialogical and polyphonic. The hidden dialogue that is the active mental life shifts without notice. That is, the other voices that the speaker replies to, that are hidden in their own dialogue, may sometimes become the overt voice of the speaker at some later date while the once manifest subject may withdraw itself into hiddenness (it may fall into a tomb). The milieu where the multitude of voices come into dialogue repeats the dynamic of the individual voices themselves; or, and I do not think it matters here, the individual voices repeat the dynamic of the milieu. The quasi-cogito of the double voiced hero, language, is likewise the quasi-cogito of the speaker. In both cases a space is cleared where language *happens* (comes to pass) as a dialogue—so too in the art works of Dostoevsky.[6]

To the extent that the voice or point of view suggests a kind of self-sustaining unity and autonomy, Bakhtin bids us no longer think in terms of voices and points of view. Bakhtin's radical polyphony of the social milieu and language requires that we think in terms of positions, non-self-identical relations that gain their "sameness" from their relation to the rest of the milieu, i.e. their contexts, which are always multiple. Bakhtin thinks the positionality of language as carnival:

> Carnival celebrates the shift itself, the very process of replaceability, and not the precise item that is replaced. Carnival is, so to speak, functional and not substantive. It absolutizes nothing, but rather proclaims the joyful relativity of everything. (125)[7]

---

[6] This "hidden dialogicality" is reminiscent of the experience one might have when reading telemetry logs. The overt voice is the voice of the emitted events describing the system's operations, what is covert is the voice of the user as they navigate the system and trigger the emission of those events.

[7] Bakhtin's notion of carnival may be supplemented with Freud's notion of

Subjectivity as the absolute point of view (origin of *theoria*) is thus divided into many relations in the carnival sense of the world that characterizes the polyphonic linguistic milieu. This carnival, which is a world without spectators, is the living participation of all positions in a constantly shifting and supplementary dynamic or economy of "*the pathos of shifts and changes, of death and renewal.*" (124) To have a carnival sense of the world is to renounce the absolute certainty of the cogito in favor of the positionality of the shifting ground that proclaims the "*joyful relativity* of all structure and order, of all authority and all (hierarchical) position." (124) This relativity is the essential trace structure of the milieu characterized only by the constant substitution of one position with another, a never-ending dialogue of many different voices.[8]

At this point a good deal should be apparent. First off, the dynamic of language is a social dynamic, language always happens as the relation and association of different voices. Secondly, the points of view or "subject" positions that these voices speak are always making their point and then "moving on" in iterant fashion. And thirdly, following from the first two, the integrity of the various positions is determined within the milieu of mediation, as a voice within the dialogue of language (first there is the din of the dialogue and only afterward can the individual voice be discerned). It is not the integrity or dignity of an absolute value inhering in the rational subject, but of the integral association of a position amid the others with which it connects.

Foucault's description of power resembles Bakhtin's description of language. The variety of positions, the interwoven relation of each to all the

---

festival in *Totem and Taboo*. 1950. Translated by James Strachey. New York, NY: WW Norton & Company. In both cases participation and release from constraints are central. See for example, p. 174: "A festival is a permitted, or rather an obligatory, excess, a solemn breach of a prohibition. It is not that men commit the excesses because they are feeling happy as a result of some injunction they have received. It is rather that excess is of the essence of a festival; the festive feeling is produced by the liberty to do what is as a rule prohibited."

[8]"Trace structure" of course recalls Derrida's notion of the deconstructed sign that plays within a dynamic that has no units or elements but only marks that gain their position within the "whole" through their relation to the other marks in the play (in the carnival). Cf. Derrida's "Differance" in *Margins* and *Of Grammatology*, et al. Note should also be taken of the manner in which the logic of the milieu is described as a logic of substitution and shifting change which no doubt recalls Derrida's notion of supplementarity suggested in the text above.

rest, and its nature as a milieu are all consistent with Foucault's notion of "power." Yet there is an important distinction: Foucault uses precisely this topography of the milieu to explain how it is that power is NOT a monological component manifesting itself as authority from a centralized point of view. Rather, power and hence coercive relations of one position upon another (authority) *requires* the polyphony of the milieu. Foucault writes in *History of Sexuality volume I*:

> It seems to me that power must be understood in the first instance as the multiplicity of force relations immanent in the sphere in which they operate and which constitute their own organization; as the process which, through ceaseless struggles and confrontations, transforms, strengthens, or reverses them; as the support which these force relations find in one another, thus forming a chain or a system, or on the contrary, the disjunctions and contradictions which isolate them from one another; and lastly, as the strategies in which they take effect, whose general design or institutional crystallization is embodied in the state apparatus, in the formulation of the law, in the various social hegemonies.[9]

Foucault thinks that a unity results from this multiplicity, a crystallization or hegemony evolves out of the various interwoven positions of power's expression. This unity resembles Bakhtin's monologic authority only in appearance. Foucault thinks this unity results from an inequality between the forces within the milieu, an inequality Bakhtin has overlooked. Foucault writes that the basis of power comes from

> the moving substrate of force relations which, by virtue of their inequality, constantly engender states of power, but the latter are always local and unstable. The omnipresence of power: not because it has the privilege of consolidating everything under its invincible unity, but because it is produced from one moment to the next, at every point, or rather in every relation from one point to another. Power is everywhere; not because it embraces everything, but because it comes from everywhere. (93)

Even the unity of power that results from its spread is a polyphonic unity, a locally emerging voice that passes along the message of the dominating force relations and builds a wave of coercion present in all

---

[9]Michel Foucault, *The History of Sexuality, volume I: An Introduction.* translated by R. Hurley. New York: Vintage Books, 1980. p. 93.

corners of the social milieu. The positions of power are not endowed with care for one another, nor do they respect the voices of the various participants in the dialogue. We could say, following Bakhtin, that there is no dialogue at all, but instead a kind of ventriloquism. That is, power constitutes subjectivity out of the positionality of power relations. The individuated point of view alone and separated from the milieu of things and persons, the subject representing a completely reified and objectified world, is a construct of a power that materializes as a polyphonic world-alienated intersubjectivity.

> This form of power applies itself to immediate everyday life which categorizes the individual, marks him by his own individuality, attaches him to his own identity, imposes a law of truth on him which he must recognize and which others have to recognize in him. It is a form of power which makes individuals subjects. There are two meanings of the word *subject*: subject to someone else by control and dependence, and tied to his own identity by a conscience or self-knowledge. Both meanings suggest a form of power which subjugates and makes subject to.[10]

The subject is always subjected to the whim of power, carrying out its projects, allowing its expansion and spread into further and further reaches of the world. Power here is will to power, the will for power to continually expand itself, power as the absolute thirst for more power.

Foucault can be interpreted to suggest a distinction between the polyphonic and the dialogic. Polyphony is the condition for all coercion and never free of it, while the dialogic—as described by Bakhtin—is not possible. The milieu described in terms of relations of power infiltrates and saturates what Bakhtin has described in terms of language that could be either authentic or coercive. Foucault does not think the inequalities of the substrate of relations can be dissolved, and he frequently reminds us that any rebellion seeking to do so is doomed to take up the baton of a wily and malleable disciplinary power that is promoted best when it lurks beyond its conduits' gaze. Instead he seems to advocate a recognition of this quality of power as a first step toward its subversion, where subversion does not imply dissolution but turning force back upon itself, using it against itself. This is the nature of resistance; resistance is always confluent with power; every exertion of force meets with resistance: power's force is the resistance it

---

[10]Michel Foucault, "The Subject and Power" in Dreyfus and Rabinow, *Michel Foucault: Beyond Structuralism and Hermeneutics*. Chicago: The University of Chicago Press, 1983. p. 212.

affects in/as/through its object. My favorite analogy here is the sailor's relationship with the wind and the waves. Sailors seek to enlist otherwise hostile elements to the advantage of the vessel's movement. It would be ridiculous to contemplate the disappearance of the sea and the wind while maintaining an interest in sailing. We might say that the disappearance of the elements would be contrary to the objectives of the sailors. Likewise, all resistance.

We should not, however, be quick to group Bakhtin with those thinkers of the dialogue who have been frequently criticized for their oversight of the power infected nature of discourse.[11] We would be well advised to recall the remarks we made earlier regarding the construction of the subject out of the dialogical doubt of the modern meditations. To the extent that subjectivity arises out of the dialogicality of doubt, and then proceeds to transcend the monological reality of objects, Bakhtin's carnival offers us a view of resistance that suggests not only resisting the subjugation of the subject in the moment of certainty, but a resistance in the face of the construction of the transcendental authority. From Bakhtin we gain an understanding of dialogical discourse that is not yet subject in any shape or form. The so called "subjectivity" of language, the hero of the double-voiced discourse, is a quasi-cogito that resists entering into the transcendental logic of subjectivity regardless of whether the subject is understood as the self-knowing or subjugated individual controlled from within by conscience or without by coercion, or as the transcendental organizing principle of the world—its substance or substrate.

Foucault, on the other hand, may not be so fortunate in avoiding the transcendentality of the subject. Foucault appears to continue thinking the "form" of power on the model of a subjectivity (or authority) beyond the world and acting by way of manifested relations within it. Power, as a substrate, repeats the logic of the subiectum, of the fundamental and transcendental guarantor of all that exists and that is problematical at the heart of all subjectivity.[12] The level at which Bakhtin's resistance to the subjection of the multiple positions of discourse to power takes place is, in a sense, prior to the constitution of subjectivity and therefore offers an alternative formulation of resistance. The wedge that is driven into the

---

[11] i.e. Hans-Georg Gadamer in Habermas' criticism of him. Cf. the appendix in *Knowledge and Human Interests*.

[12] In other words, the subject that has authority over the world of representations through its determination beforehand of what counts as an existing entity is being hypostatized in Foucault and renamed "power." Just as the perceptions of the subject are multiple, so too the relationships of power. Hence, Foucault's "subject" is more like Hume's than Descartes' but it still repeats the logic.

subject in Bakhtin's "dialogue" is driven into the heart of power as well, into the very source of all coercion thus letting the source overflow and, eventually, dry up.

The carnival suggests a way of life that has stepped back from the hierarchical power relations of the transcendentally organized social milieu apparently described by Foucault:

> Carnival is the place for working out, in a concretely sensuous, half-real and half-play-acted form, a new mode of interrelationship between individuals, counterposed to the all-powerful socio-hierarchical relationships of noncarnival life. The behavior, gesture, and positions (social estate, rank, age, property) defining them totally in noncarnival life, and thus from one vantage point of noncarnival life become eccentric and inappropriate. *Eccentricity* is a special category of the carnival sense of the world, organically connected with the category of familiar contact; it permits— in concretely sensuous form—the latent sides of human nature to reveal and express themselves. (123)

Resistance, not absolute resistance, that so widely saturates the milieu that it resists the imposition of a transcendental origin, suggests a social determination or way of life that is beyond the reach of power. More to the point, it inscribes resistance into the heart of power thus breaching a passageway that no longer allows for the transcendence of power. Resistance no longer "beyond" power takes up residence within a power coopted through its disruption. Both the individual author and the overarching author of existence become "quasi-cogitos" and resist all subjugation in favor of their eccentric selves.[13]

---

[13]It is no small criticism of the carnival that it has been a potentially dehumanizing environment for women (and others), portraying the female body as grotesque, etc. as pointed out by Mary Russo in her "Female Grotesques: Carnival and Theory" in *Feminist Studies/Critical Studies*, edited by T. de Lauretis. Bloomington, IN: Indiana University Press, 1986. This suggests that all voices can be allowed to ring out and articulate points of view that are saturated with powerful interests and biased orientations. To the extent that any historically occurring carnival fails to resist the subjugation and coercion of some of its participants and thus only surfaces a partial vision of the positions at work, it is likely a carnival in name only for the sake of distracting and entertaining its participants. It is interesting to note that the discussion of carnival in the Dostoevsky book does not include such discussions of the grotesque and "freakish" nature of the participants. The "eccentricity" of the self in carnival, I take it, is more a reference to its

This suggested "appearance" of the transcendental in Foucault's thinking may have been disrupted in a similar fashion. The appearance of course was that the being of power as "substrate" repeated the logic of the transcendental in the work of one whose task should have been to supersede it. That is, Foucault seems to repeat the logic of the Enlightenment in his "theory" of power when the genealogical project seems to necessitate overturning this same logic. Foucault has long since characterized the nature of power as *essentially* resistance: every exertion of force has a concomitant resistance, as mentioned above. In this way, power ceases to overcode the entire milieu of relations and becomes divided within itself as both coercion and resistance like the example of the sailing vessel demonstrated. Bakhtin helps us to de-transcendentalize Foucault, to read Foucault on resistance as a thinker of the carnival who steps back in a way that attempts to erase the hierarchies and coercive discipline of power. Bakhtin can be made to teach us to leave the transcendental reading of Foucault to its appearances. And at the same time, to resist the urge to assign any revolutionary or progressively political content to it. The dynamics of the dialogical precede any conclusions of value or ethical preference.

Bakhtin writes in "Discourse in the Novel" concerning "the contradiction-ridden, tension-filled unity of two embattled tendencies in the life of language,"[14] that language tends toward both a centripetal unifying and centralizing movement as well as a centrifugal multiplying and decentering movement. Like the telemetry event that both emits and is collected, the utterance articulates the tension between two forces. Every utterance embodies in its concrete nature both the centralizing and decentralizing capacity of language. The position or mark of the utterance is both a concrete statement and a referential and multiplying relation within a larger context.

> The authentic environment of an utterance, the environment in which it lives and takes shape, is dialogized heteroglossia, anonymous and social as language, but simultaneously concrete, filled with specific content and accented as an individual utterance.[15]

---

decentered nature, its resistance to subjugation and hence its refusal to *be* a "freak". There, in that other carnival, all desires are permitted and legitimate, all can be subject to advertisement and targeted marketing.

[14]"Discourse in the Novel" in *The Dialogic Imagination* by Mikhail Bakhtin, edited M. Holquist, translated by C. Emerson and M. Holquist. Austin, TX: University of Texas Press, 1981. p. 272.

[15] Bakhtin, *The Dialogic Imagination*, p. 272.

So long as the decentering tendency is at work, the utterance is "individual" without being subjected to an order. The disseminating power of the centrifugal, however, is materialized through the ongoing concretion of the centripetal. Therefore, the possibility of a transcendental origin is overcome by the facticity of the utterance within the polyphonic world. There is nothing beyond the utterance which alone embodies the tensions of the competing forces in its own "trace structure." An utterance may be experienced as a liberating act of resistance while simultaneously embodying the dynamics of hidden power: the emission is collected and fed back for the sake of improving upon the spontaneity of event production.

This tension explains how it is possible for the individuality of the position to yield to coercion, to become subjugated by an ordering principle that is itself, at least at first, an utterance building up force through the spread of alliances between various positions. It also explains how it is possible to consider resistance and power in some way other than a metaphysical hierarchy of realms and regions. The uncovering of the essential tensions of the utterance is already the uncovering of a resistance to the subjugation of the position, a subjection that is nothing other than the acceptance of a unifying order that dissolves all tensions into an incorporated lifeworld with all forces moving in common toward a unified aim. In Bakhtin's terms, to hear the utterance as a two-way tension is to no longer listen to the monological intentions of authority that seek a subject in every point of view, but to carnivalize the utterance as always already dialogical and decentering.

In the moment when resistance is understood to have divided power and broken up the transcendental logic of the subject, we catch a glimpse of the connection that exists between Bakhtin's discourse on language and Foucault's discourse on power. The becoming carnival of the world is a becoming language *and* a becoming power. The relativity of the carnival that disperses the hierarchy of subjectivity and its appended identity, evokes the topography of power right along with the topography of language. Language, dialogical language, is a milieu of resistance and force no less than the Foucaultian economy of power is an essentially discursive milieu, where "discursive" suggests more than just natural language, but the differentiation of gestures and positions: carnival.

Language can be merely one organization of differentiation among others. Discourse, as the articulation of signifiance (in Lacan's sense[16]), is

---

[16] In terms of the indefinite article, there is a possible opportunistic reading of Lacan such that the child's experience takes place in the context of a world-

precisely that trace structure which Foucault frequently calls "the relationship," of which there are numerous kinds: power, communication, and objective capacities. The "field" in which these various modes of relationship "overlap" is precisely what we here refer to as discourse and as the field of "transcendental" power inscribed and supplemented by resistance and immanence.[17] It is a mistake to think (a mistake equally for Foucault as for any reader of him) that a "substrate" of relations can be "transcendental." The role that the "relation" has taken in the carnivalesque forms of thought is that of the supplement of all metaphysics of substance whereby the relation is nothing substantial even if it is a measured event. The invisibility of the "relation" does not imply its transcendentality unless one is to continue to think it in terms of a metaphysical opposition between the visible and the invisible, an opposition happily exploited by telemetry as "shadow text" and which orders the hierarchy of any foundationalist analytical project for the sake of implicit social orders that are unified in their logic of association, involvement, and positioning. When we think we have broken free of it, we are most in its grasp.

---

structuring organization's desire. This awkward phrase replaces "mother" because—from the point of view of the child—"mother" is merely an organizing structure. "Mother," in the sense that any adult gives it, already presumes a set of social-family relationships that have not yet developed. This same pattern, the identification with the object of the Mother's desire so as to obtain the object of one's own desire, characterizes all organizational occupation of experience, all partial phenomenology. With organization, as a realization of zones of significance and having been cast as an intelligent being, the person as indefinite article can be refracted in an identification with the object of the organization's "desire." The phallus floats in the play of signifiers in these various organizational structures. Cf. Lacan's *Formations of the Unconscious*. 2017. Translated by Russell Grigg. Cambridge, UK: Polity Press. Chapter XII.

[17]Cf. "The Subject and Power" pp. 217-8. Note also that, following Derrida in many places (i.e. *Of Grammatology*), we seek to supplement the transcendental which (and this should be clear to anyone who thinks the transcendental in a Kantian manner of a purity, eternity and intelligibility of rules that condition the manifestation of whatever can be phenomenally) so as to erase the very possibility of the transcendental. There can be no transcendental supplement: it is a contradiction in terms.

Producing Enlightened Subjects
the rational method of power[1]

"Rational method" in the title is redundant since rationality from Descartes to Kant is always methodological and method is always rational. We think we can prove that "rational method *of power*" is also redundant in the projects of these thinkers and will try to show that "the rational method of power" is not aiming at the discovery of theoretical knowledge but at the production of facts, the most fundamental of which is that the individual inquirer is always the subject of a conditioning procedure. We hope to introduce the reader to the basis for an attack on Enlightened subjectivity; and to do so in a manner suggesting that attempts to escape this attack on subjectivity—while maintaining notions of universal procedures[2]— fail to understand the problem.

The first sentence of the "First Meditation" already suggests the historical context of the inquiry:

> Some years ago I was struck by the large number of falsehoods that I had accepted as true in my childhood, and by the highly doubtful nature of the whole edifice that I had subsequently based on them.[3]

Here there is a strong suggestion of a dawning Enlightenment. Childhood suggests what Kant would later refer to as the "self-incurred immaturity"[4] of

---

[1] This chapter was edited by Michael Roth and based on a longer version written by Laura Haber. 1997. *Enlightened Subjectivity: the rational method of power*. Urbana, IL: University of Illinois at Urbana-Champaign Archives.

[2] In other words, procedures that are given any kind of universal status like actions posited by a will or action oriented toward understanding. It is ultimately our concern that this sort of universality is the way in which "practice" has been inhabited historically by metaphysical principles. This applies to classical figures such as Kant as much as to more recent thinkers like Habermas.

[3] From *The Philosophical Writings of Descartes*, volume II, translated by J. Cottingham, R. Stoothoff, and D. Murdoch. Cambridge University Press, 1984. P. 12.

[4] Cf. "What is Enlightenment?" by Immanuel Kant in *The Philosophy of Kant*, edited by Carl J. Friedrich. Modern Library, 1977. P. 132.

"man" from which he emerges into the light of reason. Descartes'
Meditations begins with the realization that this immaturity must instigate
an attempt to more firmly establish knowledge. Enlightenment is a form of
growth, the actualization of a capacity previously denied or inhibited. The
individual gains the "courage to use one's intelligence without being guided
by another."[5] Although this reading points forward to Kant, it was Kant who
pointed backward to the Copernican revolution as the initiation of this
process of development when he offered his *Critique of Pure Reason* as a
philosophical foundation for the new science. The scientist, Copernicus or
Galileo, is an investigator making observations that are to be interpreted
without dependence on the dogmatic doctrines of the ruling tradition.
Insofar as the scientist's investigations attempt to overcome the immaturity
of beliefs based on tradition, the new science rises as an onslaught of
individual attempts to become enlightened through the employment of
rational understanding in search of fundamental truths.

The implication of an entire edifice in the dubious beliefs of the
immature thinker is not an attack on the world as such, but on the system
of beliefs and ideas that the individual has about the world. Descartes does
not think he needs to demonstrate the necessity of starting with an attempt
to verify the beliefs inquirers have about objects, since this has long been
accepted by scientists. In some sense, it is this presupposition that points at
the crisis of his age. The battle that had been raging between church and
science for nearly 150 years was implicit in the abstraction of the believer
from the content of his beliefs. The world is now at issue in a competition
between two systems of belief, putting individuals in a position where they
must decide between the theories. Thinking of them as systems of belief
already suggests that each of them is questionable, merely a theory to be
evaluated and not accepted with certainty. That one view has holes and
weaknesses has been clear for over a century, but for various reasons the
individual could not know immediately and without reflection which one
was true. The world lost any absolute or certain status and became
something viewed as an explanatory scheme that may or may not turn out
to be correct.

In this context, the term "world picture"[6] yields an image of the world

---

[5] Kant, "What is Enlightenment?", p. 132.

[6]The term comes from Heidegger and does not suggest the similar notion
of "worldview" in the least. For Heidegger, the world is a picture insofar as it is
set up opposite an alienated observer or agent. This subject is essentially
different in kind from the objective world that is only available to the subject
through representations (*vorstellen*), images that "stand before" the mind, in
much the same way that a picture appears to an observer strolling through a
museum. Cf. Heidegger's "Age of the World Picture" in *The Question*

exhausted in its relation to the individual inquirer. This entails that the history of philosophy is not one world picture following another, but that the possibility of understanding the world as something "out there" and viewed by a distanced human observer is exclusively an element of the historical epoch guided by the nascent science. There is only one way of looking at a world conceived in an essential relation to an observer trying to obtain knowledge of it, and that is the manner provided by the scientific method of inquiry. This unique manner of seeing may still direct itself toward different schemes implying that the crisis between these two positions has in some sense put "man" outside the world and looking upon it as one might look at a picture. It seems to follow that the choice between these two explanations is not a neutral one. Only a scientist would feel the power of this crisis in these terms, the traditional church's approach had not been characterized this way and any adherent would not consider opting for the scientific position as a choice between theories. From their point of view, the dynamic was entirely different and amounted to an attack on sacred tradition by secular fashion that threatened to change the very meaning of existence.

This new science offered a view of the individual's relationship to the world that attempted to give "man" a more prominent position as the subject of knowledge. "Subject," need not mean "individual observer." That is only the interpretation of it provided by modern science. "Subject"—derived from the Latin "subicere"—just means "to bring under." In its logical use, the "subject" is that element in a proposition about which various predicates are either affirmed or denied, making it the free-standing basis upon which various qualities may be said to rest. For the Church, the metaphysical subject of all qualities was God, the self-caused creator of everything that exists. To say that the inquirer had become the subject is to say that the world as picture is to be based on the foundation of the inquiring observer in his methodical and systematic activity of calculating precise representations of the world: everything that is, is an idea for "man." Once the world has been conceived as two conflicting theories, the scientific attitude has already won the battle for subjectivity: even if the inquirer publicly devotes himself to the church.

Returning to Descartes:

> I realized that it was necessary, once in the course of my life,
> to demolish everything completely and start again right from

Concerning Technology and other essays, translated by W. Lovitt. Harper & Row, 1977.

the foundations if I wanted to establish anything at all in the
sciences that was stable and likely to last.[7]

Here, the description of his beliefs as though they were a system should
become apparent: for a system is just a structure that follows in accordance
with a foundation synthetically connected to the elements of the structure.
Additionally, we learn that grounded beliefs are the most important
elements of "science" and that the subject as individual inquirer will be the
axiomatic element of this system. Stability (and perhaps predictability) have
been assigned great value and require a systematic approach to be achieved.
Finally, some suspicions concerning the coherence of this approach
become apparent. Descartes calls this Meditation "What can be called into
doubt" and says that he is going to wipe out all his unfounded beliefs for
the sake of building a new and secure system of knowledge. The
implication is that he will be neutral regarding the actual beliefs established
in his investigations, and we may now wonder whether he can really do this.

In his *Principles of Philosophy*, Descartes says that "we possess only two
modes of thinking: the perception of the intellect and the operation of the
will."[8] In the description of this principle, he claims that "desire, aversion,
assertion, denial and doubt are various modes of willing."[9] At the outset of
his *Meditations*, Descartes does not destroy his confidence in doubt for
withholding belief, in the systematic structure of beliefs, and in the light of
reason. The act of doubting is a modification of the will that is engaged in
the procedure of doubting beliefs and thus performing methodical inquiry
with the use of reason. These presupposed elements in the *Meditations* are
not beliefs but procedural activities associated with the method and manner
of inquiry. The what of the world is in question whereas the how is not.

This amounts to a characterization of two different modes of thinking
where beliefs are only associated with the intellectual modification of
thought or "perception." Since the will may be involved in activity without
being the content of a belief, it need not be called into question along with
the veracity of all beliefs. The entire project of the *Meditations* is not at all
concerned with calling volition into question. Descartes never says he will
annihilate everything that exists, only that he will destroy all his beliefs.
What is presupposed in the *Meditations* is a method or rational activity of
the will for proceeding in systematic fashion in investigations for the sake
of securing beliefs through the establishment of axioms.

The Second Meditation, with the subtitle "The nature of the human

---

[7] Descartes, *Volume II*, p. 12.

[8] Descartes, *Volume I*, p. 204 #32.

[9] Descartes, *Volume I*, p. 204 #32.

mind, and how it is better known than the body," is initially oriented by the question as to whether anything remains after the previous development of a hyperbolic doubt. Descartes cannot doubt that he exists. Insofar as it is his will that asserts itself in the skeptical arguments, his own existence is guaranteed. The first and certain fundamental belief of the Cartesian system of knowledge is the belief in the certainty of a thinking thing's existence through an act of doubt. The argument is that the one belief I cannot doubt is the belief in which the willing/thinking thing is the content. In saying that this belief cannot be doubted, he turns the willing and inquiring thinker into an object of belief. And this is a belief he can have with certainty since it is not possible to assert the will in doubt while asserting a doubt about the existence of the will: one cannot doubt that one is doubting if doubt is a modification of the will.

Descartes establishes the thinking thing as the subject and axiomatic foundation of all knowledge. When he discovers that his activity as thinker cannot be doubted and thus can be asserted with certainty, he discovers that the activity of thinking is itself the foundation of all knowledge concerning the existence and nature of things. Descartes sets himself into the picture. That is, in the second meditation Descartes places the willing/thinking thing into the world of things as the object of a belief, the content of an assertion of the will. "I think, therefore I am" is not the construction of a world picture, but the insertion of objectified human being into that picture. The picture itself was established through the method of the will; the systematic way reason carries out its calculating activity relative to every content of belief. This first and most certain of beliefs is the foundation for knowledge that guarantees the effectiveness of the scientific approach to the world. It is because this procedure of the will allows a certain and fundamental belief upon which all further beliefs can be built that its method can be trusted to yield truth.

This reading of Descartes more thoroughly situates him relative to his era, more convincingly presents him as a philosopher dedicating himself to metaphysical arguments for the sake of securing an epistemological basis for modern science. He rejects the theological position that abides by Aristotelian and Ptolemaic conceptions of motion which place God at the center of creation and as the guarantor of everything that exists for human experience and understanding. God is the supreme being and the universe is accessible to any human attempt at understanding it only because God acts as a purveyor of underlying principles. Rejecting this threatens the world with anarchy, it sets the world up as picture and threatens to undermine any claim to truth in favor of perspectives concerning what appears in the picture. Only our rational method can protect us from this relativism.

As a philosopher of the new science, Descartes is not inventing the scientific method of inquiry. He is merely utilizing it in philosophical reflection for the sake of showing that such a method does admit of certainty and principles that can guide and ground knowledge. He wants to undermine the church's charge that the new science and its method cannot provide true beliefs. This should further explain why it is an error to think that a crisis of world views is being decided by a neutral observer. The new science's attack on the Church's project created the crisis insofar as method enabled an ontological orientation toward world as picture. Descartes never attempts neutrality in this way of thinking. Instead, he began with the will and set up doubt—the withholding of the assertion of the will—as a form of scientific neutrality that distances the observer from the world and enables better results in any investigation. *Neutrality* is itself a facet of the scientific attitude where the world is understood as a place where autonomous individual observers carry out procedures of calculation and measurement for the sake of securing truths about the objects of belief constituting the world picture. An actor employing such methodology is neutral by definition.

What the Cartesian project seems to suggest, if we are reading him right, is that the subject can be an object. That is, the foundation and guarantee of all knowledge is itself the content of a belief, which means that the thinking thing is objectified as the content of the fundamental belief of epistemology. A strange situation follows since Descartes has all along suggested that it is a belief that lies at the bottom of all systems of knowledge. The truth that lies at the bottom is discovered only because of a right use of reason in the method of carrying out the scientific project. "I think, therefore I am" lies at the bottom of all knowledge, but "I will" conditions all activity in the sciences in pursuit of knowledge. Both appear to be essential to the truthful nature of science, for the new science to acquire knowledge it must use the right method and base its results on the right foundation: the scientific method is necessary for arriving at the truth and, as Descartes claims to have proven, is capable of arriving there. Yet, Descartes does not prove the first element, the necessity of the method for truth. He cannot prove it since all attempts at such a proof would employ the method in question to say something about a belief itself distinct from methodical activity.

It seems like there is an insurmountable problem here. The scientist wants to be able to claim that his own will, methodically employed, is the subject of knowledge; whereas the Cartesian proof only allows him to claim that his will—understood as an object or content of belief, is the subject. Without this assurance of the scientific method's claims to the establishment of truth, it seems that the scientific approach will constantly be in danger of failing to provide anyone with exhaustive knowledge. What is in question here is the *necessity* of the will's relationship to truth. In other words, are there other kinds of truth than the kind offered by the rational scientific approach or does the methodology guarantee a unique status for the sciences and their characteristic form of inquiry?

The scientific method is supposed to be derived from something that is essential to the whole of nature. It is supposed to represent a universal dynamic of that nature wired into the ground plan of the new science. The project of mathematically calculating and measuring the world hypothesizes that the world is ready and willing to be measured and calculated so that these activities are calibrated by the very dynamics and principles through which nature operates. For this reason, method in the new science cannot be one approach among others, it must be universal and the success of science in rendering explanations about natural phenomena is the strength of that hypothesis. The philosopher must be able to show, somehow, that the willing inquirer is himself, in and through his activity, the subject of what is true and the embodiment of the method.

If we have explained this clearly enough, it should be apparent how important Kant's philosophy was to the project of insuring the claim to universality by the new science. Kant, in his *Critique of Pure Reason*,[10] develops a new form of "proof" for establishing this claim without turning the inquirer into an object. This "transcendental deduction" has two steps: 1) a deduction of the necessary unity underlying all experience; and 2) a deduction of the necessary concepts employed in experience.

In the first step, Kant shows that experience is a continuum of intuitions linked together in appearance by an observer who is not experiencing the world as an assortment of unrelated and scattered perceptions. In experience the world appears meaningful, full of objects and things. These representations must be put together from across space and time out of a "manifold of intuitions" (or raw and scattered sense data) to form synthetic unities for representing agency or activity. The world does not unify itself in giving itself to experience but must be unified by an active procedure of synthesis whereby "objects" come into existence as meaningful components. These "objects" are nothing other than the formation of a representation appearing based on the activity of a faculty of synthesis called the "unity of apperception."

In the second step of the deduction, Kant tries to describe what the unity of apperception must be doing in order to achieve a representation of the manifold of intuition. The synthesis of the manifold is established by the unity of apperception through the employment of a priori categories. These concepts are not ideas given to us through experience or innate and

---

[10]Immanuel Kant. *Critique of Pure Reason*. Translated by N. Kemp Smith. St. Martin's Press, 1965. Cf. especially the A edition of the Transcendental Deduction.

distinct from experience, but are conditions, or rules to be followed, for having any experience at all. Thus, they are always involved in synthetic or empirical relations to objects. Kant recognizes that this position must sound strange since one of the implications is that "nature" is in some way constructed by the observer. This means that it would be non-sense to speak of nature as "out there" independently of experience. "Nature" is a construct of the human mind, conceived formally, and its status independent of observation is opaque by definition. Because our interpretations of nature are always derived through our cognitive capacity to experience it, "nature" is always relative to the human apperception of it. This means it is a contradiction to talk about the way nature is in itself *for* an observer. The employment of these categories no longer admits of being called laws of the inherent dynamic of the world, but only rules for the sake of experiencing the world.

Several conclusions can be drawn from this discussion of Kant's transcendental deduction of the necessary conditions for experience: 1) Like Descartes, Kant is working within the framework of the world as picture where the representational nature of entities is their essential relatedness to an experiencing agent who applies itself to the sense data so as to picture the world. 2) Unlike Descartes, Kant is not looking for a belief that is the foundation of the system of knowledge obtained in experience; rather Kant is trying to establish the activity of the observer as the subject of all experience and all picturing of the world. The alienation of method from the subject of knowledge, so problematic for Descartes, is overcome by Kant. That is, the only conditions that yield truth claims in the realm of experience are derived from the rule-based activity of the self-conscious unity underlying all experience: the method is hard-wired into human cognition. The agent for the acquisition of knowledge is the foundation for all research and empirical investigation into the truths of nature. This is just one more way of saying that the activity of the will in its procedural inquiry (or method) is the universal form for achieving knowledge about the world. 3) Again, in opposition to Descartes, for Kant this activity is never the object of a belief but maintains only a transcendental efficacy in relation to the objects of experience. To make such an activity into an object of a representation is always to divorce it from its essentially procedural state. Kant thinks this can happen, but that such a belief formed about the subject is not a foundation for knowledge and need not be. Instead, it is an essentially empirical ego that is never the subject of knowledge, but always an object for knowledge, an object about which the active understanding can have knowledge. To put this in terms that will suggest the work of Michel Foucault: the empirical ego is not a subject for knowledge but is subjected to knowledge, imprisoned in a picture formulated by the transcendental ego's theoretical gaze.

Foucault, in *The Order of Things*, calls this the doubling of man: "Man, in the analytic of finitude, is a strange empirico-transcendental doublet, since he is a being such that knowledge will be attained in him of what renders all knowledge possible."[11] The transcendental ego conceived as the subject of knowledge is a constituting activity lending coherence to the systematic deployment of categories in experience. As such, it extends beyond the boundaries of finitude enclosing the empirical world. The empirical ego, on the other hand, has been transformed with the transference of subjectivity to the transcendental realm. According to Foucault, this is the finite man who is always an empirical object and is in the process of being constituted by the activity of human sciences (including psychology). Kant's attempt to "fix" Descartes seems to have mystified the subject of knowledge by placing it beyond experience. The transcendental subject is the agent of all scientific investigation, but it is unfamiliar to those same investigations while reducing the familiar or known "man" to an object of science.[12]

The unfamiliarity of the transcendental being of the will is not a problem to Kant because it resides very close to us insofar as it has a constitutive role to play in the dynamic of our empirical knowledge of the world. Systematic method cannot be conceived as an object of experience, it still cannot be evaluated as one would evaluate a belief or a truth claim, but it is impossible to have any beliefs at all without it insofar as scientific method has now become inextricably identified with the willful understanding of "man." This doubles man as subject and object where the subject is what he never sees and never thinks about (because concepts can only attach to objects). Strictly speaking, the subject is the unthought being of man.

---

[11] Michel Foucault. *The Order of Things*. Vintage Books Edition, 1973. P. 318. The implied reference to Heidegger is out of scope here, but in the following chapters the issue will be revisited.

[12] Another way to spin this might be to show that Descartes dismantles privacy for an individual investigator by situating their knowledge in a persistent relationship to an all-knowing, all-seeing, and all-powerful deity. Such a "surveillance state" is transcendent to the subject. In the Kantian maneuver, the individual investigator and the certainty of the deity have disappeared in favor of a universal set of categories immanent in all rational beings across all of their experience. The all-knowing and all-seeing power is transcendental and thus occupies any agency where the individual investigator achieves its status through its empirically constrained objectivity. Privacy is not violated by a deity coming from above, but is inhabited by universal categories shared by all such beings capable of cognition.

> In this form, the *cogito* will not therefore be the sudden and
> illuminating discovery that all thought is thought, but the
> constantly renewed interrogation as to how thought can
> reside elsewhere than here, and yet so very close to itself;
> how it can *be* in the forms of non-thinking. The modern
> *cogito* does not reduce the whole being of things to thought
> without ramifying the being of thought right down to the
> inert network of what does not think.[13]

The dynamic of the cogito is a double movement whereby the thing which
we know to think, does not think at all (because it is an object); while the
thing we do not have the capacity to think about at all (because it is
transcendental) is what performs the act of thinking.

This mystification of thought in the doubling of "man" destroys any
possibility of "man" becoming self-present to himself as "man." The days of
the simplicity of the "I think, therefore I am" have been destroyed. When
"man" asserts his existence, he does so as an object that does not think
whereas the assertion itself, where thinking takes place, does not yield any
concrete existence for "man." Kant has resolved the problem of the
universality of the scientific method only to inextricably alienate "man" from
himself. Foucault goes on to read the whole of "modernity" as man's attempt
to overcome this alienation:

> For though this double may be close, it is alien, and the role,
> the true undertaking, of thought will be to bring it as close to
> itself as possible; the whole of modern thought [modernity?]
> is imbued with the necessity of thinking the unthought—of
> reflecting the contents of the *In-Itself* in the form of the *For-
> Itself*, of ending man's alienation by reconciling him with his
> own essence, of making explicit the horizon that provides
> experience with its background of immediate and disarmed
> proof, of lifting the veil of the Unconscious, of becoming
> absorbed in its silence, or of straining to catch its endless
> murmur.[14]

Foucault thinks this state of alienation scares or threatens "man," it is
somehow dangerous to him. How so?

When the Cartesian and Kantian support for the fundamental role of
the will or understanding in scientific method is demonstrated it becomes
apparent that the nature of science as the pursuit of knowledge for its own

---

[13] Foucault, *The Order of Things*, p. 324.

[14] Foucault, *The Order of Things*, p. 327.

sake is questionable. Because science is essentially a universally willful procedure, its characteristics are like those commonly assigned to the will: (self-)control and mastery (over nature). When science treats the world as a picture it understands the existence of everything exclusively in terms relative to the human agent. There is nothing else to things in the world than what humans can find there in their investigations. This picture is not at all destroyed by Kant. Instead, its universality is demonstrated. Kant shows that the world would be meaningless without the active employment of categories. Furthermore, Kant conceives of these categories as rules for understanding. Understanding itself becomes a kind of action that manipulates objects into meaningful form. Because this "man" is a doublet, he is not only in control, he is—in his more familiar being, the object of such control: that is, he is unfamiliar with that thinking part of himself which performs the dominating activities while he is most familiar with that unthinking part of himself that is dominated as an object set into the picture of the world.

In *Dialectic of Enlightenment*, Adorno and Horkheimer claim that the instrumental rationality essential to the Early Modern age is first and foremost a technique for control.

> The system the Enlightenment has in mind is the form of knowledge which copes most proficiently with the facts and supports the individual most effectively in the mastery of nature. Its principles are the principles of self-preservation. Immaturity is then the inability to survive. The burgher, in the successive forms of slaveowner, free entrepreneur, and administrator, is the logical subject of the Enlightenment.[15]

To the extent that "coping" becomes reason's greatest aim, reason is instrumental with utilitarian aims of preservation where that suggests the struggle against pain or suffering in favor of the pursuit of pleasure or happiness. What is more, the "subject" of this form of rationality is an agent who is in the pursuit of control, but not only over nature, over his fellow "man" as well. The burgher or bourgeoisie as slaveowner or as capitalist is the true subject of the Enlightenment will to knowledge since knowledge is always for the sake of a surplus whether that be understood as profit or as progress. Adorno and Horkheimer, at least here, seem to agree with Heidegger's characterization of the methodology of modern science as subservient to technological interests which are always employed and

---

[15] Horkheimer, Max and Adorno, Theodor. *Dialectic of Enlightenment.* Translated by J. Cumming. The Continuum Publishing Company, 1991. P. 83.

deployed in markets. When science reveals itself as nothing other than technology, its concerns are no longer conceived as "purely speculative" but oriented toward the production of goods, the entities of the world which are not merely objects of inquiry, but resources for use in manufacturing, marketing, and—ultimately, consumption. Speculation becomes an essentially economic activity.

Adorno and Horkheimer focus on Kant's first critique to demonstrate how Kant's formalistic conception of transcendental categories upholds this view of the Enlightenment.

> The conceptual apparatus determines the senses, even before perception occurs; *a priori*, the citizen sees the world as the matter from which he himself manufactures it. Intuitively, Kant foretold what Hollywood consciously put into practice: in the very process of production, images are pre-censored according to the norm of the understanding which will later govern their apprehension.[16]

The way the categories "produce" experience is essentially related to the citizen or burgher making all experience into a censored form into which all specific content must be placed. The images and experiences of the world are normalized in the very forms that experience takes when it has been subjected to this conception of human understanding.

> Science in general relates to nature and man only as the insurance company in particular relates to life and death. Whoever dies is unimportant: it is a question of ratio between accidents and the company's liabilities. Not the individuality but the law of the majority recurs in the formula.[17]

The formulaic nature of experience, the statistical and aggregate understanding of the world, deprives the world of concreteness. The concern for subsuming the concrete to laws and formulas is ultimately the data scientific statistical understanding of a world in which only the formula for successful production matters and the individuals who take part are totally subservient to them: the subject is always subject to the laws of formal activity, especially the formulas for manufacture, distribution, and

---

[16] Horkheimer and Adorno, *Dialectic of Enlightenment*, p. 84.

[17] Horkheimer and Adorno, *Dialectic of Enlightenment*, p. 84.

consumption. And if they were writing today, they would likely have replaced their use of the word formula with the word algorithm.[18]

In terms of Enlightenment, Adorno and Horkheimer want to show a tension within Kant, a way in which the Enlightenment comes into opposition with itself in its latest articulation. That is, science—given the principles of its universality established in the first critique, is at odds with the "self-understanding" required by the critique. What Kant shows in the first critique is that there are speculative limits to the forms of the understanding employed in scientific understanding. Because science as method has been reduced to a technique employed in the manufacturing of experiences, the self-understanding of its limitations transcends the realm of science through regulative ideas. And this can only be condemned as a kind of dogma from the standpoint of enlightened scientific reason.[19]

The Enlightenment was nothing if not an opposition to the dogma of religion and tradition. The regulative ideas of pure reason may be dogmatic insofar as they point beyond the productive conditioning of the inquirer's own understanding. It may not be the case that they rely on some other's understanding of things, or on some traditional understanding, but the fact that they point beyond the phenomenal world of the scientific understanding already entangles them in a mythical dynamic by which they cannot be proven with means available to the individual inquirer having a concrete and specific personality.

The contents of these dogmatic and regulative ideas contrary to the Enlightenment project are: God, immortality of the soul, and freedom of the will. The technical rationality of the Enlightenment does not permit such ideas since God is not an object of experience, immortality requires a conception of simple substances that transcends experience, and material causality guided by physical laws does not admit of a causality outside the necessary chain of relations in nature. When Kant turns away from these positions and toward the pragmatic possibility of such ideas, he turns against the Enlightenment conception of reason. Adorno and Horkheimer point out that this is characteristic of that same Enlightenment, albeit in an historical rather than a methodological sense.

They point out that it was a common ploy of the bourgeoisie to attempt

---

[18] The material world runs on a shared digital illusion. Take it away and what do you have? Whatever is physically in your possession? Your money is really a set of socially defined procedures that you have to execute in order to meet needs, satisfy desires, and have experiences. It enables the quantification of your personal limits in a single number. The illusion props it up and without it you would be dead in a few weeks.

[19] Cf. Horkheimer and Adorno, *Dialectic of Enlightenment*, p. 85.

to establish a morality that went beyond the purely calculative components of the scientific understanding of the world. Ultimately this attempt must be viewed as "propagandistic and sentimental" and the writings on these subjects (Kant's moral writings in the *Groundwork* and second critique) have no justification from the point of view of the scientific understanding. Such a citizen, a moral one, would be a fool from the point of view of reason and Kant was known to have expressed the need for his morality under the grounds that without it, a moral barbarism or nihilism results. The rejection of a conclusion (provided by his own first critique) is hardly evidence for this alternative moral framework. Adorno and Horkheimer claim Kant suggests that

> in the face of scientific reason moral forces are no less neutral impulses and modes of behavior than the immoral forces into which they change when directed not to that hidden possibility but to reconciliation with power. Enlightenment expels the distinction from theory.[20]

Meaning that moral or immoral, such concerns are equally irrelevant to the procedures of scientific understanding. Kant's purpose in the first critique may have been to make room for moral deliberation, but he is accused of having done the exact opposite.

What Adorno and Horkheimer only suggest at this point is that this dogmatic and mythical moral conception in the age of Enlightenment is not a distinct universal form of rational endeavor. As propagandistic, its practical validity may be subsumed to an instrumental economy of social life in which the moral consciousness is itself an unquestionable faculty in the hands of a formal policy guiding the movement of the society as its law and represented by a dominant class of individuals who are the true exponents of practical reason. Morality for Kant is a modification of a will where that will is consistent in its expression relative to some possible universal formula. As such, the conditions for understanding the will's goodness in terms of its adherence to a Categorical Imperative requires evaluation in terms of universality and the law of non-contradiction suggesting the employment of the categories of the understanding. For us to know if our acts are driven by moral rules or maxims, we must be able to manufacture an understanding of our activity as moral. Contrary to Kant's claims that morality and immorality are *neutral* to the concerns of any scientific understanding, they appear as products of that same scientific understanding. Such production of morality is not completely independent of empirical concerns but synthesizes them with certain mythical and

---

[20] Horkheimer and Adorno, *Dialectic of Enlightenment*, p. 86.

dogmatic concepts that are available to us (empirically through the traditional or religious apparatuses that make up our factical history). As moral agents, we act in the empirical world as it has been conditioned by the categories of experience and are charged with the universal imperative to be moral within that setting.

In this way, Kant's efforts at giving the principles for a morality that would temper the Enlightenment emphasis on scientific procedures would be revealed in its truly bourgeois nature. The morality that is produced in opposition to the threat of scientific nihilism or barbarism, is not only "justified" (that is, evaluated) by that same scientific understanding, but it continues to uphold it as a universal principle that in some way exceeds its bounds through its necessary employment in moral evaluations. Such an approach does not call into question its own operative principles and thus continues to uphold them as standards of activity in both the moral and the non-moral spheres of reason.

Of course, there is plenty of room for variation in the content of these moral principles and there will continue to be debates about what is the right thing to do. The range and nature of the debate will never exceed the boundaries of the method essential to making any such debate coherent or meaningful, anyone who rejects these essential principles for debating the moral content of laws will be effectively condemned as irrational or delusional. This is the salient point and the details of the morality do not matter that much. What does matter is that the subjects of inquiry and moral debates are always subjected to a procedure that stems from the individual inquirer's moral or theoretical agency and that this point of view prevents them from considering anything that transcends that point of view.

To the extent that this agency is driven by the interests of manufacturing, distribution, and consumption, it will always be a technological (that is, telemetric) agency. An underwritten power of procedural influence remains to guide the moral as well as scientific reasoning of the inquirers; and such a power, invested in that procedure, will never be open to critical attacks by its inquirers. This recalls a discussion by Foucault that articulates a direct assault on the intellectual and procedural framework of the Enlightenment.

In Foucault's description of Bentham's *Panopticon*, a figure is presented to describe the nature of the subject entangled in reason as universally applicable procedure. Here the individual agent is described on a microscopic level as well as a macroscopic one: the former accords with the relation of the transcendental ego with the objects of experience insofar as they are grasped by an inquiring agent in relation to which all entities gain their ontological status; the latter accords with the relation of the formal elements of subjectivity per se insofar as any social organization committed to the existence of subjects embodied with such a formal structure is responsible for a normative constraint that limits the range of possible experiences and legitimate concerns for such individuals. In other words, we will try to show through the figure of the Panopticon how the universality of the scientific method carried out in the individual's experience is inextricably caught up in the dynamic of an overarching telemetric/technological formalism that subjects the individuals to a universal understanding that is alien to that body and invests him or her with a coercive power: the individual in the Age of Reason is both subject to and subject of an inter-subjective power.

Foucault's concern in *Discipline and Punish*[21] is the abnormal individual who does not fit into the ordinary bounds of rational discourse. Such an individual may not act in accordance with the basic rules of rational society and, in some sense, has failed to be subjected to the techniques of rational method that would more appropriately order that individual's activities. In this sense, the goal of the panoptical prison would be the creation or manufacture of rational subjects:

> Bentham's *Panopticon* is the architectural figure of this composition. We know the principle on which it was based: at the periphery, an annular building; at the centre, a tower; this tower is pierced with wide windows that open onto the inner side of the ring; the peripheric building is divided into cells, each of which extends the whole width of the building; they have two windows, one on the inside, corresponding to the windows of the tower; the other, on the outside, allows the light to cross the cell from one end to the other. All that is needed, then, is to place a supervisor in a central tower and to shut up in each cell a madman, a patient, a condemned man, a worker or a schoolboy. By the effect of backlighting, one can observe from the tower, standing out precisely against the light, the small captive shadows in the cells of the periphery. They are like so many cages, so many small theatres, in which each actor is alone, perfectly individualized and constantly visible. The panoptic mechanism arranges spatial unities that make it possible to see constantly and to recognize immediately. In short, it reverses the principle of the dungeon; or rather of its three functions—to enclose, to deprive of light and to hide—it preserves only the first and eliminates the other two. Full

---

[21]Michel Foucault. *Discipline and Punish*. Translated by Alan Sheridan. Vintage Books, 1979.

> lighting and the eye of a supervisor capture better than darkness, which ultimately protected. Visibility is a trap.[22]

Although designed as a prison, Foucault sees this apparatus as a means for achieving much more broadly applicable disciplinary ends. Our use of the figure will go further than his stated applications: the invisible center which is unseen but will become familiar to the inhabitants of the "cells" is that same transcendental ego that Foucault earlier described as the invisible element in the Kantian doublet. The inhabitants of the cell may be understood as different empirically graspable intentional relations between a perceiving consciousness and the objects of its perception. In this way, the Panopticon offers a view of the world as picture where the individual inquirer is set into it as an objectified and constantly visible element of inquiry.

The self-understanding of the individual under panoptical conditions will always be manufactured by a methodologically rigorous activity of objective discovery. The individual's own practical activity will always be understood and evaluated as a scientist understanding the data of their own investigations. The states of being of the individual are always subjected to the central power mechanism, to how such states are understood. In this process, following Foucault, the "centralized power" reveals itself as something other than central, rather this power is articulated in the forming of each of the different states of the objectified subject. This element of power is present in some sense in each of the modifications of the individual. *In some sense* because, as such, power is invisible; that is, invisible as power. Individuals, who are unable to critically evaluate the conditions of their own self-understanding (because they employ themselves in this same self-understanding through which the "common sense" of the individual operates), might think of themselves as autonomous and free and whatever else. Meanwhile, the meaning and nature of any of these qualities is modified by the invisible technologies of power which ultimately only let them be the qualities of object-egos that, by definition, are never free—although they may come to appear as autonomous precisely because of the ordering capacity of the panoptical transcendental ego. Such

---

[22] From *Discipline an Punish*, p. 200. This might suggest to the reader of the "Corporations are People" chapter in *Telemetry Phenomenology Commonwealth: Corporate Surveillance and the Colonization of Personality* the assertion there that the incarceration of corporations deemed "persons" would have a radical impact on their potential behavior. To subject the corporation to this form of visibility would have the same radical impact on a corporate subjectivity as Foucault claims it had on human subjectivity.

an individual "is seen, but ... does not see; he is the object of information, never a subject in communication."[23]

Thus far this only partially attacks the Enlightenment conception of subjectivity since the transcendental ego still may be understood as individual (although it is hard to know what this might mean given that "individuality" is itself a rule for the objectification of experiences by the transcendental ego). How then can we understand the panoptical subject as achieving the major effect of "induc[ing] in the inmate a state of conscious and permanent visibility that assures the automatic functioning of power,"[24] where that power is an "impersonal" power, the kind associated with the overarching understanding of Being essential to an epoch?

Addressing this question is the stated component of Foucault's project: as method, this transcendental practice that structures the self-understanding of subjectivity belongs to no one, it is the form of a universal activity that belongs to "the rational being." In saying this, the distinction between rationality and power is obscured, at least insofar as rationality is understood as practice or, more traditionally, capacity. Action, insofar as it constitutes objects (including the subjected empirical ego which is an object), further rationalizes the world by wrapping—through inquiry—more and more of the world into the circle of panoptical objectivity. This extends the realm of reason through more investigations that go further and further in knowing the world, the so-called objective world of nature. Since nothing can exist without it being an object of inquiry, the acts of the individual inquirer enlarge the world by discovering more objects and bringing more entities into existence. This emergence is always the taming of entities into a ground plan projected by rational endeavor.

The story in Kant's ethics concerning rationality was that either the agent is going to be guided by nature or by reason; and the truly moral, that is free, individual is the one whose acts are guided by reason. By surrendering the natural component of some given individuality to the guidance of a universal reason, the person can establish a moral freedom in herself that is something other than the wild license of nature. The first critique had already established that "nature" is nothing other than that strange conditioned objectivity where the transcendental ego in its formality was responsible for its determination. And since the empirical ego is an object, the natural elements of the individual are already subjected to the determinations of reason. The already normalized individual is, in ethical action, subjected still further to a rational choice between rationally conceived nature and rationally conceived morality. Like we saw in

---

[23] Foucault, *Discipline and Punish*, p. 200.

[24] Foucault, *Discipline and Punish*, p. 201.

Descartes' framing of the question concerning two theories, this decision only pretends to be *neutral*. The decision as to whether nature or reason is to guide action is already projected as a decision between two different rationally constructed options. The power of method no longer admits of a limit between theoretical and practical concerns (in Kant's sense). And what is more, it has become increasingly more difficult to claim that the transcendental ego is a capacity of an individual.[25]

Foucault initially described the Panopticon as an institutional apparatus or "machine" where individual persons inhabit the cells visible to the "tower" where an invisible power keeps watch. As such its effect is the creation of a strange prison community of distinct individuals who might be thought as autonomous where this now suggests that they are *self-regulating* insofar as they appropriate the positions of power to govern their behavior. The Panopticon is

> a machine for creating and sustaining a power relation independent of the person who exercises it; in short, that the inmates should be caught up in a power situation of which they are themselves the bearers. To achieve this, it is at once too much and too little that the prisoner should be constantly observed by an inspector: too little, for what matters is that he knows himself to be observed; too much, because he has no need in fact of being so.[26]

Because the prisoner does not know when or if he is being watched, he must assume that he is always being monitored and thus govern himself accordingly. He takes over the disciplinary activities of power by constantly enacting them upon himself. It is in this sense that the prisoner becomes autonomous, like a wound-up automaton.

In a society where individualism is King and everyone's "common sense" tells them they are individuals with the "autonomy and freedom" this suggests, power has most thoroughly gained an invisible control over all action, theoretical or practical. It may never occur to the individual that he or she is being watched since the apparatus has fixed these qualities so long

---

[25] That is, the so-called "individual" is essentially an ego without determinations but responsible for all determinations. In this sense, it is the absolute infinite (in Hegel's sense) and shared by all who claim to be rational agents. At this point it would be possible to insert a reading of Hegel that attempts to show how his phenomenology of spirit is the "truth" of the Enlightenment. That is, it is the synthesis left over from the movement through the contradictory moments of Descartes and Kant.

[26] Foucault, *Discipline and Punish*, p. 201.

ago and so deeply that the power positioned in the individual is completely and thoroughly invisible. This may happen in a variety of ways and means through different kinds of institutions in which the child finds herself: the family, the school, the church, and language.

It would be a mistake to think that Foucault or the authors are advocating a release of restraint that would enable "prisoners" to go free. One of Foucault's major aims in *Discipline and Punish* is to show that the prison's purpose is not rehabilitation or punishment ordinarily understood. Rather, the prison is an institution meant to constitute human individuals as criminals. That is, they serve the function of convincing miscreants that they are criminals thus enabling them to develop the appropriate self-understanding. Like Kant's view of natural inclination, the prison is an attempt to subsume criminality to rational understanding. This is not for the sake of creating a morally good person since, on our interpretation, both good and evil are in some sense rational and both equally serve the interests of rationality. Objectifications of individuals, subjecting them to rational conditions of experience, promote and further the measurement and rational understanding of the world and, therefore, "man's" control over nature. Digital telemetry and the data science consuming it, on this reading, marks the highest realization of Enlightenment methodology.

The bully at school, the agnostic, the schizophrenic, the criminal, etc. are all rational determinations that can be given to subjected individuals who, as such, continue to advance the aims of power/reason. A sociological question that may arise from this claim is whether disciplining students at school requires bullies, whether Protestant faith requires agnostics, whether intellectual discipline requires schizophrenics, and whether legal and moral discipline require criminals? In other words, in what sense does the rational society of individuals require "abnormal" individuals for the sake of promoting its aims and interests? These questions may also suggest a manner in which communities can be understood in some way other than disciplinary: can there be a community that is no longer defined in instrumental terms of aims, methodological terms of individuals and citizens, or in theoretical terms of objects giving rise to interest? The possibility of posing these questions in a thoughtful way requires at the very least that their *solution* not be *conceived* as *attainable* through *investigations,* and that the premise of individuality and subjectivity cannot be understood in opposition to the totalitarian and universal domination of power: where there are inquiring and rational "individuals" in search of solutions, there is a coercive and normalizing power.

We think, finally, that this description of the collective attack on the Age of Reason coming from Frankfurt and Paris has shown that it is not subjectivity per se that is problematic, nor is the problem one of instrumentalism as an exclusive interest or goal for the rational society.

Instead, we think we have shown that the problem is that practice, when comprehended as rational and methodical activity, is coerced through a subjection to universal form serving the interests of contemporary apparatuses of power: all behavior has been subsumed by the telemetric.

On Becoming (what one is)

The Lens Grinder

The standard line on the epoch of technology is that all distances are bridged and whatever is far away is brought near. "Every day the urge grows stronger to get hold of an object at very close range by way of its likeness, its reproduction."[1] Benjamin associates this mechanical intervention with a removal of the "aura" from things as they are so that they might be seen up close. In Heidegger, a similar pattern emerges at the heart of his project.

> "Desevering"* amounts to making the farness vanish—that is, making the remoteness of something disappear, bringing it close. Dasein is essentially de-severant: it lets any entity be encountered close by as the entity which it is. De-severance discovers remoteness; and remoteness, like distance, is a determinate categorial characteristic of entities whose nature is not that of Dasein. De-severance*, however, is an existentiale; this must be kept in mind. Only to the extent that entities are revealed for Dasein in their discoveredness [Entferntheit], do 'remotenesses' ["Entfernungen"] and distances with regard to other things become accessible in entities within-the-world themselves.[2]

---

[1] Walter Benjamin, "The Work of Art in the Age of Mechanical Reproduction" in *Illuminations*. Translated by Harry Zohn. New York: Schocken Books. 1968. P. 223.

[2] Martin Heidegger. *Being and Time*. Translated by John MacQuarrie and Edward Robinson. New York: Harper Perennial Modern Thought. 1962. P. 139. De-severance comes back around when Heidegger gets to resoluteness, thus inciting spatial orientation into the notion of authenticity. P. 346: "In the term "Situation" ("situation"—'to be in a situation') there is an overtone of a signification that is spatial. We shall not try to eliminate this from the existential conception, for such an overtone is also implied in the 'there' of Dasein. Being-in-the-world has a spatiality of its own, characterized by the phenomena of de-severance and directionality. Dasein 'makes room' insofar as it factically exists." ... "...the situation has its foundations in resoluteness." And "...the situation *is* only through resoluteness and in it." In what follows, problems are revealed in Heidegger's offset of the authentic and inauthentic, but the reader should not

By his reckoning, bringing close is embedded in the existential fabric of human being, it is part and parcel of the this that is there. Not essentially connected to a technological way of Being or of understanding whatever is in the world, desevering indicates a basic structural component and is that characteristic that makes Dasein susceptible to the corruption that technology may incite. In his later work, he asserts the proximity of the poetic and the technical as both the greatest danger and the saving power, suggesting that it may be this very existential structure of human being that makes it both vulnerable to the dangers of technology and capable of saving itself.[3] The lenses that we grind are both constraining and liberating.

To some extent, it is standard to view telemetry in this same way since the remote measurements made by instrumentation are performed for the sake of bridging the distance between the point of analysis and the point of execution, rendering the system's inner workings visible to a non-participating observer. Yet, the function of telemetry is best achieved when that distance is maintained as a separation of concern by both the measuring devices themselves, which attempt to remain unseen, and by the measuring outcomes, which use statistical aggregation to remain distinct from any individual member of the population under observation.

> Seeing and hearing are distance-senses [Fernsinne] not because they are far-reaching, but because it is in them that Dasein as deseverant mainly dwells. When, for instance, a man wears a pair of spectacles which are so close to him distantially that they are 'sitting on his nose', they are environmentally more remote from him than the picture on the opposite wall.[4]

The spectacles are so integral to seeing that they are no longer seen. Telemetry, as the eyes and ears of organizational power, is so close to our agency that we no longer see it. Remote measurement itself has been situated far away from human awareness and it requires this condition to be the desevering* mechanism extraordinaire. Here we turn the tables and employ the existential analytic to draw out the structural framework of the

---

conclude that my point is completely at odds with Heidegger's although I do argue that there is a tension between the existential structure of Dasein unfolding in the analytic and the "slogans" of authenticity and inauthenticity.

[3] Martin Heidegger, *The Question Concerning Technology and Other Essays*. Translated by William Lovitt. New York: Harper Torchbooks, 1977. P. 34.

[4] Heidegger, *Being and Time*, p. 141.

remote seeing that watches human being in its natural habitat, without impacting the decision-making and deliberation by any awareness of the metering presence. The Dasein at issue is the being of the organizational practices that keep tabs, aggregate data, and come to understand the human population as a set of agent-oriented extensions for carrying out the objectives of the organization. And humans are just the sort of creatures that act differently when they know they are being watched. The aims of telemetric organization are to employ and deploy the human resources being metered without those resources impacting the results through an awareness of the measurements. By coming up close and 'sitting on his nose,' telemetry retreats into the remoteness of invisibility that comes with being part of sight itself.

Telemetry is the lens in the spectacles. And the standard pattern for firing a telemetry event is via delegation. The telemeter defines a helper component that sends the event off to whatever store is configured to collect the data. Instead of writing a line of code that directly calls into a dependent method, the developer will wrap the method call in an instrumentation provider's delegate operation that executes the method with a surrounding block of code that captures, for example, the number of milliseconds the method took to execute, the name of the method, and whatever outcome resulted from the call, including the exception that it might have thrown or the error code that it might have returned. When this pattern is used, the telemetry becomes an invisible part of the operation that is integral to it, that wraps it and becomes its basic condition of possibility. The method does not execute without the operation of the delegate but this *middleware* itself is remote to the execution insofar as it is no part of it, extraneous to it, and thus able to observe its execution and outcome without itself having any impact. To the extent that human beings act in context and for the sake of organizational objectives and operations, we execute our lives in a delegated form that fires telemetry events alongside every movement that we make. This indicates a power dynamic in which observation is not directly coercing the agent into a specific reflective sense, rather the observation is a data collection event that feeds the resulting data back into data stores where those metrics can be used to effect opportunities and contexts elsewhere. The coercion is invisible and, because it comes from an unseen delegate at work in the agent's experience, it evades critical reflection: there is no reference to the delegate available to the acting agent. This is not a simple Panopticon, rather it is the organizational delegate wrapping itself around the experience so that it can share in it and co-opt it for the sake of its own aims, associations, and interests. In digital domains, the delegate uses the operation's resources (computing and memory) to do its work. Through telemetry's lens, the organization functions as middleware constituting a medium through which all execution takes place.

The sooner that such measurements find their way into human development, the greater the saturation of human experience with organizational vision. The most obvious way in which this appears is in the form of growing adeptness at consumer behavior. Human beings growing up within conditions of dominant corporate organization, for example, develop consumer capable habits and abilities very early on in their lives. Learning to speak and gaining familiarity with the marketplace of commodities become one and the same. Desire saturates such experiences and, through telemetric delegation, is metered and transported into stores where it can be aggregated with measurements captured from the activity of others with attributes cultivated from those same experiences. Data is correlated both positively and negatively to enable conclusions being drawn about other directions that this same desire might offer as guideline for future activity. You can be directed and prodded implicitly and integrally to that very desire and, since it happens invisibly, it need not enter any possible critical reflection that you might achieve for that experience. The desire is shaped and for the agent's part this shaped desire surfaces as vision and interest, curiosity and response: natural involvements arising as conditions for the possibility of perceiving anything at all. Telemetry does not just steer, it harnesses and directs. You want this and that, you enjoy this and that, and this enjoyment itself is the very actualization of the middleware that inhabits the experience, the delegate that wraps the operation and fires the event, and the telemetry that measures it all.

> Magician and surgeon compare to painter and cameraman.
> The painter maintains in his work a natural distance from
> reality, the cameraman penetrates deeply into its web. There
> is a tremendous difference between the pictures they obtain.
> That of the painter is a total one, that of the cameraman
> consists of multiple fragments which are assembled under a
> new law. Thus, for contemporary man the representation of
> reality by film is incomparably more significant than that of
> the painter, since it offers, precisely because of the
> thoroughgoing permeation of reality with mechanical
> equipment, an aspect of reality which is free of all
> equipment.[5]

Are you interested? Will you read on? Where does that come from and how much money has it cost you? Every human being is cultivated.

---

[5] Benjamin, *Illuminations*, pp. 233-34.

And it is possible that at some point the individual arises and takes over that cultivation. This expresses a desire and an interest that have themselves been cultivated. As such, this may be characterized as the wind-up antics of an automaton more so than the liberated action of an autonomous agent.

> Only because the Being of the 'there' receives its Constitution through understanding and through the character of understanding as projection, only because it is what it becomes (or alternatively, does not become) , can it say to itself 'Become what you are', and say this with understanding.[6]

In what follows, we start from the position described by an inverted reading of this notion: that becoming what you are amounts to the achievement of a personality that is itself a delegated form for experience, middleware that has wrapped itself around any operation producing measurements for use in aggregate computations that "understand" the world in a way that promotes the interests of the organizing agents. The consensus that results is the telemetric lifeworld that, under current social and historical conditions, is the domain within which corporate persons act in commerce with each other via the employment of human resources. If it is true that "in the greatest danger the saving power lies," then the way in will likewise be the way out.

Love of Wisdom

Commodity fetishism and the making of experience into fetish may appear overtly in the lives of younger people and children, but the coercive immersion that we are trying to uncover deepens over the years and through the accumulation of experience. Those with wisdom are more at risk and those who love wisdom, the philosophers, are most at risk. This position depends on an assignment of wisdom via the understanding. To the extent that the understanding is the projection of meaningful possibilities, the associations that have substantiated it over the developmental progression of the human being are prone to deeper appropriation by the interests that lie behind those associations. The "wise" person in this sense is more familiar with possibilities, with various outcomes based on given contexts, and they are more inundated with

---

[6] Heidegger, *Being and Time*, p. 186.

organizational contributions to these contexts and to the outcomes that can be anticipated based upon them. Wisdom connotes a growth in experiences that provide ample background to how things work, how people tend to act, what their motives tend to be, and how the worldly conditions are likely to unfold given such motivations and actions. This familiarity amounts to an absorption in those worldly states of affairs. To the extent, therefore, that the wise individual better understands how things work in the real world of human involvement, that same individual lays claim to a greater absorption in the meaning contexts that underlie those experiences. Experience is not an absolute good to be lauded or relied upon in all circumstances. Instead, it may constitute a trap that lulls the agent into thinking everything is familiar, and that the likely outcome is easily predictable given a set of variable inputs or arguments.

Philosophy, however, is not the same as wisdom itself and should not be equated with experience as such. Rather, the philosopher, or so the historical tendency suggests, is one who maintains a critical attitude toward their experience, who has come to know that it should not be trusted and considered exhaustively evaluated once and for all after some small set of deliberations have taken place. Instead, the philosopher knows that any new experience, any ongoing experience, has the possibility to derail or undermine previously achieved notions or previously attained understanding. This view of philosophy as the love of wisdom can be opportunistically characterized using both Heidegger's and Habermas' notions of 'understanding'. In both cases, the characterization is futural, the understanding—for Heidegger—amounts to the projection of possibility, whereas for Habermas it amounts to an achievement of integrated and interpersonal action. As such a future oriented structure, the understanding must be open to revision, to changes in meaning and to the impact of new occurrences and how they will effect already known, already experienced, sets of information that are likely to flavor the established attitudes or states-of-mind of the individual in action.

> In the understanding of the "for-the-sake-of-which", the significance which is grounded therein, is disclosed along with it. The disclosedness of understanding, as the disclosedness of the "for-the-sake-of-which" and of significance equiprimordially, pertains to the entirety of Being-in-the-world. Significance is that on the basis of which the world is disclosed as such. To say that the "for-the-sake-of-which" and significance are both disclosed in Dasein,

means that Dasein is that entity which, as Being-in-the-world,
is an issue for itself.[7]

On the reading that I am suggesting, Heidegger's point is that the
understanding does not point backwards into a set of already
comprehended rigid and established notions that define the "sight" of the
agent. Rather future orientation is the substance of the understanding and
this understanding is constantly at work reconsidering the factical states
from which those future orientations emerge. An agent who is only driven
forward by what is already known is closed off to new possibilities, is unable
to experience anything new that does not fit with what has already been
seen and comprehended in its details. "Understanding is the existential
Being of Dasein's own potentiality-for-Being; and it is so in such a way that
this Being discloses in itself what its Being is capable of."[8] And this holds in
both being closed off to anything new and open to a novel event. The state
of the understanding, its condition and conditioning, determines how the
world will come to pass for the experiencing agent. If the understanding is
rigid and absorbed in what is already known, then new events will be
understood in terms just like everything that has happened already, and
which seems just like it. If the understanding is flexible and open to re-
evaluation and reconsideration of what it thinks it has come to understand
in past experience, then whatever comes to pass can be seen with fresh eyes
that consider the possibility that everything that has come before is at odds
with the new thing that is happening now. Philosophy, as the love wisdom,
is how I name this openness that understands its condition and the
possibility that the condition may result from a set of associations that have
reified rigid vision into a dogma. The next thing that the philosopher
experiences may be what breaks the rule that has governed all experience,
it may be the extraordinary occurrence of something unique. Not
necessarily, but the potential is there.
    There is a structurally social element of this orientation, since all
understanding is based on projections in terms of associations that have
been acquired and accumulated. We understand things just the way that
"they" understand them.[9] Experience is part and parcel of a shared world
and set of commonly available associations and organizational participation
that applies to groups and populations. The shared understanding of those

---

[7] Heidegger, *Being and Time*, p. 182.

[8] Heidegger, *Being and Time*, p. 184.

[9] Heidegger, *Being and Time*, p. 167: "The 'they' is an existentiale; and as
a primordial phenomenon, it belongs to Dasein's positive constitution."

with common associations and group memberships may be deemed a form of communication.

> In this more general kind of communication, the Articulation of Being with one another understandingly is constituted. Through it a co-state-of-mind [Mitbefindlichkeit] gets 'shared', and so does the understanding of Being-with. Communication is never anything like a conveying of experiences, such as opinions or wishes, from the interior of one subject into the interior of another. Dasein-with is already essentially manifest in a co-state-of-mind and a co-understanding.[10]

The shared understanding amounts to a common sense among those who have traversed a set of shared experiences. They commune with each other insofar as they already understand those things which they have in common. Communication, in this sense, amounts to a shared set of associations: an existential state-of-mind oriented toward possibilities based on a set of shared involvements common to those who have come to have such an understanding.

Already understanding each other, however, does not imply that the individuals sharing this understanding agree with one another on all assertions of fact or matters of belief. The factical state of being of individual persons, those with specific experiences in common, will vary along the lines of other axes and matters. The shared understanding puts them in the same place, in the same context, but they each bring other contexts and placements with them. And these other contexts and placements enable variation. Two philosophers will not necessarily agree on anything at all. Their shared form of understanding and the ease with which they can communicate with each other does not necessitate agreement. At least part of any disagreement they have may come from a likelihood to reify their past understanding as the basis against which all future actions must be evaluated and considered. The philosopher is vulnerable to dogma in some subset of actions or operations. And this dogma can lead to violent disagreement between individuals equally devoted to the love of wisdom.

> Every process of reaching understanding takes place against the background of culturally ingrained preunderstanding. This background knowledge remains unproblematic as a whole; only that part of the stock of knowledge that

---

[10] Heidegger, *Being and Time*, p. 205.

> participants make use of and thematize at a given time is put
> to the test. To the extent that definitions of situations are
> negotiated by participants themselves, this thematic segment
> of the lifeworld is at their disposal with the negotiation of
> each new definition of the situation.[11]

This passage can now be offered in a new context to invite a renewed critical understanding. The impact and upshot of our experience can always be called into question given a new set of conditions discovered in experience with others. We are embedded together in our experience and we are set apart.

> The focus of the investigation thereby shifts from cognitive-
> instrumental rationality to communicative rationality. And
> what is paradigmatic for the latter is not the relation of a
> solitary subject to something in the objective world that can
> be represented and manipulated, but the intersubjective
> relation that speaking and acting subjects take up when they
> come to an understanding with one another about
> something. In doing so, communicative actors move in the
> medium of a natural language, draw upon culturally
> transmitted interpretations, and relate simultaneously to
> something in the one objective world, something in their
> common social world, and something in each's own
> subjective world.[12]

Likewise here, we begin to sense the futural nature of the understanding and the way in which it binds us together with the pre-understanding or factical conditions that we carry with us into an experience with others, the communication that takes place there, and the understanding that is achieved in the process of everyday being alongside others.

This opportunistic merger of Habermas' notion with Heidegger's is meant to boost a sense of the meaning behind "becoming what one is" insofar as it relates to philosophy. Becoming what one is amounts to the accumulation of experiences that give one a set of characteristics in common with those who have shared in that understanding. This may amount to different population segments with different orientations. The appearance of uniqueness in each of us comes from arbitrary sequences or

[11] Jurgen Habermas. *The Theory of Communicative Action, Volume 1: Reason and the Rationalization of Society*. Translated by Thomas McCarthy. Boston. Beacon Press. 1984. P. 100.

[12] Habermas, *The Theory of Communicative Action, Volume 1*, p. 392.

combinations of associations characteristic of that life. The commonality does not breed uniformity, instead it can result in identifiably distinct forms of dogma. Not only that. Insofar as the common sense is characterized by more than just wisdom itself but by the love of it, there is a chance that the disagreements and conflict between the variably situated members of these commonly interleaved associations will enable a common medium of critical openness making it possible to evaluate the future events and experiences in the light of past occurrences, all in such a way that it is not predetermined which will yield to the other. Such a medium is always at risk of executing via middleware.

Truth be told, I am not entitled to any declaration of rank order in value here. I do not mean to suggest that the love of wisdom present in one individual at various times under various conditions makes that person somehow superior in moral standing to a person who is merely wise. There is no trap of authenticity here either. We become who we are either as wise humans or as philosophers. And the becoming itself may vary from context to context in whatever medium holds sway. An individual may be a philosopher in some areas of their lives, whereas they remain merely wise in other areas. Phenomenologically, these are basic existential characteristics of experience. As such, however, no ethical claims or hierarchies are associated with them, they merely characterize human agents as either oriented toward constant recharacterization of their interpretations of the world based on new experience, or as those who already know what to say about whatever happens to them as pertains to specific facets of their lives. The nature of conversation and the associations that follow from these orientations are likely to be deeply impacted, of course, but there is nothing in what I have said so far that entitles a conclusion preferring one orientation over the other.

Unrequited Love

> Dasein can fall only because Being-in-the-world understandingly with a state-of-mind is an issue for it. On the other hand, authentic existence is not something which floats above falling everydayness; existentially, it is only a modified way in which such everydayness is seized upon.[13]

In *Telemetry Phenomenology Commonwealth*, the actual struggle

---

[13] Heidegger, *Being and Time*, p. 224.

between wisdom and the love of it replaces any schematics of authenticity and inauthenticity. This is possible because there is understanding in both the wise act and the act that embodies the philosophical. When something happens, both immediately imply attempts at associating it with what has been experienced before. The wise person can easily interpret the event in terms of what they have seen. The philosopher may come to the same conclusion, but only after they have truly attempted to interpret the event in all possible contexts, considering the possibility that this new experience may undermine everything with which they were previously familiar. The two acts are distinguished along these lines, but we are not setting the philosopher, or the acts of loving wisdom, above the wise person or their concomitant acts of wisdom. Nor are we claiming that some traditionally conceptualized individual is more rigorously preserved according to their *own* rule or their *own* pattern of existence through one or the other of these act orientations. If personality as such is characteristic of the wise action and the rejection of it more closely affiliated with the acts of a philosopher, then the realization of the offset does not place any one of the two above the other. The seizure of personality in either case may be aligned with a coercive fabrication process that belongs to the lifeworld of those corporate persons or larger context-providing organizations whose right to privacy and power of association are most thoroughly preserved by modern day legislation. The articulation of wisdom or philosophy, should it evade such coercive effects on personality, falls into a different trap laid by that same organizational middleware: the error of thinking itself requited, the notion that the pursuit and attainment of wisdom will somehow promote the wellbeing of those who seek it. This danger is so deeply engrained in wisdom and philosophy that those who most brutally practice these behaviors are most likely perceived as sceptics or nihilists.

> Our task is not to prove that an 'external world' is present-at-hand or to show how it is present-at-hand, but to point out why Dasein, as Being-in-the-world, has the tendency to bury the 'external world' in nullity 'epistemologically' before going on to prove it. The reason for this lies in Dasein's falling and in the way in which the primary understanding of Being has been diverted to Being as present-at-hand—a diversion which is motivated by that falling itself.[14]

Both the wise and traditionally trained philosophers succumb to this. The relationship between wisdom, its pursuit, and its tendency to find expression in telemetric delineation of a world present-at-hand or

---

[14] Heidegger, *Being and Time*, p. 250.

theoretically understood, amounts to the highest achievement of human being's absorption in the world. Raising doubts about one's wisdom, challenging it for the sake of one's love of it, amounts to a cancellation of that absorption and a purge of whatever success that might lie in its achievement. The cost associated with this is the despair of not knowing or, worse, of knowing and not being able to do anything about it. The cognitive act that achieves the bridging of the distance between the world and oneself, that apprehends the social complexity of spatio-temporal historical relationships in one's ideas and feelings, brings on hesitation and doubt. Such a sage would cease to recommend and explain, would back off from assertions and commands. Such a person in such a moment would have gained insight into the operations of an other who does not care about them, but with whom such a person is so deeply disadvantaged because of their extreme love and adoration for that other. Socrates is the model.

Care may emerge as the existential structure of understanding factical Dasein, but the ontological foundation which is disclosed does not care at all. And therefore, understanding only comes to light through its Habermasian communicative turn. Interpretative action aimed at understanding and communication amounts to commiseration among agent actors under given conditions and contexts. There is nothing to be said any longer between two such agents expressing deeply philosophical orientations and yet governed by a common middleware. True philosophy runs out of things to say because the interlocutors find themselves together in agreement and comprehending an impossible set of circumstances in which human communal fabrication aims at producing a state of affairs that is of no significance at all to the world within which they are attempting to establish it. To continue, they must leave their philosophy behind and act on the wisdom itself. This amounts to acting based on the context of experience accumulated as factical states of mind. Only such wisdom can overtake the impasse that the pursuit of it necessarily entails. Arguments between philosophers always reify wisdom as supplement to the love of it that would have sufficiently isolated the participants and prevented any dispute.

There is a movement in modern academic philosophy aiming at making "the love of wisdom" useful to some set of conversations or domains of inquiry. The philosopher can contribute to investigations in physics and psychology, human behavior and productivity, as well as biology and human social organization. No doubt, there are many who have successfully brought their wisdom in such matters to the benefit of others likewise engaged. In those contributions, make no mistake that philosophy has been left behind. These wise persons enter the fray and in so doing take a stand for this position or that one, they defend themselves and they establish terrain and professional influence. None of this articulates the philosophical, although they still manage a moment of it here and there throughout their work week. The philosopher is always an amateur and always incapable of helping move things along productively toward a beneficial outcome. A group of such persons, acting communally, are totally useless. All they can see is how wrong it has all gone, how the conditions of emerging space and time are in deep conflict with the apparatuses of the past that stand against what is coming.

> I use the term culture for the stock of knowledge from which participants in communication supply themselves with interpretations as they come to an understanding about something in the world. I use the term society for the legitimate orders through which participants regulate their membership in social groups and thereby secure solidarity. By personality I understand the competences that make a subject capable of speaking and acting, that put him in a position to take part in processes of reaching understanding and thereby to assert his own identity. The dimensions in which communicative action extends comprise the semantic field of symbolic contents, social space, and historical time. The interactions woven into the fabric of every day communicative practice constitute the medium through which culture, society, and person get reproduced. These reproduction processes cover the symbolic structures of the lifeworld. We have to distinguish from this the maintenance of the material substratum of the lifeworld.[15]

We may replace "medium" with "middleware" so that in this characterization of the understanding and its relationship to communication and social forms, the true dystopia of human existence becomes clear regardless of whether that is Habermas' point. The structural wisdom that we acquire is our adaptation to our world, it is our becoming rational members of a society. The systematic structure acquired over time provides the conceptual boundaries for human technology and "...these technologies make possible the formation of public spheres..."[16] In the face of such structures, the questioning act that takes nothing for granted, that stands in wonder against the accident of human nature as human social ordering, is impotent and unable to achieve anything at all. If

---

[15] Jurgen Habermas. *The Theory of Communicative Action, Volume Two: Lifeworld and System: A Critique of Functionalist Reason.* Translated by Thomas McCarthy. Boston: Beacon Press. P. 138.

[16] Habermas, *The Theory of Communicative Action, Volume Two*, p. 184.

multiple individuals come to this understanding near the high city in Athens, there will be nothing for them to do with it or about it. It is not clear that they would be able to instruct those around them on the methods and procedures that best yield this result. How does one perform a philosophical act? Step one? The standard line is to begin the study of examples: Descartes, Aristotle, Hume, Kant, etc. The bridge between epistemology and philosophy as the love of wisdom, however, is not achieved in steps. No philosophical act that takes for granted its essential nature is worthy of the name. This makes a near impossibility of the process.

Philosophy, as I have been describing it, would seem to be a sort of birth where the act amounts to an emergence from an otherwise holistically sealed structural totality of social fabrication and coordinated human agency for the sake of it. It is a standard realization of the myth where the womb represents safety and security and the world outside a hostile place where nothing remains to support the act other than the source from which it emerged. The maternal power in the myth is the power to protect the individual amid a cold and hard world. Your social roots, the civilization within which you were born, the citizenship that holds you up every day wherever you might go, constitutes one side of the story on how to alleviate the trauma of birth. The paternal power lies in the urge to conquer that trauma, to venture out and take a stand on your own to dominate the conditions that would otherwise threaten you. A proper mixture of the paternal and the maternal make for the healthy baby and ensure a productive life that has ventured out on its own while carrying with it the original power of its parental source. This myth, however, is the absorbed condition of a wise person and not representative of philosophical action. An act of loving wisdom might express recognition that the mythologies around birth are some of the most historically optimized mechanisms for establishing and maintaining the power of those structures responsible for all the fabricating acts Habermas described in his notion of culture. The structure itself amounts to a form of infantilization that lays claim to the agent throughout the most independent instances of its agency. These foundations are essential for keeping the agent functional throughout its navigation of the human world, whereas philosophical acts thwart any possible effectiveness of the act itself.

> A subjectivity that is characterized by communicative reason resists the denaturing of the self for the sake of self-preservation. Unlike instrumental reason, communicative reason cannot be subsumed without resistance under a blind self-preservation. It refers neither to a subject that preserves itself in relating to objects via representation and action, nor

to a self-maintaining system that demarcates itself from an
environment, but to a symbolically structured lifeworld that
is constituted in the interpretive accomplishments of its
members and only reproduced through communication.
Thus communicative reason does not simply encounter
ready-made subjects and systems; rather, it takes part in
structuring what is to be preserved. The utopian perspective
of reconciliation and freedom is ingrained in the conditions
for the communicative sociation of individuals; it is built into
the linguistic mechanism of the reproduction of the
species.[17]

Communicative reason, as such, amounts to the highest form of
wisdom, it is the thorough and complete absorption of the individual in the
social structure that lies at its origin. Reflectively aware of those conditions
from which we come, only intersubjectively positioned reason can properly
respond to the world in which we find ourselves alongside each other.
Wisdom, therefore, has an advantage over naivete which may be associated
with a traditional Cartesian view of the universe, an eternal subsistent and
independent subject metaphysically distinct from its world. This advantage
over the naïve perspective, however, is not enough to merit a "critical
understanding" capable of higher order construction of ideal living
conditions for enlightened agents. Rather, it amounts to the highest form
of colonized understanding achieved while basking in the love of the
civilization within which it takes place. The philosophical act, on the other
hand, marks a true incision into this social foundation and leaves one truly
and completely alone. And this cognitive solitude is not an idealized state
nor is it desirable even if it offers the most structurally comprehensive
perspective on human existence.[18] The "beast or the god" that emerges in
such philosophical acts is an abomination, a monstrous outcome of human
agency taken to its most extreme potential. This act of love is unrequited,
for there is no one there to requite it, and thus shares in none of the poetry
associated with truly human love, the love that only the wise can know.

---

[17] Habermas, *The Theory of Communicative Action, Volume One*, p. 398.

[18] Cognitive solitude and the solitary nature of this romanticized notion of
philosophy should not be confused with physical isolation. The opposite may
be the case. A prisoner in solitary confinement would not be alone in this sense
specifically because it is the power of exercised political forces that put the
prisoner there. The "cognitive" solitude in the philosopher is specifically meant
to suggest a breaking free of any such political or social power. Given the
intrinsically social nature of wisdom, the love of wisdom is monstrous.

Behold the Man

To emulate Nietzsche is to misunderstand him. He is a form of existence; he is a possible world and more so a cautionary tale than a role model. He should be read as though he were an historical event as should any true philosopher. A "follower" of Nietzsche is not very different from Menard and Menard is insane.[19] Any writer is never more ridiculous than when they write about Nietzsche. To reach an understanding with Nietzsche is to shut up about him. And I will leave my ridiculous homage at that.

Human being builds a cocoon around itself to insulate it against the cruelty of chance and necessity. Doing so has transformed nature into an artifact. "And even Nature is historical. It is *not* historical, to be sure, insofar as we speak of 'natural history'; but Nature is historical as a countryside, as an area that has been colonized or exploited, as a battlefield, or as the site of a cult."[20] The external world with which we interact from birth to death is mediated by human social production and the historically accumulated goods and services of the human world. "*The historizing of history is the historizing of Being-in-the-world.*"[21] Your explanations of the brutal natural reality of the stars amount to data collected from telemetric devices and instruments, designed and manufactured by enterprises around the world and throughout history. Those who work to advance "ethics" in matters of the technological always allude to the great advantages brought by invention, the diseases to be cured, the disabilities to be corrected, and the brute necessity to be overcome. This too is a part of the fabrication of a human gloss on the world at large. Just as the oil refineries and the factories make synthetic clothing, so too the artificially intelligent limbs that restore what has been lost to a person who suffered an accident or disease. The advantages we reap from our fabrication are interleaved with the destruction that it sews, they are the pattern of human world-making and they have become the dominant domain of large scale associations that lay claim to the formation of all and any future association: the corporate being

---

[19] Jorge Luis Borges. "Pierre Menard, Author of the Quixote" in *Labyrinths*. Translated by James E. Irby. New York: New Directions. 1964. Pp. 36-44.

[20] Heidegger, *Being and Time*, p. 440.

[21] Heidegger, *Being and Time*, p. 440.

or golem we have fashioned to save the species from its natural habitat. And in the saving power, the greatest danger lies.

Insofar as the cult of individuality and authenticity hold the agent in awe, it offers up itself as salvation to the condition of being absorbed in a world where the organizational other occupies cognitive forces through the most intimate of daily processes and procedures. To be in the grip of organizational powers and yet consider oneself autonomous and engaged in rational action is to be distracted from the very condition of one's distraction. To strive to get behind this presumption would be just as warped as failing to consider it a presumption. Becoming what one is cannot be a matter of emerging from an ambiguous existence into a purified state of excellence as though the truly human specimen must separate from the herd. Yet we seem to have discovered this exact aim in the unrequited love of wisdom. The deconstruction of privacy and the entanglements of social being in any and all human practice, amounts to a failure of language to transcend socialized existence in the imaginary private domain. We are absorbed in each other and we may be striving to establish ourselves as proper individuals, and yet our individual existence would become meaningless if we were to successfully separate from everyone else.

Philosophy as the love of wisdom is an impossible objective. It aims at isolation, it aims at undermining the 'they' in consciousness and throughout one's personality, it aims at undermining personality. It is, however, distinguished from any assumption that such solitude is already achieved as a starting point for action. At least part of the rarity of the philosopher's project is the rarity of any sense that it is a project for one to have. And by philosopher, I mean the instantiated subject of the act of loving wisdom, it is merely a positional declaration that belongs to any actor enacting such love. The flipside of the impossibility of the project is that if the objective were to be reached, there would be nothing left to do once one arrived *there*. By attempting to leave behind the social occupation of the self, the philosopher attempts to arrive at a place where there is no longer any need of wisdom or understanding, where communication has come to an end and where there are no longer colleagues to share in it. Phenomenological authenticity has nothing to offer. If understanding itself is the aim, then an already held understanding becomes the aim of a self-reflective process of making that understanding explicit in its shared meaning. In that case, the lover of wisdom pursues what they already have, as though in a circle, aiming at realizing the previously apprehended condition in a shared reflective sense. To the extent that all the participants in the conversation are enacting the philosophical, such may become the subject of their understanding. And to the extent that the participants live in different eras or different places, this becomes a conversation across space and time. More than just asynchronous, it may include participants who never meet.

And yet they arrive in a shared place. And in so *being there*, they share in understanding, and they communicate.

The pattern is revealed as a line of flight maneuver. The orientation toward an outside is non-sensical when detached from its inner origins. The existential quality of the 'they' means that authenticity is non-sense, but the line of flight maneuver that orients toward authenticity *is* authentic to the extent that the authentic has taken on a verbal quality just like Being itself seems to have acquired through the existential analytic of Dasein. The goal is not an endpoint, but a circumspectly immersive condition that takes over the actor and undermines any possibility of goals. This means you can love wisdom wherever you might happen to find yourself. You need not be a genius who transforms world history by reconceptualizing basic notions enabling historical revolutions across disciplines. Instead, the philosopher can be pedestrian and struggling to understand notions that are quite clear to others and have been for a very long time. A philosopher may achieve their goal—in the sense being explained—without saying or thinking anything wise. Some may think it true to say that although I am not Aristotle, being able to read him and see what he saw is a great intellectual achievement that allows one to walk in the shoes of the great thinker. Add to this the sense that one might immerse oneself in the process of thinking, of contemplating conditions of human existence, in such a way as to live as a great thinker might live for a stretch of time. Although the content of that thought fails in achieving wisdom, the philosophical will have been actualized. And if one can read and understand Aristotle while also being able to spend time periodically absorbed in matters of significance, what more is there to it? Aristotle was not aware of the grand impact of his work. He did not live to see the centuries that followed upon his achievements. What could these events possibly matter to his experience of loving wisdom, of doing philosophy? And if they do not matter for Aristotle, why do they matter to anyone else?

This is a wearing away of standards. I feel the objection as I articulate the position. I am deriding the greatness of Aristotle when I take this away from him. He was great, but he was a great human being. His experience is not so alien to me in virtue of the very fact that we were both socialized in human communities, both articulating the 1000 years and the 1000 villages that gave rise to each of us. True, his is a voice worth hearing and mine may not be, but that belongs to the experience of loving wisdom enacted by others not by me. What matters the adulation, appreciation, or impact upon others when my phenomenological experience of doing philosophy is at stake? I am not belittling his accomplishment; I hold that I am putting it on the highest of pedestals. Once we settle upon the unrequited nature of the love of wisdom, this erosion of standards is bedrock as the standard itself becomes nothing other than the phenomenological experience of the agent. When the ordinary person strives in this way, they do so only for themselves as individuated from their social condition and with no communal adornments such that narcissism may form the applied basis upon which such philosophy is enacted. To the extent that such acts are the modus operandi of becoming what one is, of achieving an autonomous individual stature disjointed from the aboriginal bond with others, what we behold in ourselves in such becoming may be an abstraction of any involved personality that we might possess. The framed reflective abstraction makes it seem as though we are inspecting ourselves in a mirror.

Ecce Populus

> Being-with-one-another in the "they" is by no means an
> indifferent side-by-side-ness in which everything has been
> settled, but rather an intent, ambiguous watching of one
> another, a secret and reciprocal listening-in. Under the mask
> of "for-one-another", an "against-one-another" is in play.[22]

A Heideggerian understanding where the light of Being unconceals, where the clearing comes to pass, is the event and it is a mission: emergent Habermasian understanding as achievement, that upon which action projects, upon which it is projected in/as/through that selfsame understanding. From childhood on, this pattern occupies us in the existential framework that correlates biology with sociology. The bubbling source of significance is this very projecting upon each other saturated through and through by that *mitsein* associative context.[23] This is the

---

[22] Heidegger, *Being and Time*, p. 219.

[23] Heidegger, *Being and Time*, p. 160-161: "...Being with Others belongs to the Being of Dasein, which is an issue for Dasein in its very Being. Thus as Being-with, Dasein 'is' essentially for the sake of Others. This must be understood as an existential statement as to its essence." ... "In Being-with, as the existential "for-the-sake-of" of Others, these have already been disclosed in their Dasein. With their Being-with, their disclosedness has been constituted beforehand; accordingly, this disclosedness also goes to make up significance— that is to say, worldhood. And, significance, as worldhood, is tied up with the existential "for-the-sake-of-which"" ... "Being-with is such that the disclosedness of the Dasein-with of Others belongs to it; this means that because Dasein's Being is Being-with, its understanding of Being already implies the

existential structure that persists the world of others and enables each to communicate with the other across the ages and the meridians. It is an action oriented toward achieving understanding. It need not be void of personality, interest, and power.[24] And its impulses may be tracked through their surfacing residuals resident in the minds and bodies it occupies. The failure of the "authentic attempt at extraordinary individuation" that we see in the narcissistic reading of the philosophical act is a failure rooted in this very understanding.

Let us call this failure a reductio ad absurdum of the notion of the philosopher cast as one who strives for authentic personal being detached from any social involvement.[25] The achievement of understanding orients us toward a love of wisdom that realizes the absorbed condition of the practitioners. Becoming what one is amounts to a realization of practices that are socially based, a realization of oneself amid others and absorbed by the kinds of action and practice that others may also be absorbed in. And how does such becoming enact the philosophical over and against a simplified wisdom that demonstrates excellence in whatever practices one performs? Now that the flavors of authenticity are properly cast into

---

understanding of Others." ... "It operates proximally in accordance with the kind of Being which is closest to us—Being-in-the-world as Being-with; and it does so by an acquaintance with that which Dasein, along with Others, comes across in its environmental circumspection and concerns itself with—an acquaintance in which Dasein understands."

[24] Heidegger, *Being and Time*, p. 336: "Everydayness takes Dasein as something ready-to-hand to be concerned with—that is, something that gets managed and reckoned up. 'Life' is a 'business', whether or not it covers its costs." And p. 339: "Dasein is regarded as an entity with which one might concern oneself, whether this "concern" has the sense of 'actualizing values' or of satisfying a norm." And then again p. 312 "With Dasein's lostness in the "they", that factical potentiality-for-Being which is closest to it (the tasks, rules, and standards, the urgency and extent, of concernful and solicitous Being-in-the-world) has already been decided upon." On the reading developing here, the characterizations, standards, and norms at work in such everydayness and lostness in the 'they' amounts to personality, interest, and power.

[25] For an early indication of this view, cf. Martin Heidegger. *Phenomenological Interpretations of Aristotle: Initiation into Phenomenological Research*. Translated by Richard Rojcewicz. Bloomington, IN: Indiana University Press. P. 75 where he discusses the relationship of philosophy to world and life: "The most convenient thing would surely be to perch oneself, outside of the world and of life, in the land of the blessed and of the absolute. Yet it would then be difficult to understand why anyone who had progressed "so far" would still philosophize at all."

suspicious conditions, we turn to see the enacting of such love in the action oriented toward the achievement of understanding where that refers to a critical orientation where acting agents work through their interactions explicitly with regard to their social absorption.[26] Insofar as I am a product of my world, I act philosophically when I do not merely hand myself over to the excellent performance of some practice, but attempt to fully comprehend the preconditions of that understanding in my social involvements. My projections, my thrownness, my being alongside, all my real worldliness must be socially founded since that is the issue that the love of wisdom demands.

No one chooses the conditions of their birth, no one has complete control over the other persons who will populate their childhood or youth and provide influence or inspiration in the various possible orientations and actions they might take on. The populus is always already at work in all actions, and we must investigate our continued absorption and reciprocal impact with the intersubjective facets of our worldly orientations. As university students or apprentices in a trade, we may run across others who help us along or who attempt to hinder us. Each of us cannot lay claim to complete authority over such conditions. Often this fact is allocated to 'luck' where 'luck' is a mystification of the social conditions that we encounter. Deeply engaging the historical causes and forces at work in such 'luck' will show that it is a set of integral conditions. Just as human beings are 'lucky' to find air to breath and water to drink, they are 'lucky' in finding positive or negative reinforcement to their aims and operations as they attempt to navigate the world of their concern.

> As we have seen, the object-oriented subject of the theory of knowledge is just the wrong model [for a theory of interaction]. The structure of action oriented to reaching understanding is a better model for studying how culture, society, and personality work together in determining action orientations. By attending to the formal properties of the interpretive performances of actors who harmonize their actions via communicative acts, we can show how cultural traditions, institutional orders, and personal competences— in the form of diffuse taken-for-granted features of the

---

[26] Effectively, I am relying on a reading of *Being and Time* that eliminates the analysis of authentic and inauthentic Dasein and focuses on the existentialia, the existential structure necessary for raising the question concerning the meaning of Being.

lifeworld—make possible the communicative interweaving and stabilizing of action systems.[27]

The largest corporations of modern life are built on top of a stable civil society that has been under construction by human social and political agency for centuries. The fact that norms govern behavior and that regularities can be anticipated in common behaviors are crucial to the prosperous results that such corporations achieve. They are not acting independently of neighborhoods with streets and traffic lights, they do not build without the permission of zoning boards and they cannot incorporate without sanction by the state. Furthermore, there are educational systems and family mores that establish populations with enough training and cognitive capacity to continue the work of the organization in its efforts to maximize revenue and reap profits. As I sit in my living room, my neighbors are not barging in to appropriate the items and space that is here. There are police in the city where we live, but none are immediately present to safeguard this normalcy. Rather, my neighbors have been thoroughly socialized to accept various principles of action that preserve, by and large, the peacefulness of my day in my home. Not all such neighborhoods are so constructed. The distinction between these neighborhoods is not merely 'luck', but rather can be analyzed and investigated through historical conditions, actions concerning the past life stories of people who came to populate my neighborhood rather than the other ones, and so on.

Such an orientation should not take anything for granted and should not presume that the rational agent capable of ordered communication and meaningful action is a natural occurrence. Rather, such a person is a product of the work of many distinct contributors. And not just individual contributors, but organizations and institutions that provide a framing for all that takes place within the distributed domain of their operations. The influence of all practical domains is generated, spread out, and distributed across space and time. There are many different people whose actions support and promote the function that the institution is meant to provide. Such institutions and organizations are containers of historically and spatially distributed meaning content that exists for the sake of being accessible to individual persons working to realize specific aims in the context of life among others.

Through its material substratum, every lifeworld is in an exchange with its surroundings, formed by the ecology of

[27] Habermas, *The Theory of Communicative Action, Volume Two*, p. 221.

external nature, the organism of its members, and the structures of alien lifeworlds.[28]

This constitutes an inversion of the form of the philosophical act that breaks one free of the social order. Rather, here the actor pursues an understanding of one's shared communicative domain, of the preconditions at work in all action orientation. The Socratic credo of being wise only to the extent that you come to understand that you know nothing at all is now displayed in the recognition of those 1000 generations and the 1000 villages that contributed and continue to contribute to the ongoing realization of your talents and capabilities, of your involvements and your absorption. The most radical invention of some extraordinary and world historically transformative process or body of knowledge is dependent on a set of preconditions that made the skill necessary to produce that radical event emitting a socially or communally effective set of traits and properties. Being 'intelligent' or 'competent' is not merely some set of qualities in the agent but connotes a set of relationships to the things that it is possible to do and the things that it is possible to be. If such a person were not born into a world needing such a change, then the creation of the change itself would not have been possible. We are so deeply interdependent that it is not possible to think at all without the ongoing and constant integration and relationship that we have with every single other person that is and every single other person that there has ever been or will be.

Associations and Interests

The standard version of the Graph data structure is an array of edges where each edge indicates a source node, a target node, and a directionality constraint between them. This adjacency list amounts to the set of direct associations that comprise the graph linking one member to another. The policies or constraints that govern the traversal of any one edge will, in its most rudimentary form, indicate whether the flow of association moves both ways or in only one way. This is the simplest form of directionality, but such a linking policy can cover more complex conditions that constrain the association. The graph can represent a flow of impact, the traversal of a pathway through the graph, and some edges may only permit the realization of an association if certain nodes were previously crossed during the current traversal. We would say then that in order to facilitate

---

[28] Habermas, *The Theory of Communicative Action, Volume Two*, p. 231.

movement along a route, the agent realizing the association has an interest in a set of preconditions being in place to facilitate the movement. An interaction with a friend may involve expressing some emotional attachment to that friend, letting them know how you feel or what the ongoing relationship means to you. In order to express that emotional attachment a set of preconditions must be in place. You must have cultivated a capacity of expressing yourself, of letting yourself be vulnerable to your friend, in order to perform the act in question. In the moment of enacting the relationship to the friend characterized by the emotional expression, you would have an interest in the precondition of properly cultivated capacities. This is what I meant when I suggested that associations and the making of them always bear an interest on preconditions to enabling the act. The association itself is thus conceptualized as an act which is both headed somewhere and accords with a policy declaring what preconditions are necessary for the movement in that direction. The thrown projection of understanding is always already realized as associations and interests. The philosophical act and the act of wisdom itself are both conceptualized as associative motion laden with interests.

Heidegger characterizes this associative process in terms of either an implicit authenticity or an inauthenticity where this base policy makes use of a notion of public or private orientation. Public interpretation is bound to the "they" which suppresses everything unfamiliar and constitutes the worldly orientation in which Dasein is mostly absorbed and at home.[29] Anxiety and the pursuant being-towards-death become the singular jolt that individualizes and, I suppose, privatizes Dasein. Despite his remarks that *mitsein* is existentially primordial along with any Being-in-the-world, he seems to be building a case for Dasein as lover of wisdom extracted in some sense from its relationship to others. The authentic Dasein turns away from

---

[29] Heidegger, *Being and Time*, p. 233 [On the one hand there is the being at home of the absorption in the 'they'.] "On the other hand, as Dasein falls, anxiety brings it back from its absorption in the 'world'. Everyday familiarity collapses. Dasein has been individualized, but individualized as Being-in-the-world. Being-in enters into the existential 'mode' of the "*not-at-home*"." And p. 234: "When in falling we flee into the "at home" of publicness, we flee in the face of the "not-at-home";" which continues later "When Dasein "understands" uncanniness in the everyday manner, it does so by turning away from it in falling; in this turning-away, the "not-at-home" gets 'dimmed-down'." And p. 237: "...since the publicness of the "they" suppresses everything unfamiliar" and p. 264: "Its absorption in the "they" signifies that it is dominated by the way things are publicly interpreted."

its public absorption to fully realize its being-there.[30] The phenomenologist takes a point of view that enables this anxious breaking free that is driven by one's deepest attestation of finitude as a boundary condition to this public absorption. The philosopher's position must encompass this policy of individualization making it possible for fundamental ontology to include a holistic analytic of all such structures and their interrelationships. Dasein does philosophy in order to carry out the existential analytic that enables clarity of insight into the publicness of inauthentic absorption and the privacy of authentic individualization. The wise Dasein expects death whereas Dasein that enacts a love of wisdom anticipates it and so gets to work in spelling it all out.

Our previous discussion demonstrated that this philosophical act is a meaningless outcome insofar as the existential conditions of understanding and communication would have been destroyed in the process of achieving it.

> Resoluteness, as *authentic Being-one's Self,* does not detach Dasein from its world, nor does it isolate it so that it becomes a free-floating "I". And how should it, when resoluteness as authentic disclosedness, is *authentically* nothing else than *Being-in-the-world?* Resoluteness brings the Self right into its current concernful Being-alongside what is ready-to-hand, and pushes it into solicitous Being with Others.[31]

Dasein, so to speak, can have no interest in foregoing all association to achieve this individualized or private state. Rather, it is unclear what such interest might look like. We would be looking for a set of conditions that enable anxiety and the turning away from absorption in the public "they"

---

[30] Heidegger, *Being and Time*, p. 294 "If Dasein stands before itself as this possibility, it has been *fully* assigned to its ownmost-potentiality-for-Being. When it stands before itself in this way, all its relations to any other Dasein have been undone. This ownmost non-relational possibility is at the same time the uttermost one." Here it becomes clear that the authentic "turn" is in ontological conflict with the role of the "they" as existentiale. The non-relational being-towards-death which sparks Dasein's authentic potentiality for being a whole amounts to a form of existentielly motivated meaninglessness and silence, an abstraction from those associations and that significance which guide and govern Dasein throughout its thrown projection. "...*this reticent self-projection upon one's ownmost Being-guilty, in which one is ready for anxiety—we call "resoluteness"*" p. 343.

[31] Heidegger, *Being and Time*, p. 344. And a bit later, on p. 345-346: "Even resolutions remain dependent upon the "they" and its world."

self; and we would be looking for something that disrupts the entirety of the existential structure of *mitsein* or mit-Dasein. Since interests are built upon the same associative movement that characterizes this very publicness, we would be looking for a set of conditions that both enact that publicness while also facilitating its elision. The crowds in this public world embodied in a conscience or in a "wanting to have a conscience" must be the cause of the attempt to turn away from it. The characterization of human existence that we get is of one that, as it comes to understand itself as being with others in the midst of a shared world, also experiences a drive to remove itself from this set of associations.[32] We might investigate the preconditions for such a drive. Must one have read Heidegger? Nietzsche? Experienced the rise of a popular culture following the Great War? What is the role of industrial production in the formation of this tendency? Electrical streetlamps? Automobiles?

"The turning-away of falling is grounded rather in anxiety..."[33] The suspicion that I am raising is the suggestion that insofar as anxiety is the trigger for this turning away—where anxiety constitutes Dasein's concern for itself in the face of its being lost or absorbed in the publicness of the "they"— it is already characterized by Dasein's absorption in the "they" through numerous associations that are crucial to the description of anxiety as a state-of-mind.[34] The associative ontology of *mitsein*, existentially equiprimordial with all other structural components of Dasein's being, indicates that the experience of anxiety would have been characterized in association with others, been understood with those others, and enacted

---

[32] Heidegger, *Being and Time*, p. 314. Also p. 334: ""Understanding the appeal" means "wanting to have a conscience"." We are individuated by a call coming from somewhere else.

[33] Heidegger, *Being and Time*, p. 230.

[34] Heidegger, *Being and Time*, p. 232: "Anxiety thus takes away from Dasein the possibility of understanding itself, as it falls, in terms of the 'world' and the way things have been publicly interpreted. Anxiety throws Dasein back upon that which it is anxious about—its authentic potentiality-for-Being-in-the-world. Anxiety individualizes Dasein for its ownmost Being-in-the-world, which as something that understands, projects itself essentially upon possibilities. Therefore, with that which it is anxious about, anxiety discloses Dasein *as Being-possible*, and indeed as the only kind of thing which it can be of its own accord as something individualized in individualization." Heidegger admits, in a footnote on p. 494, that he learned a lot from reading Kierkegaard's work on anxiety. The footnote is enough to cause some concern as to whether Heidegger's discussion of anxiety is based on phenomenology or upon his scholarly engagement with a predecessor.

with them. Proximally and for the most part, Dasein experiences itself as individuated and an understanding of its being with others and their being with Dasein is far from its everyday experience. They all think they are individuated, and they all think they stand apart. And yet, they too are easily predictable through aggregated data fed into models using common attribution to explore the relevant associations for the sake of making those predictions. Such oblivion may repeat itself in the anxiety of the professor of philosophy working to make himself stand out from the rest of his colleagues and predecessors by publishing a book to help his mentor recommend him for a university chair. The existential analytic bears with it a destruction of the history of philosophy, a historically understood enactment of the love of wisdom come upon its limits, realized in the partiality of those humans who have undertaken its pursuit. As such, it is always conditioned by that same history just as authentically disclosing Dasein turns in a way that is always conditioned by its being among others, associated with "them", and anxious about itself just as "they" are.[35]

The associations at work in the model we are experimenting with cannot be meaningfully assigned a "public" or a "private" ontological condition. If the purpose of the "private" is instead an "individualizing" tendency, then it too is a publicly conformed and identified set of actions. The shared communicative domain of being with them as they are and as our associations with them require us to be, is built into the existential structure that Heidegger's hermeneutical phenomenology has unearthed. It may be that "...anxiety individualizes"[36] but it does so from Dasein's position alongside one another, with others. This amounts to a dismantling of the public and the private spheres through the rise of sets of associations guided by policy like those we would find in the graph structure defined at the outset of this section. The actions of a human agent are associations with preconditions or aims that have an interest in preconditions and as such are always bound to the living pathways of action that constitute the real thrown projection of each agent insofar as they are the emission of a temporal sequence of events.[37] The breakdown of the domains occurs as

[35] Heidegger, *Being and Time*, p. 229: "That in the face of which Dasein flees, is precisely what Dasein comes up 'behind'. Only to the extent that Dasein has been brought before itself in an ontologically essential manner through whatever disclosedness belongs to it, can it flee in the face of that *in the face of* which it flees. To be sure, that in the face of which it flees is *not grasped* in thus turning away in falling; nor is it experienced even in turning thither. Rather, in turning away *from* it, it is disclosed 'there'."

[36] Heidegger, *Being and Time*, p. 235

[37] This summarizes an argument from *Telemetry Phenomenology*

the rise of a singular domain of association commonly characterized as generically 'social' so as to capture both the psycho-individualizing characteristics and the absorbed public characteristics. Being authentic or being inauthentic are thereby recast as slogans to initiate associations and interests in the possibilities of a human agent seeking to distinguish itself from its peers.

> No one is officially responsible for what he thinks. Instead everyone is enclosed at any early age in a system of churches, clubs, professional associations, and other such concerns, which constitute the most sensitive instrument of social control.[38]

Likewise, philosophical orientations learned in school, discussed with colleagues, and read in the work of others such as Edmund Husserl and Max Scheler. Arguably such a transformation of the public and private or authentic and inauthentic requires the perfect confluence of historical conditions involving capitalist production and democratic political order. Telemetry-driven advertisements, in this case, become the common currency for both economic and political action. The "political ad" takes on a colossal role in the public life of all persons living under such conditions. And the political ad is fabricated by the same conditions and according to the same rules as the advertisement for any product or service that is for sale. The response to the ad is measured and analyzed over and against the attributes of the consumer, models are built to understand the

---

Commonwealth: Corporate Surveillance and the Colonization of Personality. Kirkland: Lensgrinder, Ltd. 2019. The pattern of emission, analysis, feedback, and residual marks the extent to which action in a context submits to that context in ignorance of its higher order objectives, but in such a way as to assert its partiality as a set of interests and valued associations. Such partiality can be tied to Heidegger's notions of anxiety and death in *Being and Time* p. 287: "Thus if we are to be able, by comparison, to define that *Being of the "not-yet"* which is of the character of Dasein, we must take into consideration entities to whose kind of Being *becoming* belongs." (emphasis added) It can also be tied to the absorption that any interest and association demand for their proper realization in concert with the agency of the previously described middleware to which the action context has been delegated. We are collectively partial to our own individualizing behavior regardless of what social associations they demonstrate. And what is more, we cannot see it, our view is obscured, it is a partial view.

[38] Max Horkheimer and Theodor Adorno, *Dialectic of Enlightenment.* Translated by John Cumming. New York: Continuum. 1991. P. 163.

response, and feedback is returned to the campaign to improve its efficiency and optimize its likelihood of reaching its target. The sense in all such cases is to demonstrate to a viewer the necessity of a given set of associations and the interests that facilitate and condition them, all of which can be learned from the statistical data being collected and analyzed. This potential is realized when this or that toothpaste is advocated because of its whitening power and the effect it will have on the consumer, as well as when the pundit indicates that this or that agenda will have such and such an effect on the quality of life of the citizen voters. The details are left to the specific engagement based off the model of how discovered associations map to likely outcomes deemed desirable to the advertiser. In all such matters, the associations are under scrutiny. The demand for attention amounts to a demand to engage, to associate, and to recognize the preconditions of one's interests in those associations. We advertise for sets of associations, attempting to make links in the agent's action such that an orientation toward the promoted ends will be instigated.

> Advertising and the culture industry merge technically as well as economically. In both cases the same thing can be seen in innumerable places, and the mechanical repetition of the same culture product has come to be the same as that of the propaganda slogan. In both cases the insistent demand for effectiveness makes technology into psycho-technology, into a procedure for manipulating men. In both cases the standards are the striking yet familiar, the easy yet catchy, the skillful yet simple; the object is to overpower the customer, who is conceived as absent-minded or resistant.[39]

The allure could exploit the old categories for the sake of reinforcing the new ones, use the idealized beauty of the noble Cartesian subject for the sake of pushing and pulling the distributed personae constructed out of associations and interests. In order to truly individuate yourself, you must vote for the right candidate or consume the right product. The pundit or the product individuate themselves and project a resolute individuation as promised should the audience attend to them, associate with them, and attach their interests to them in their solicitous exchange. The effectiveness of these influences in people's lives would not be likely to go unnoticed in the evaluation of election committees strategizing about the best ways to get their candidate into office or keep them there. Whatever it is that the culture industry is fabricating, the ads are trying to get you to buy it. Lifeworld, Inc. is an omnipresent social domain without boundaries that

---

[39] Horkheimer and Adorno, *Dialectic of Enlightenment*, p. 163.

would permit a public or private characterization of the existential and ontological structure of human existence.

> Ever since the marketing of the editorial section became interdependent with that of the advertising section, the press (until then an institution of private people insofar as they constituted a public) became an institution of certain participants in the public sphere in their capacity as private individuals; that is, it became the gate through which privileged private interests invaded the public sphere.[40]

And

> One may speak of re-feudalization of the public sphere in yet another, more exact sense. For the kind of integration of mass entertainment with advertising, which in the form of public relations already assumes a 'political' character, subjects even the state itself to its code. Because private enterprises evoke in their customers the idea that in their consumption decisions they act in their capacity as citizens, the state has to 'address' its citizens like consumers. As a result, public authority too competes for publicity.[41]

The private sphere is that which has been left to the business concerns for colonization independently of public political concern. Privacy was already inhabited by social mechanisms and the contemporary transformation brought on by telemetric middleware amounts to this invasion of the public sphere by such private social forces. Habermas, of course, still thinks some version of authenticity remains possible to an agent under such conditions, although it is not the form seized upon within the existential analytic (viz. a phenomenological authenticity).

> The political public sphere of the social welfare state is marked by two competing tendencies. Insofar as it represents the collapse of the public sphere of civil society, it makes room for a staged and manipulative publicity displayed by organizations over the heads of a mediatized public. On the other hand, to the degree to which it

---

[40] Jurgen Habermas. *The Structural Transformation of the Public Sphere: An Inquiry into a Category of Bourgeois Society.* Translated by Thomas Burger. Cambridge: The MIT Press. 1991. P. 185.

[41] Habermas, *The Structural Transformation of the Public Sphere*, p. 195.

> preserves the continuity with the liberal constitutional state, the social welfare state clings to the mandate of a political public sphere according to which the public is to set in motion a critical process of public communication through the very organizations that mediatize it. In the constitutional reality of the social-welfare state, this form of critical publicity is in conflict with publicity merely staged for manipulative ends. The extent to which the former type prevails gauges the degree of democratization of an industrial society constituted as a social-welfare state— namely, the rationalization of the exercise of social and political authority.[42]

The difference is clear in that individualization is not the goal, but instead we see the beginnings of the gesture in the direction of communicative action where wisdom prevails. There is a common pattern. We have a conflicting set of conditions at work and the tension must yield the conditions for their own overcoming or any resulting turning away. The means of communication have been saturated with a corrupted notion of the 'public' while the liberating communication of rational agents aimed at achieving understanding must venture through that very same media or middleware. The welfare state is no longer a purified public political domain but is invested in the social conditions of citizens. The social domain becomes the appropriate locus for enacting a consensus oriented toward understanding and thus all the originally affective private forces pose a continued threat to any liberating maneuvers. In both this orientation and in Heidegger's the dynamic of a saving power and a greatest danger are integrally fabricated.

The tension at work here raises the possibility that any escape plan will repeat the pattern of what it is escaping from.[43] As regards the notion of

---

[42] Habermas, *The Structural Transformation of the Public Sphere*, p. 232.

[43] Dasein in fully resolute communication with others, for example, may turn out to be a terrifying event: "But if fateful Dasein, as Being-in-the-world, exists essentially in Being-with Others, its historizing is a co-historizing and is determinative for it as *destiny*. This is how we designate the historizing of a community, of a people. Destiny is not something that puts itself together out of individual fates, any more than Being-with-one-another can be conceived as the occurring together of several Subjects. Our fates have already been guided in advance, in our Being with one another in the same world and in our resoluteness for definite possibilities. Only in communicating and in struggling does the power of destiny become free. Dasein's fateful destiny in and with its 'generation' goes to make up the full authentic historizing of Dasein."

"becoming what one is", we come upon the basic reflexive problem that a disingenuous moment of detachment will proclaim itself liberated while acting under the opaquely positioned functions and conditions of that same set of associations. The intellectual complexity of such liberating agency is not a safeguard against coercion but is an indication of its immanent possibility. The cognitively sophisticated reasoning of wise human beings seeking to transform themselves into lovers of wisdom are more deeply involved in sets of associations that are likely to spring this trap. And what is more, since their associations may be durably supported with extremely complicated conditions with all kinds of complex relationships and derivations, the likelihood of an invisible influence in the realization of their end is significantly higher. More moving parts amounts to more parts that can be moved through telemetry's feedback loops. With any added complexity in the associative experience of an agent, the likelihood of concealed forces and conditions increases: the more nooks and crannies that there are in a worldview, the more places there are for the middleware to wrap execution.

The realization of a philosophical act cannot reliably advocate an end state of associations and interests. It cannot project a totality or rationalized structure, an end state representing an achieved understanding. Such would be the idealized state of a projected authenticity or of a communicative understanding. Any philosophical maneuver that distances the specimen from the species is ideological. Similarly, any maneuver that unites all members of the species in a common configuration of associations and interests is utopian.[44] Instead, the pattern that each of these mistaken orientations follow can reveal the ongoing necessity of uncovering conditions at work in the formation of associations, including critical reflection aiming at grasping the delegate that fires the event wrapping the current cognitive operation. Not so much an instance of the hermeneutical circle where the pre-understanding is made apparent in any consequent understanding, but where the hidden middleware is executing the action and driving all efforts at discovery through it. The enactment of such

---

Heidegger, *Being and Time*, p. 436. The shadow of the Heidegger affair makes possible a chilling reading of this passage.

[44] Karl Mannheim. *Ideology and Utopia: An Introduction to the Sociology of Knowledge.* Translated by Louis Wirth and Edward Shils. New York: Harcourt. 1936. P. 40: Ideology: "...ruling groups can in their thinking become so intensively interest-bound to a situation that they are simply no longer able to see certain facts which would undermine their sense of domination." And Utopia: "...certain oppressed groups are intellectually so strongly interested in the destruction and transformation of a given condition of society that they unwittingly see only those elements in the situation which tend to negate it."

practices at work in any becoming of what one is can only take as its objective the understanding of the associations and interests at work in such understanding. This circular motion constitutes a pattern of departure that can never leave the domain from which it originates, it becomes questioning, a perpetual anxious circling and orienting, an ongoing effort at achieving understanding of the conditions at work in one's efforts at achieving understanding. Such is the fullest realization of hermeneutical circularity and interpretation. Enacting this, like it or not, articulates how one becomes what one is.[45]

---

[45] It remains to be seen whether a non-individuating state of anxiety or experience of finitude takes place outside of an organizational context independent of its boundaries, or whether it is precisely in the personified phenomenological interleaving of the organization's operations that anxiety has its meaning.

Anxiety and Death
the hinge in *Being and Time*

The Turn

In the "Letter on Humanism", Heidegger writes:

> The adequate execution and completion of this other thinking that abandons subjectivity is surely made more difficult by the fact that in the publication of *Being and Time* the third division of the first part, "Time and Being", was held back. Here everything is reversed. The section in question was held back because thinking failed in the adequate saying of this turning and did not succeed with the help of the language of metaphysics. The lecture "On the Essence of Truth", thought out and delivered in 1930 but not printed until 1943, provides a certain insight into the thinking of the turning from "Being and Time" to "Time and Being". This turning is not a change in standpoint from *Being and Time*, but in it the thinking that was sought first arrives at the location of that dimension out of which *Being and Time* is experienced, that is to say, experienced from the fundamental experience of the oblivion of Being.[1]

1) The reference to an "other thinking" is supposed to suggest that kind of thinking that thinks the question concerning the meaning of Being, the question that has been forgotten in the history of ontology or metaphysics. 2) This thinking is not the thinking of a subject, that belongs to a subject as a faculty or capacity inhering in it. This traditional manner of conceiving "thought" is what *Being and Time*[2] seeks to destroy in raising and posing the forgotten question. 3) The context of these remarks is a letter Heidegger is writing in which, among other things, he is rejecting any humanistic or anthropological reading of his project. This reading was the

---

[1] Martin Heidegger. "Letter on Humanism" in *Basic Writings*. Translated by Frank A. Capuzzi and J. Glenn Gray. New York: Harper Perennial Modern Thought. 2008. PP. 207-208.

[2] Martin Heidegger. *Being and Time*. Translated by John MacQuarrie and Edward Robinson. New York: Harper Perennial Modern Thought. 2008.

most popular one that met *Being and Time* when it was first published, and it stuck to it throughout the twenty years between then and the letter. The reading that is a misreading—according to Heidegger, is justified because of the missing parts, most notably this third division of part one called "Time and Being". 4) Heidegger suggests here that this division of *Being and Time* was "held back" and it was held back because the language employed in *Being and Time* (a self-described fundamental ontology) was too deeply indebted to metaphysics to perform the "turning" that such a division would have required. 5) This "turning" is not a change in the standpoint taken up in *Being and Time* and has been further articulated in a lecture that addresses the essence of truth much as *Being and Time* does shortly after the discussion of anxiety in chapter six of Division One.

What does "held back" mean in this context? Are we to understand that Heidegger wrote a third division but did not publish it? Was it Heidegger who "held back"? The section in question was itself a turning, a turn: the inversion or turn from "Being and Time" to "Time and Being." And this section where such a turn takes place was held back because "thinking failed in the adequate saying of this turning." Thinking failed to say or articulate this turn. And, as he goes on to say, the language of metaphysics—which was assisting in "thinking's" attempt to say the turn, was of no help at all. The problem is that, despite the remarks in the introduction suggesting the contrary as a requirement, *Being and Time* was too dependent on the language of metaphysics.

Maybe it was not Heidegger who held back the third division of part one, but Being.[3] And Being refused to grant the turning to the extent that the language Heidegger used to set up the discussion was too deeply indebted to the grammar of traditional metaphysics, making it impossible to properly articulate a newly conceived non-metaphysical approach. If *Being and Time* were properly on the path toward the event of the question, the metaphysical assistance (the language of ontology) that it carried with it made the event's arrival impossible. I cannot help but think that the explanation of the fourth and fifth points in the commentary is linked in some way to the first three points. Namely, that the failure of thinking that took place in *Being and Time* was communicated to Heidegger through the readings the book received after it had been offered

---

[3]This may hold true even if Heidegger did send a manuscript called "Time and Being" to a publisher, only to withdraw it later. That a manuscript was given a title does not suggest that the project proscribed for that manuscript took place in it and it may very well have been Heidegger's realization that the material had been held back (where 'held back' was euphemism for 'missing from the exposition') that led him to omit whatever material he had developed for that part of the book.

for public consideration. And this may be linked to the statements about subjectivity and its hostility toward the other thinking. That is, the anthropological reading of *Being and Time* as a modified form of human being, continued to subject Dasein to a metaphysical understanding. When interpreters like Husserl and other "professional" philosophers read Dasein as though it meant something like "the self" where that self is in the world as opposed to being alienated from it, like in Descartes, they continue to think of Dasein as a subject or thinking thing. Heidegger has always maintained that the subject is not an entity but a metaphysical way of understanding the role that some entity has relative to every other entity. Whatever entity functions as a foundation for knowledge, existence, value or whatever, it is functioning as the subject. Dasein understood as a self who discovers the question concerning the meaning of Being in its own existence, continues to function as a subject, as the subject of the question. Such an understanding of Dasein cannot undergo a turning toward "Time and Being" but only thinks "Dasein and Temporality" and "Dasein and Being".

This reading of *Being and Time* fails to understand the meaning of Dasein's death. It robs Dasein of its defining act in the same instant that it robs it of its mortality and finitude. This happens because Dasein conceived as a subject continues to be that in the light of which everything has meaning, value, existence, etc. Dasein would be, in that case, the conditioning agent of everything that exists, making it impossible to raise the question concerning the meaning of Being and leaving us with some pale question concerning the meaning of Being for Dasein. In other words, such a Dasein is without limits, is unlimited by Being, and hence, infinite.[4] And such an infinite Dasein cannot die, nor think that it will and would never take itself as an issue for itself, would never question concerning itself. And what is more, such a Dasein can never decide concerning its limit,

---

[4]The basis of Dasein's finitude, realized in its Being-towards-death is its thrownness into the world. That is, Dasein is essentially determined by the element of facticity—that it is without having chosen to be. Dasein, at least as human existence, is fabricated through no control of its own. The historical conditions that project Dasein on its way are something other than Dasein and lie beyond Dasein's control; as such, they provide the basis of that same finitude. This suggests to me that there is a high risk of being fooled when one understands oneself in terms of one's most authentic Being. If only "authentic" Dasein can initiate an existential analytic, then anyone who initiates such a project is likely to think they see political and social discourse with the utmost clarity, making them capable of developing their own work in terms of a rising mass movement spinning what "they" say into an authentic philosophical inquiry.

concerning its own thrownness, such a Dasein cannot turn toward the thrown projection of its own disclosedness, and so would never recognize itself as having been born and cultivated among and by others in accordance with the ways in which "they" existentielly *are*. Such a Dasein would never question concerning the meaning of its Being.

It has often been suggested that Dasein disappeared from Heidegger's work because of a "turn." This is a commonly posed commentary on Heidegger's corpus in which the period of the "turn" (1931-1935) is supposed to suggest a turn from Dasein to Being.[5] This would mean that Heidegger discarded Dasein when his thinking turned from the metaphysically assisted existential analytic to the other thinking of Being. This further hints at an understanding of *Being and Time* that makes it fundamentally, and not just stylistically, corrupt. That is, the corrupt element in *Being and Time* was the route through Dasein, as if Heidegger had made it impossible to recall the question concerning the meaning of Being by beginning with an entity that ultimately could only have the status of a subject and thus present us with still another version of traditional metaphysics. This approach is inconsistent with Heidegger's remarks in the *Letter*. It may be the case that a renewed reading of *Being and Time* offers a deeper understanding of this "turn" and makes it possible to reject Heidegger's claim that the turn from "Being and Time" to "Time and Being" was held back, suggesting that the proposed project of *Being and Time* could be fulfilled through a re-reading. Can the success of *Being and Time* be found in the text itself and does Heidegger's rejection of it, in the *Letter* and elsewhere, result from his forgetfulness in relation to what "they" were saying about his work?[6]

Polemically, Dasein's death marked a wrong turn, since ultimately it is the adequate thinking of this turning that will bring an end to the traditional role Dasein plays in the history of philosophy. Dasein's death and the anxiety associated with it, provides a methodological turning that hints at a reading of *Being and Time* undermining the everyday understanding of the work and the existentiell material that fills it. Because Heidegger began with the existential analytic of Dasein, he obscured the possibility of appropriately posing the very question which the early work sought to raise,

---

[5]Wheeler, Michael, "Martin Heidegger", *The Stanford Encyclopedia of Philosophy* (Winter 2018 Edition), Edward N. Zalta (ed.), URL = <https://plato.stanford.edu/archives/win2018/entries/heidegger/>.

[6] More than a juvenile play on words, this is paradigmatic of my position: they are everywhere, and they are not to be outstripped. They are a factical certainty. They are the boundary condition of Dasein's determinateness, Dasein's finitude.

unless the methodology for his approach is correctly understood by its readers. Regardless of whether this complies with his remarks in the *Letter* on what has been "held back," it may yet be possible to offer a different way of understanding *Being and Time* such that it makes its way toward the turning that will bring about the end of Dasein, the turning that is "Time and Being".[7]

The Hinge

Throughout *Being and Time*, Heidegger is fond of examples and images from carpentry: most notably that hammer that keeps propping up his discussion of instruments ready-to-hand for their employment in projects. Following Heidegger, I am offering an image from carpentry to initiate this new reading: the hinge. Hinges, of course, are devices for making a plank of wood that fills a passageway from one space to another, or from the inside of a dwelling to the outside, turn out of the way when such a passage is desired. The hinge makes the ensemble into a doorway. Depending on how heavy the door, hinges might be responsible for making that place into a passageway as opposed to a blocked route. The turning of the hinges on a door is the opening of a pathway between the inside and the outside of a place, they are essential to any way-making between inside and outside. As such, they mark the threshold between two places, their limit or boundary. If there is a hinge in *Being and Time*, it could be used to open a way while maintaining a limit. And what is more, this would be done through the carrying out of a turn.

Consider the mechanism further: a hinge will have one side or leg bolted to the door jamb and another bolted to the door. Between these two

---

[7] I do not know what it would take to prove this, but I am coming more and more to think that my reading contradicts Heidegger's claim that the third division of Part One was "held back". Instead, if the "hinge" succeeds in making the turn within the Being of the entity Dasein, it will have transformed the linear structure of divisions one and two into a rotating structure of which it would be possible to discover an elaborate and labyrinthine subtext devoted to "Time and Being". I suspect that if this commentary could be performed explicitly enough, the third division would become superfluous and would instead be the "belonging together" of divisions one and two. (NB: "belonging together" is a term that I have interpreted elsewhere as a supplementary notion like Derrida's *Différance*. Cf. *The Poetics of Resistance: Heidegger's Line*, Evanston, Northwestern University Press, 1996.)

sides or legs is the central cylinder that rotates allowing the door to open and close. Looking back at the table of contents in *Being and Time*, it is possible to check for a hinge: divisions one and two of part one are all that we find there. The last chapter of the first and the first chapter of the second division are positioned much like the legs of the hinge that I described, they form the middle of the "manuscript." Division one, chapter six is called "Care as the Being of Dasein" and it contains discussions of totality, anxiety, care, truth, and the problem of reality. Division two, chapter one is called "Dasein's Possibility of Being-A-Whole and Being-Towards-Death" which concerns a variety of different issues relevant to Dasein's orientation toward its impending death and the ontological role it plays in Dasein's constitution.

In these two chapters, we find an overall concern with the place where Dasein comes upon its limit and begins to understand what that means. This limit should not be narrowly conceived as a time in the future in which Dasein will die, but that the finitude apprehended in the limit is always with Dasein, intrinsic to its ongoing existence. This is the hinge in *Being and Time* and we can proceed to a detailed commentary to unpack its role as such. As context for this commentary, note that the second division is supposed to open a dimension of temporality that it will be possible to place backward into the existentially structural elements discussed in the first division. As such, Heidegger spends a lot of time in the second division retrieving terms and concepts from the first division to engage them in the additional movement that the discovery of temporality will bring. One could see this as a kind of circling back to the first division with the addition of what has come in the meantime. If the second division is to turn back to the first division, there must be some way for it to turn, and something that has made this turn possible both in terms of its conception and its performance. Considering the discussions of anxiety, truth, and being-towards-death (among other elements) to be the hinge in the book, addresses both the programmatic and material concerns of this circling back. The following commentary will attempt to show this.[8]

The first five chapters of the book provide a conceptual map of the various structural elements of Dasein. The existentialia provide a structural analysis of Dasein's existence, producing a schema that lets us know *who*

---

[8]Notice the way that the hinge suggests the crucial synonymy of retrieval and turning toward the other thinking of Being. One element of this early project that Heidegger never seems to have changed his mind about is the way in which the destruction of the history of ontology and the replacing of that same history with the region of an other thinking belong together. Of course, it has since become standard to refer to this belonging together of destruction and replacement as "deconstruction."

Dasein *is*. Dasein is meant to contain everything essential and exceptional in conscious being and most readers will be at least partially inclined to identify at least some facets of their existence with the description. And then chapter six begins with the claim that Dasein's structure makes up a whole, a kind of totality. This totality is not the sum of the parts that have been presented in the course of the last five chapters. Instead, Heidegger says:

> The Being of Dasein, upon which the structural whole as such is ontologically supported, becomes accessible to us when we look all the way *through* this whole *to a single* primordially unitary phenomenon which is already in this whole in such a way that it provides the ontological foundation for each structural item in its structural possibility.[9]

Here we acquire evidence of the assistance Heidegger's project is receiving from the language of metaphysics. Dasein's 'totality' is more than a sum of its parts, rather it is a 'totality' that is determined by something that is ontologically basic to every element that is discovered in Dasein's structure. No doubt such a passage promotes that humanist reading of the book that makes Dasein into a subject. What could be clearer, this foundationally derived 'totality' is the Dasein entity as subject using a Kantian model where existentialia are synonymous with categories?

Dasein's function in *Being and Time* is to serve as way-making to further the project of formulating the question concerning the meaning of Being. There is something peculiar about Dasein that allows an existential analysis to reveal Dasein's ways of Being and to do so in such a way that the movement from Dasein's Being to Being itself will become possible. This peculiarity of Dasein is its own interest and concern for its own existence. "An understanding of Being belongs to Dasein's ontological structure. As something that is, it is disclosed to itself in its Being."[10] The way in which Dasein discloses itself to itself is through a state-of-mind that Heidegger calls "anxiety" (angst). The Being of Dasein revealed in anxiety is this fundamental totality called "care." The problem has been set up for us here. Regardless of whatever humanistic implications the above statements about Dasein may have, if "anxiety" and "care" cannot be made to function in the form of a subject entity, then the humanist reading will have been made incoherent and a turning begun.

---

[9] Heidegger, *Being and Time*, p. 226.

[10] Heidegger, *Being and Time*, p. 226.

Dasein moves through the world ordinarily in a kind of oblivion, thinking itself to be an individual and yet thoroughly conditioned by its relationship with others and the organized world within which its personality has been cultivated. That is, the everyday concerns of Dasein are directed at specific entities that are relevant to Dasein's projects. Dasein fetishizes itself and its projects thus failing to see the extent to which its concerns are their concerns, are the standard concerns of any random Dasein that exists within the world and alongside the countless others there with it. In "anxiety," however, Dasein is wrenched out of this everyday existence through the disclosure of its own essential Being as something vulnerable to destruction and whose destruction is singularly relevant to itself as a Dasein distinct from all others. Ordinarily, there is a "*fleeing* of Dasein in the face of itself"[11] where Dasein "turns *away from* itself in accordance with its ownmost inertia of falling."[12] Dasein turns away from itself where this turning away, this falling, can only be understood as a failure to face up to its existence as a finite entity distinct from others and as a fleeing *as such*. Dasein, in its everyday way of existing, escapes itself, enacts a fleeing in the face of itself which therefore already discloses, albeit in a privative sense, that away from which Dasein is turning and fleeing.

> From an existentiell point of view, the authenticity of Being-one's-Self has of course been closed off and thrust aside in falling; but to be thus closed off is merely the *privation* of a disclosedness which manifests itself phenomenally in the fact that Dasein's fleeing is a fleeing *in the face of* itself. That in the face of which Dasein flees, is precisely what Dasein comes up 'behind'. Only to the extent that Dasein has been brought before itself in an ontologically essential manner through whatever disclosedness belongs to it, *can* it flee *in the face of* that in the face of which it flees. To be sure, that in the face of which it flees is *not grasped* in thus turning away in falling; nor is it experienced even in turning thither. Rather, in turning away *from* it, it is disclosed 'there'.[13]

Not only is "it" disclosed there but, as the playful language suggests, the 'there' itself (da) is disclosed in its Being (Sein): as fleeing in the face of

---

[11] Heidegger, *Being and Time*, p. 229.

[12] Heidegger, *Being and Time*, p. 229.

[13] Heidegger, *Being and Time*, p. 229.

itself, da-sein.[14] The 'there' is always partial and offset as a boundary marking the situatedness of Dasein within a larger organizational totality.

It is in this context that anxiety is introduced as the state of mind of Dasein that discloses its Being in its totality. As opposed to fear which is always directed at some entity in the world, anxiety grounds the whole of Dasein's fallen Being within the world and thus its relationship with entities as such and not any specific entity. "*That in the face of which one has anxiety is Being-in-the-world as such*"[15] and "*the world as such is that in the face of which one has anxiety.*"[16] Anxiety is always related to nothing, no entity, and comes in the form of a great emptiness of significance: it is the apprehension that whatever Dasein has been will cease to be. We see in anxiety a confrontation with the abyss, the world as such over and against any entity in it. Falling is a turning away from, a fleeing in the face of, the abysmal nothingness of the world as such. Dasein's fleeing is an essential relation to an abyss which is unconcealed and casts a shadow over everything that Dasein has ever been.[17] Recalling this, calls out the fact that proximally and for the most part Dasein is in a condition of fleeing in the face of itself. And it is this disclosure of the abyss that Heidegger is referring

---

[14] Many have pointed out that this structural description need not be exclusively determinate of human beings. Any conscious creature that can be anxious and flee from itself in this way opens being 'there'. The terminological gymnastics of "Dasein" would seem to commit Heidegger to an existential functionalism although any deeper analysis of this topic is outside the present scope and is the intended purpose of my work in progress: *Artists of Despair: The Existential Analytic of Organizations.*

[15] Heidegger, *Being and Time*, p. 230.

[16] Heidegger, *Being and Time*, p. 231.

[17]"Unconcealedness" is the translation usually assigned for Heidegger's *Unverborgenheit* which is supposed to translate *aletheia* which, through its Latin translation into *veritas*, came to be known in modern English as "truth." Heidegger opts for this term over the more standard *Wahrheit* because of its negative prefix which parallels the Greek. Truth, according to Heidegger, when understood as unconcealedness is always saturated with negativity. That is, it is not pure revelation or clear and distinct, but every revelation is essentially interwoven with concealment. Furthermore, unconcealedness is not some relationship between two entities (like the correspondence of a thing to an assertion about it) but is rather the coming into existence of any thing at all (whether it be an assertion or an entity in the world). Before any assertion can be made about an entity, there must be an entity, etc. This *process* through which entities come to be is called "unconcealedness" or, in the next few paragraphs, "disclosedness." This is described both in section 44 of *Being and Time* and in the previously mentioned lecture "On the Essence of Truth."

to as the 'there' of Being that comes up behind Dasein and chases it while it flees.

Dasein's everyday being is forgetful and unquestioning of its original Being because that origin is horrifying, it is an abyss, an ab-origin (nicht ein grund aber ein abgrund). The abyss disclosed *there* in anxiety individuates Dasein in a way that its other existential structures cannot. The elements of Heidegger's Dasein analysis have all been presented as ways in which Dasein is essentially involved with the entities it comes across in the world. Anxiety, on the other hand, alienates Dasein from all entities so that it may be brought face to face with the world as such, and the world is not any thing in the world, it is no-thing, nothing. Anxiety therefore plays a similar role in Heidegger's work as hyperbolic doubt played for Descartes; it presents Dasein as a 'solus ipse':

> But this existential 'solipsism' is so far from the displacement
> of putting an isolated subject-Thing into the innocuous
> emptiness of worldless occurring, that in an extreme sense
> what it does is precisely to bring Dasein face to face with its
> world as world, and thus bring it face to face with itself as
> Being-in-the-world.[18]

Since this point is supposed to attack any humanist reading of anxiety, it is worth spending more time here.

There are two elements in Heidegger's thought that may allow this claim to do what he wants it to do. First, unlike Descartes' skepticism, anxiety does not leave Dasein in a position to pronounce its own existence as a thing, neither as a *res cogitans* nor as anything else. Throughout the book, Heidegger has tried to show that Dasein is the same as Being-in-the-world and thus Dasein has always understood itself in terms of those entities with which it has been and will be involved. Then anxiety shows Dasein, or discloses it, to itself as no thing at all since in its fallen state Dasein may have been tempted to understand itself as an individual entity much like those other entities with which it has been related.[19] Descartes' project,

---

[18] Heidegger, *Being and Time*, p. 233.

[19] It is precisely because Dasein is "proximally-and-for-the-most-part" an entity and yet also the disclosedness of entities that makes it the first and only example for use in the existential analytic aimed at posing the question concerning the meaning of Being. Dasein is not only *Being and Time*'s focus, but we see that it is through destiny that it acquires this role: no other entity can perform this task. Notice that the conception of history that a reader would take from *Being and Time* will be radically altered if this claim is understood humanistically with Dasein functioning as a subject.

therefore, would be revealed as an everyday occurrence of a modern Dasein reflecting on its own being as a thing or entity. As such, the Cartesian attitude would be an attitude typical of the everyday falling of Dasein. In the book, Heidegger refers to this as the theoretical standpoint of a Dasein who looks at entities that were once ready-to-hand for employment in projects as merely present-at-hand as objects of investigation or observation. There is more than one way to flee in the face of Dasein. On the one hand, Dasein flees by throwing itself into a world of practical activity; while on the other hand, Dasein sits back and observes those same entities from a distance. Given this latter standpoint, it was only a matter of time before Dasein turned its objectifying gaze upon itself and proclaimed itself an individual worthy of study and analysis.[20] Anxiety, to the contrary, is not concerned with any entities or things at all, it is not a state of mind that sets Dasein up as a subject, instead, it "individuates" Dasein by pulling it out of the world of entities and leaving it confronting worldhood as such: "...anxiety individualizes."[21] But individualization cannot be rendered as an aspect of an entity, rather it must be the articulation of a boundary condition between that entity and the world from which it is offset, from which it flees.

This suggests the second element that makes Heidegger's claim more coherent. We saw that anxiety discloses the Being of Dasein insofar as it discloses Being *there*. That is, the 'there' itself is disclosed 'behind' Dasein in its fleeing, thus fleeing itself places the 'da' of Dasein behind it. We cannot read this as some thing disclosed there, but rather thereness itself is disclosed, or rather disclosure is itself disclosed. That it is 'like' something to exist becomes characteristic of any entity which is 'there'. At the outset of chapter five, Heidegger referred to the 'there' (da) of Dasein as that clearing of Being where entities come to reside as the entities that they are in Dasein's involvements or projects. The entities revealed in this clearing have the status of being ready-to-hand or present-at-hand (instruments for use in projects or objects studied in inquiry) and Dasein, insofar as it understands itself as an entity, may be either an agent engaged in praxis or an observer engaged in theory. When Dasein turns away from these entities in anxiety, it loses contact with determinate entities of any kind and instead comes into contact, comes face to face with, the determining "origin" itself. That is, disclosure which discloses entities that are in some way either ready

---

[20] The extreme form of this being the 'telemetric' organizational existence that is described in *Telemetry Phenomenology Commonwealth: Corporate Surveillance and the Colonization of Personality*. Kirkland: Lensgrinder, Ltd. 2019.

[21] Heidegger, *Being and Time*, p. 235.

for use or present for observation is no longer the concealed origin of entities but appears as disclosedness to Dasein. And what is most uncanny for Dasein in this experience is that Dasein discovers that this disclosure at the origin of entities is Dasein itself, the 'there' of Being, the clearing of Being.[22] Whatever there is, is tempered through Dasein's involvements with it and relationship to it.

If this is a form of idealism, it is the strangest form anyone has ever seen, since it is an idealism based in ecstatic temporality and without any ideas since ideas themselves are founded on a specific way in which Dasein can be. What is more, it is an idealism without a thinking thing in which those ideas inhere since the cognition and thinghood both are founded on a specific way in which Dasein can be.

> If the 'subject' gets conceived ontologically as an existing Dasein whose Being is grounded in temporality, then one must say that the world is 'subjective'. But in that case, this 'subjective' world, as one that is temporally transcendent, is 'more Objective' than any possible 'Object'.[23]

Dasein has come face to face with the origin of the meaningful world and discovered itself *there* staring back at it. This nothingness of the origin of the world, this speculative ab-original disclosure, whatever it is, is nothing human. There is no other way in which a human being can be thought than as an entity existing within the world and characterized by attributes and conditions. Dasein may have a lot in common with a human being, but it most certainly is not a human being. The uncanny or *unheimlich* experience of anxiety not only wrenches Dasein out of its involvements with entities, but estranges it from its everyday manner of Being in the world as an entity, which might mean, as a self-conceived human being understood in a certain way in relationship to entities understood in a certain way (homo faber and tools or homo sapiens and objects).

---

[22] Heidegger, *Being and Time*, p. 401-402: "The entity which bears the title "Being-there" is one that has been '*cleared*. The light which constitutes this clearedness of Dasein, is not something ontically present-at-hand as a power or source for a radiant brightness occurring in the entity on occasion. That by which this entity is essentially cleared—in other words, that which makes it both 'open' for itself and 'bright' for itself—is what we have defined as "care", in advance of any 'temporal' Interpretation. In care is grounded the full disclosedness of the "there". ... *Ecstatical temporality clears the "there" primordially.* It is what regulates the possible unity of all Dasein's existential structures."

[23] Heidegger, *Being and Time*, p. 418.

Anxiety reveals two possibilities of Being for Dasein, Dasein may be authentically or it may be inauthentically. "These basic possibilities of Dasein show themselves in anxiety as they are in themselves—undisguised by entities within-the-world, to which proximally and for the most part, Dasein clings."[24] Authenticity suggests a way of Being in which Dasein is distinguished from the things in the world and thus suggests that authentic Dasein has in some way faced up to that in the face of which inauthentic Dasein flees. The difference between the two possibilities is not understood by falling Dasein since this fleeing is always a fleeing from its authentic Being. The failure to grasp that privative disclosedness revealed in fleeing is also the failure to understand that there is some alternative to it. Therefore, only a Dasein that has turned to face itself has these possibilities before itself as possibilities. Only authentic Dasein understands that it is mostly inauthentic and absorbed by the things and others that populate the world.

Heidegger opens the section on care by recalling that the phenomenon of anxiety was supposed to disclose Dasein's totality to it. Can it do this? He answers this question affirmatively by recounting the three elements of anxiety in systematic fashion: anxiety is a way of Being in the world that is anxious in the face of Dasein's being thrown and anxious about Dasein's potential. These elements of anxiety are meant to recall some of the basic elements of Dasein's structure described throughout the first five chapters. Put simply, they suggest that Dasein is anxious in the face of its origins for the sake of its worldly possibilities. When Dasein tries to outrun that in the face of which it flees, it is trying to elude that which discloses the conditions of its Being in the world. When I said that this aboriginal Being of Dasein was the disclosive power of the world itself, this indicated that Dasein would discover in its original state its own conditions for existence as an entity in the world. Discovering this shakes Dasein to its core because of its possible effects on its potential existence, on its relationships with those others that it loves and those projects with which it concerns itself. By discovering its own origin, Dasein risks no longer being able to concern itself with those same projects and those same others that it has been concerned with while fleeing.[25]

---

[24] Heidegger, *Being and Time*, p. 235.

[25]This abstract point can be made clearer through a slightly different phrasing: imagine that you discover that your self-understanding is the result of the constitution of a subjectivity by socially emergent power relations. Through a critical mechanism, you then attempt to get behind this social construction to discover what you "really are." What you find, of course, is nothing: the loss of

Anxiety therefore has an existential (the way Dasein is as anxious in the face of that which it flees), factical (the origin of Dasein's thrown Being in the world from which it is fleeing), and fallen (its rigid insistence on adhering to its everyday concerns) nature. This threefold characterization enables anxiety to reveal the totality of Dasein because the context created by the synthesis of these three facets already is the origin of Dasein disclosed privatively. Therefore, that which anxiety discloses will be a positively grasped account of this same origin.

Heidegger goes on to describe the threefold nature of care as that positive description of the Being of Dasein: "ahead-of-itself-Being-already-in-(the world) as Being-alongside (entities encountered within the world)."[26] Ahead of itself suggests that Dasein is concerned with its potential to be this or that, already in the world suggests that Dasein has been thrown into the world and finds itself already there, and being alongside entities within the world suggests Dasein's involvement with those things that make up its projects. When Dasein turns to face itself so as to discover the source from which it has been fleeing in anxiety, it discovers that it is not fleeing on accident, but that its fleeing is its falling away from that which has thrown it out into the world. The care structure of Dasein is the structure of a Dasein that is always in some sense falling or fleeing in anxiety. Anxiety is how Dasein lives its finite boundary as a partial being offset by an organizational existential context where it finds itself.

In order to pursue this issue to clear up any confusion that is likely to follow from it, it is necessary to skip ahead to the chapter on death, bypassing an isolated look at the section on truth and the problem of reality which have been designed to avoid any possible misunderstanding of Heidegger's proximity to the Cartesian subject and any humanist reading of *Being and Time* based on it. I will only say in passing that the hinge turns on this notion of truth as disclosedness just as the legs of the door's hinge turn on the cylinder inserted between them. Commentaries available on *Being and Time* rarely give any clear sense of the structure of chapter six and omit any detailed investigation of how disclosedness, reality, and truth bridge the discussions of anxiety and being-towards-death's relationship to care. It is to be hoped that my reading here has at the very least suggested why it was essential for Heidegger to proceed in the way that he did.

In turning toward death, I will start by deepening our awareness of what the problem is at this point. Anxiety reveals care as the structure of Dasein. In so doing, however, it makes it difficult to understand how Dasein ever becomes anxious. That is, why would a thrown Being in the world

---

everyone and everything that matters to you. What then? This is the question confronting Dasein at this point in the commentary.

[26] Heidegger, *Being and Time*, p. 237.

concerned with its own potential and alongside entities within the world ever sense the origin that it is fleeing from, ever sense the existence of something in the face of which it flees? That is, how is it that there is anxiety at all and not rather complete oblivion? Secondly, there is a problem as to how anything other than inauthenticity is possible given that anxiety discloses the care structure which may only be conceivable in terms of a fleeing or turning away. In other words, what constitutes Dasein's turning toward that which it flees? Or put still another way, how could Heidegger have articulated the care structure given that its illumination required a turning back toward the origin that seems impossible given the nature of care? One more way of putting it: is it possible to fall authentically?[27]

The question as to whether it is possible for authenticity to be a modification of falling may strike some readers as obvious and immediately answered with a negative, but this would be rash. Equating inauthenticity and falling requires that authenticity surrender any kind of relations to entities within the world, since fallenness is that element of Dasein's Being that places it alongside entities. The question essential for authenticity and inauthenticity seems to be how Dasein goes about interpreting its own way of Being? Should Dasein interpret itself through the entities it finds itself alongside within the world, Dasein is inauthentic. Given the discussions in *Being and Time*, this might mean inauthenticity is Dasein understood as present-at-hand or that Dasein understands itself as an instrument ready to hand. Authenticity, to the contrary, would occur when Dasein owns up to itself (eigentlich -ownness, properness) and begins to understand worldliness (world) through its own Being disclosing clearing 'there'. This world that each of us is absorbed by is the set of significant relations that our very Being is capable of, making each of us a partial filter of what is happening there. Looking ahead to the later writings, I might say that when Dasein understands itself this way, its Being-in-the-world is alongside "things."[28] On this reading of the two, they both turn out to be modifications

---

[27]Continuing with the language of a previous footnote, I might ask: why would a subject be constructed such that it could question its own construction? Has "power" built the capacity to deconstruct into the design of the subject? Why would it do this? Note that the power/resistance problematic coming from Foucault is only a restatement of Heidegger's problem concerning the turn from inauthentic to authentic Dasein (at least in the way that I have been interpreting it). Cf. *The Poetics of Resistance: Heidegger's Line* for a further discussion of the "Derridean criticism" of propriety relative to Heidegger's notion of Authenticity / Inauthenticity / Ereignis.

[28]On this reading, the thing is always disclosed in terms of a care structure including anxiety and a being-towards-death. This means that things are incarnations of a not yet dead turning to and fro (fort/da) relative to the

of falling, that is, modifications of Being-in-the-world and alongside entities that may or may not be ready to hand, present at hand, or anything else.

> But now that falling has been exhibited, have we not set forth a phenomenon which speaks directly against the definition we have used in indicating the formal idea of existence? Can Dasein be conceived as an entity for which, in its Being, its potentiality-for-Being is an issue, if this entity, in its everydayness, has lost itself, and, in falling, 'lives' away from itself? But falling into the world would be phenomenal 'evidence' against the existentiality of Dasein only if Dasein were regarded as an isolated 'I' or subject, as a self-point from which it moves away. In that case, the world would be an Object. Falling into the world would then have to be re-Interpreted ontologically as Being-present-at-hand in the manner of an entity within-the-world. If, however, we keep in mind that Dasein's Being is in the state of Being-in-the-world, as we have already pointed out, then it becomes manifest that falling, as a kind of Being of this Being-in, affords us rather the most elemental evidence for Dasein's existentiality. In falling, nothing other than our potentiality-for-Being-in the world is the issue, even if in the mode of inauthenticity. Dasein can fall only because Being-in-the-world understandingly with a state-of-mind is an issue for it. On the other hand, authentic existence is not something which floats above fallen everydayness; existentially, it is only a modified way in which such everydayness is seized upon.[29]

This is the discussion that draws chapter five to a close. Then we turn to the discussion of anxiety which is at the seat of all falling and which discloses the disclosiveness of Dasein to it as it falls. That is, falling is the way in which the existential Being of Dasein (which will lead to the posing of the question) is disclosed, albeit in a privative sense. The key then is to circle back (execute a turn) pivoting on the disclosiveness that discloses Dasein in its fallenness (its thrown projection). Is it only a matter of which way Dasein turns as it falls? When falling inauthentically, Dasein turns

---

aboriginal disclosure of their thinghood. One could follow Hegel here and say that the thing has overcome the opposition of subject and object, which makes sense of claims I have made elsewhere concerning the thinghood of human being (whereas Dasein is never a thing, human being may be). Without this relationship, the man, Martin Heidegger, could not have written the book *Being and Time*.

[29] Heidegger, *Being and Time*, pp. 223-224.

toward the world and away from that which it is, that in the face of which it flees into the world; whereas authentically falling Dasein turns back toward itself.[30] Now the question is, how does it do this?

In chapter one of division two, Heidegger tells us that "the possibility of this entity's [Dasein's] Being-a-whole is manifestly inconsistent with the ontological meaning of care."[31] Because one of the elements of the care structure was being-ahead-of-itself, there is always something projected in Dasein's being that overflows the boundary of any possible wholeness. Although anxiety revealed the whole structure of Dasein as care, doing so equally made conceiving Dasein's structure as anything like a "whole" impossible. It seems that if Dasein is, there is always something, some possibility or element of Dasein, that is still outstanding, that has yet to take place. Dasein's wholeness is characterized by partiality.

What marks the end of Dasein's projections, of everything still outstanding for Dasein, is Dasein's death. Since death marks Dasein's limit, it suggests its totality where that totality "can constitute *Being-a-whole* for the entity which exists."[32] But this end must function as a marker and not as an actual state for Dasein, dead Dasein is Dasein no more (but only a corpse thing present-at-hand to the mourner or ready-to-hand for the mortician). As such, the existential meaning of Dasein's death is achieved only when it is considered as something that has not yet happened, as an event that has not yet taken place but that marks Dasein's Being with a projected limit.[33]

---

[30] The difference between authenticity and inauthenticity, therefore, is the ontological difference between Being and beings. In a more complete commentary on *Being and Time*, it would become possible to show how the realization of this difference taking place in authenticity (which also comprehends the meaning of inauthenticity for the first time) is that element of Dasein which composes its most basic existentiell activities. When Dasein becomes authentic, it comprehends difference (it becomes the ontological difference per se by encircling it), and thus makes possible the posing of the question concerning the meaning of Being from the position of the ontological difference (itself). Authentic Dasein is difference insofar as authenticity is always the revelation of the to and fro (fort/da) motion between authenticity and inauthenticity. This to and fro motion is the turning back and forth of Dasein that results in the conclusion that Dasein is the hinge between Being and Time.

[31] Heidegger, *Being and Time*, p. 279.

[32] Heidegger, *Being and Time*, p. 286.

[33] The child's knowledge of death may begin with what "they" say about it (Mom and Dad, for example), but the anxiety the child experiences originates in the incorporation of the meaning of their description.

This "not-yet" *belongs* to Dasein, characterizes its every condition, it is Dasein's projected limit incorporated into the whole Being of Dasein. One might say that, in some sense, the "not-yet" incorporates Dasein as its limit, so that Dasein may be understood as always already defined by its death as a limit that saturates it through a total investment of the limit. I might go so far as to say that Dasein is always already not yet dead at its birth, since recently incarnated Dasein is already approaching its death (birth is the incarnation of the not-yet, it is the incorporation of an existential finitude). "Factical Dasein exists as born; and, as born, it is already dying, in the sense of Being-towards-death."[34] This suggests that Dasein's death is not some end that it comes to have at some moment, unknown, in the future, but that death is Dasein's being towards its end. Death is Dasein's essential partiality, its death inevitably comes but has not yet arrived and thus possibilities remain. Dasein has not yet died and so death marks a limit that is not there in its very manner of being there as limit.

Dasein's totality is a strange kind of whole since it is a structural totality that is not all there, but only anticipated as coming toward it through the stretch of time as an *issue*. "Anticipating" death is not a kind of morbid waiting for it as an actual occurrence that will one day befall Dasein. Heidegger suggests that anticipation is a form of Being-towards-death that relates to it as an essential possibility where the meaning of possibilities themselves are realized. Possibilities are always possible ways for Dasein to be into the future, ways Dasein's potential can be modified in the course of its movement through time and in the course of how it interprets itself as an *issue* for itself in questioning. The true understanding of possibility already pushes Dasein away from an inauthentic falling that views the future as worldly modifications. Anticipating Dasein no longer views its future in terms delineated by the world, a world that is then used to inauthentically interpret the Being (present, past, and future) of Dasein; instead, such a Dasein views its possibilities as emanating from itself as authentic Being-in-the-world disclosing clearing in thrown projection. That is, Dasein that anticipates its death, is Dasein turned back toward the disclosive Being of Dasein from which it has been fleeing and for which it has been anxious.[35]

> Dasein is authentically itself only to the extent that, as concernful Being-alongside and solicitous Being-with, it projects itself upon its ownmost potentiality-for-Being rather than upon the possibility of the they-self.[36]

---

[34] Heidegger, Being and Time, p. 426.

[35] i.e., Dasein stops running and becomes what it is.

[36] Heidegger, *Being and Time*, p. 308.

This reinforces the claim that authentic Dasein is falling, since it is a manner of concernful Being alongside and solicitous Being-with which means that authentic Dasein is still related to the entities of the world and the other Dasein it belongs together with there. Its concern and solicitude are existentielly modified by the anticipation of death which turns Dasein back toward its disclosure. Heidegger expresses this by writing that "in anticipating the indefinite certainty of death, Dasein opens itself to a constant *threat* arising out of its own 'there'."[37] Opening itself up in this way, can only take place—given the structure of movement described so far, through turning. Dasein has been closed off from itself in its fleeing as inauthentic falling. Opening itself up, therefore, amounts to its turning back toward its own original disclosure.

> How is it existentially possible for this constant threat to be genuinely disclosed? All understanding is accompanied by a state-of-mind. Dasein's mood brings it face to face with the thrownness of its 'that it is there'. *But the state-of-mind which can hold open the utter and constant threat to itself arising from Dasein's ownmost individualized Being, is anxiety.* In this state-of-mind, Dasein finds itself *face to face* with 'nothing' of the possible impossibility of its existence.[38]

In anticipation, the threat of death is realized as an outstanding limit that threatens the whole of Dasein's Being. And this anticipation is, ultimately, a turning back toward that which Dasein has been fleeing, namely itself. This turning back is what places Dasein face to face with the 'nothing' that is its own disclosive Being.

This description may recall again the image of the hinge. Death, discussed after anxiety, care, truth as disclosedness, and the fallacy of the Cartesian worldview, brings about a turn back toward anxiety and its nothingness. Looking at the structure of the book from this point on, it is evident that Heidegger takes up a new discussion of "care" from the point of view of authenticity (anticipatory resoluteness), then comes a temporal discussion of everydayness including understanding, state-of-mind (thrownness), falling, etc. (i.e. the topics discussed in the fifth chapter of the first division). Then comes a discussion of history understood as the way in which human Dasein is in the world with other Dasein (paralleling the topics of chapters three and four in division one). Finally, there is a

---

[37] Heidegger, *Being and Time*, p. 310.

[38] Heidegger, *Being and Time*, p. 310.

discussion of Temporality and Within-Time-Ness as essential to the Being of Dasein and suggesting a parallel to the discussion in chapter two of division one where Being-in-the-World is described as Dasein's basic state. The conclusion I draw from this is that *Being and Time* has turned back upon itself and that rather than proceeding in a linear manner from start to finish, the second division is folded back and laid on top of the first: the turning of the hinge and the establishment of a threshold has made this possible.

But how exactly has this hinge worked? Dasein's Being-towards-death has opened it to the meaning of its ownmost-potentiality for Being as anticipated possibilities. Dasein begins to show itself as a care structure that is essentially temporal, its projections are always future possibilities of its state of Being. Furthermore, in Being-towards-death, Dasein has turned back toward the nothingness of the world and seen itself as that same disclosive nothingness, that nothingness which discloses the temporal care structure. In its most essential Being, Dasein is a temporal nothing. Not only, "the null basis of a nullity," but a temporal one. The null basis that grants Dasein's Being as such, is temporality: Being (i.e. not a thing) is time. In Dasein's confrontation with its own nothingness, it confronts the nothingness of the world where the world is no thing at all. Dasein's death not only brings it face to face with its own possible impossibility, but with that possible impossibility which is the world, Being as the primordial world granting and, now, temporal movement.

To speak, therefore, (as Heidegger does) of an individuated Dasein, is to speak of a Dasein that has, in some sense, ceased to be itself in becoming completely and totally that which it *is*. The problems in understanding this claim may arise from a tendency to continue with that same anthropological humanistic reading of this work that, in some sense, views Dasein as a subject and its individuality as its fundamental assertion of subjectivity. This also suggests why it is so important to discuss the Cartesian world view in articulating the hinge of the "manuscript" and what Heidegger meant when he pointed out that the mistaken view of falling which sees fallenness as always inauthentic is a view of Dasein that maintains itself in a humanist reading. Dasein's individualizing capability can only mean Dasein's Being insofar as that Being is an issue for it, where that is the turning of Dasein back toward the null origin in the face of which it flees. What this means, is made no clearer in saying so.[39] It does, however, raise once more the

---

[39] The existentiell content of this turning could very well fall victim to a comparison with volkish ideology and the heroic historical role of an authentic understanding of a leader's relationship to his people and their destiny. Analysis along these lines is, however, beyond the scope of the current essay although raising its questionability is well within that scope. Cf. section 74 of

question concerning the meaning of Dasein and points us once again back toward Dasein's unmentioned (and unmentionable) death. The full force of this is at least within reach in coming to see that the hinge in *Being and Time* is also the anxious care structure of Dasein's Being-towards-death: Dasein's Being-a-whole, Dasein. Dasein is the hinge in *Being and Time* and through Dasein a turning may take place, letting thinking Being come in a future event.

The Story

> Existence can be questionable. If it is to be possible for something 'to be in question', a disclosedness is needed.[40]

Being and Time is not a book, not really: it is only an imagined book. Heidegger begins with a question. It is a question that will not be asked explicitly and according to any average understanding of what counts as "asking" a question. It is a question he says has been forgotten, so much so that Heidegger himself may have forgotten it: "This question has today been forgotten."[41] What does this mean, "today"? As the rest of the first paragraph of the introduction suggests, Heidegger is chastising those philosophers of his era who "deem it progressive to give... ...approval to 'metaphysics' again." But he includes himself in this group, these are the philosophers of "our time" who have given "our" approval, etc. Heidegger seems to include himself among those who have fallen victim to this forgetting. As an attempt to remember the forgotten question, *Being and Time* may present itself as Heidegger's effort at distinguishing himself from this "we" which has forgotten the question. If Heidegger wrote this introduction after he had written the rest of the book, odd as it may be to introduce a book that has not yet been completed, he may have been trying to provide some direction beyond what he was able to present for publication. In that case, when Heidegger says that "[t]his question has today been forgotten", he may be apologizing. Heidegger today, that day when he sat down to write the introduction after having written all he could for publication, apologizes to the reader for himself having forgotten the

---

Being and Time, as a brief indication of where this analysis might begin: "...may choose its hero..." and "...makes one free for the struggle of loyally following...". Heidegger, *Being and Time*, p. 437.

[40] Heidegger, *Being and Time*, p. 385.

[41] Heidegger, *Being and Time*, p. 21.

question. "You see," he might say to clarify. "I intended to raise the question but have forgotten to do so. Here is the book that has attempted to recall a forgotten question, a book that means to repeat the history of philosophy in the light of this forgotten question, and a book which has itself forgotten the question."[42]

A little further on Heidegger, as befits an introduction, attempts to explain why Dasein is going to be the focus of the investigation to come.

> If the question about Being is to be explicitly formulated and carried through in such a manner as to be completely transparent to itself, then any treatment of it in line with the elucidations we have given requires us to explain how Being is to be looked at, how its meaning is to be understood and conceptually grasped; it requires us to prepare the way for choosing the right entity for our example, and to work out the genuine way of access to it. Looking at something, understanding and conceiving it, choosing, access to it—all these ways of behaving are constitutive for our inquiry, and therefore are modes of Being for those particular entities which we, the inquirers, are ourselves. Thus to work out the question of Being adequately, we must make an entity—the inquirer—transparent in his own Being. The very asking of this question is an entity's mode of Being; and as such it gets its essential character from what is inquired about—namely, Being. This entity which each of us is himself and which includes inquiring as one of the possibilities of its Being, we shall denote by the term "Dasein". If we are to formulate our question explicitly and transparently, we must first give a proper explication of an entity (Dasein), with regard to its Being.[43]

Heidegger's forgetfulness may have reached its saturation point here. There is some indication that he is anticipating the analysis to come: all the constitutive factors mentioned as an element of any inquiry turn out to be

---

[42] As late as division two, chapter five Heidegger is still working to formulate the question: "Only after this entity has been Interpreted in a way which is sufficiently primordial, can we have a conception of the understanding of Being, which is included in its very state of Being; only on this basis can we formulate the question of the Being which is understood in the understanding, and the question of what such understanding 'presupposes'." Heidegger, *Being and Time*, p. 424.

[43] Heidegger, *Being and Time*, p. 27.

the basis of Dasein presented in chapter five, "Being-in as such." And yet, Heidegger here insists that Dasein is an entity. Not just here. Both in the introduction and in chapter five, Heidegger refers to Dasein as an entity. But in chapter five, he clarifies this claim by calling Dasein that entity which "is its disclosedness."[44]

> Dasein, as constituted by disclosedness, is essentially in the truth. Disclosedness is a kind of Being which is essential to Dasein. 'There is' truth only in so far as Dasein is and so long as Dasein is. Entities are uncovered only when Dasein is; and only as long as Dasein is, are they disclosed. Newton's laws, the principle of contradiction, any truth whatever— these are true only as long as Dasein is. Before there was any Dasein, there was no truth; nor will there be any after Dasein is no more. For in such a case truth as disclosedness, uncovering, and uncoveredness, cannot be.[45]

Dasein presupposes truth and truth presupposes Dasein. That is, "the kind of Being that is essential to truth is of the character of Dasein, all truth is relative to Dasein's Being."[46] Here "presuppose" suggests "understand[ing] something as the ground for the Being of some other entity."[47] And in this case, both Dasein and truth are presupposed, they do not merely presuppose each other. Dasein presupposes itself as the disclosedness of whatever is in truth. This means that Dasein is the presupposed ground of some other entity; or rather of every entity that can be said to exist at all. Without Dasein, there is nothing.

Heidegger claims that Dasein is both Being and an entity, both the ground that lets beings be in their truth (the disclosedness of what is) and the entity that is as such. Dasein is therefore an entity *and not* an entity. "Being cannot have the character of an entity."[48] So Dasein is supposed to be an entity and yet "entities are uncovered only when Dasein is." Dasein is presupposed in the uncovering of Dasein. This cannot be the presupposition of an entity; it is not an entity that is presupposed. The Dasein that is presupposed in the Being of the entity Dasein, has the character of disclosedness or truth. And truth is not an entity.

---

[44] Heidegger, *Being and Time*, p. 171.

[45] Heidegger, *Being and Time*, p. 269.

[46] Heidegger, *Being and Time*, p. 270.

[47] Heidegger, *Being and Time*, p. 270.

[48] Heidegger, *Being and Time*, p. 23.

> Da-sein is not the kind of reality of any and every being, but
> is itself the being of the there. But the there is the openness
> of beings as such in the whole, the ground of the more
> primordially thought aletheia. Da-sein is a way to be which,
> in that it "is" (actively and transitively, so to speak), the there,
> is a unique being (what presences in the presencing of being)
> in accordance with this distinctive being and as this being
> itself.[49]

Stambaugh's translation is troubled: "is a unique entity (what presences in
the presencing of Being) in accordance with this distinctive Being and as
this Being itself." That is, there is something about Dasein, the entity, that
allows it to come to be in terms of its own presupposed Dasein,
disclosedness.   But the passage from *Beiträge* tells us something more
about this contradictory Dasein which both is and is not an entity. In section
173, Heidegger is drawing a comparison between Dasein understood in
two separate ways: Dasein understood from the point of view of the first
beginning, which suggests the metaphysical tradition, and Dasein
understood from the point of view, of the other beginning.   "The
significance and matter of the word Da-sein is completely different in the
thinking of the other beginning, so different that there is no mediating
transition from that first usage to this other."[50]
     What if Dasein, the entity, were the Dasein familiar to the history of
metaphysics, the tradition that has forgotten the question concerning the
meaning of Being? And what if that other Dasein, that Dasein that is other,
that is not an entity, that is not in any traditional sense, is the Dasein with
its Being in disclosedness? I quote again from *Beiträge*, this time it's my
translation:

> In *Being and Time*, Da-sein still gives the illusion of the
> Anthropological, Subjectivistic, and Individualistic, and so
> on; nevertheless it is the opposite of everything in that view:
> certainly not as the first and only intention, but only as the
> *necessary consequence* of the resolute change of the Being
> Question from the questioning guided by the question
> concerning the ground.[51]

---

[49]   Martin Heidegger. *Beiträge zur Philosophie (Vom Ereignis)*.
Gesamtausgabe 65. Frankfurt: Vittorio Klostermann. 1989. P. 296. Cited
passage has been translated by Joan Stambaugh in *The Finitude of Being*.
Albany: SUNY Press.

[50] Heidegger, *Beiträge zur Philosophie*, p. 296.

[51] Heidegger, *Beiträge zur Philosophie*, p. 295.

In keeping with the themes of *Being and Time*, 'Dasein'—the entity—is that Dasein which has traditionally been understood as the existence of something present, something that has been uncovered. As an entity that enquires into the nature of Being, such a Dasein would be the subject, the individual human observer who asks questions concerning the Being of entities. In accordance with Descartes' project, such a Dasein would be the present-at-hand version of the ego cogito that is the epistemic foundation for everything, the mind in which everything that exists takes on the form of an idea. This subject, this subiectum, is metaphysical Dasein, the traditional Dasein, in terms of which everything is. On the other hand, there is Dasein, that other Dasein, that Dasein that is not an entity, that is the disclosedness of entities as such and including Dasein understood as a subject. Any forgetfulness that may have been exposed at the outset is overturned by *repetition* in an alternative orientation toward the past, one which forces a rethinking of the history of the subject, and grips Dasein with anxiety:

> The forgetting which is constitutive for fear, bewilders Dasein and lets it drift back and forth between 'worldly' possibilities which it has not seized upon. In contrast to this making-present which is not held on to, the Present of anxiety is held on to when one brings oneself back to one's ownmost thrownness. [52]

That is, when one turns back toward it, "...*bringing one face to face with repeatability*..."[53] Anxiety thus draws together the dynamic of repetition that surges in both the historical and the existential analyses that mark the outline of the move from Being and Time to Time and Being.

"Has Dasein as itself ever decided freely whether it wants to come into 'Dasein' or not, and will it ever be able to make such a decision?"[54] Has Dasein, the entity, ever decided to disclose itself? Could it? Notice that the interpretation here makes this question meaningful, it asks after the nature of Dasein's thrownness and whether that thrownness could possibly be something that belongs to Dasein, the entity. What kind of a relationship can an entity such as Dasein have toward its own disclosedness? This is the direction in which the question forces thinking to move and yet this same interpretation of Dasein is at work in this movement of thought. Without

---

[52] Heidegger, *Being and Time*, p. 394.

[53] Heidegger, *Being and Time*, p. 394.

[54] Heidegger, *Being and Time*, p. 271.

this interpretation, the question merely asks whether Dasein can decide to be Dasein, and the impossibility of the decision seems to be necessitated by the tautology. Dasein is Dasein, no decision or deliberation necessary. What must Dasein be like for a decision to be possible for Dasein, the entity, relative to its own disclosedness? It must be split, self-divided, it must be a living, projecting, thrown contradiction, a Dasein that both is and is not an entity.

This long excursus is ultimately an attempt to show why Dasein takes center stage in *Being and Time*, why Dasein is to be the entity that is investigated in the attempt to articulate and pose the question that has been forgotten but which may now be repeated. And I mean to say Dasein the entity, for ultimately it is Dasein the entity that is being investigated in the Dasein analysis. It will be Heidegger's aim to uncover that which is presupposed in the entity Dasein and, in so doing, to investigate the meaning of this presupposition, the meaning of disclosedness, and, ultimately, the meaning of Being as the disclosedness of beings (the 'there' of Being, Da-sein). It begins with a forgotten question.

History

What secures the story is the telling of it. Section 63 of *Being and Time* describes a condition such that the telling of the story is what precipitates that existentiell movement that enables Dasein to turn upon its hinge.

> ...and, now that we have concretely worked out the structure of Dasein's Being, its peculiar ontological character has become so plain as compared with everything present-at-hand, that Dasein's existentiality has been grasped in advance with sufficient Articulation to give sure guidance for working out the *existentialia* conceptually.[55]

Insofar as authenticity does not indicate a structural transformation of Dasein, the dynamic motivation of the movement is characterized by some facet of Dasein's life as it is being projected onto possibilities from a given thrown factical state. And to the extent that this condition speaks from the point of view of the phenomenologist trying to raise the forgotten question, the philosopher asserts himself and his project in the same event, the same momentary eliciting of a question that has, for the most part, been

---

[55] Heidegger, *Being and Time*, pp. 358-359.

forgotten. "It has been shown that proximally and for the most part Dasein is *not* itself but is lost in the they-self, which is an existentiell modification of the authentic Self."[56] It is not just that the recollection of the question is discovered through the ways of Being of that being which in each case the questioner is, the questioning itself is a recollection of forgotten Being: undertaking the project itself constitutes a turning away from that fallen state which characterizes Dasein in its everydayness. Anxious Being-towards-death brings Dasein back full circle to the very raising of the forgotten question, to the instigating act that leads the philosopher to question concerning the concealed history of philosophy that yields the point of origin. "Does it not then become altogether patent in the end that this problem of fundamental ontology which we have broached, is one which moves in a 'circle'?"[57] The circularity is supported as methodology by a hinge.

> A state-of-mind is a basic existential way in which Dasein is its "there". It not only characterizes Dasein ontologically, but, because of what it discloses, it is at the same time methodologically significant in principle for the existential analytic. Like any ontological Interpretation whatsoever, this analytic can only, so to speak, "listen in" to some previously disclosed entity as it regards its Being. And it will attach itself to Dasein's distinctive and most far-reaching possibilities of disclosure, in order to get information about this entity from these. Phenomenological Interpretation must make it possible for Dasein itself to disclose things primordially; it must, as it were, let Dasein interpret itself. Such Interpretation takes part in this disclosure only in order to raise to a conceptual level the phenomenal content of what has been disclosed, and to do so existentially.
>
> Later (Cf. Section 40) we shall provide an Interpretation of anxiety as such a basic state-of-mind of Dasein, and as one which is significant from the existential-ontological standpoint; with this in view, we shall now illustrate the phenomenon of state-of-mind even more concretely in its determinate mode of *fear.*[58]

Anxiety is the methodological hinge of the project that takes issue with the forgotten question. It is anxiety that launches the phenomenological inquiry

---

[56] Heidegger, *Being and Time*, p. 365.

[57] Heidegger, *Being and Time*, p. 362.

[58] Heidegger, *Being and Time*, pp. 178-179.

and it is anxiety that brings the questioner face to face with what has been forgotten up until this moment of vision.

> Yet the factical rarity of anxiety as a phenomenon cannot deprive it of its fitness to take over a methodological function *in principle* for the existential analytic. On the contrary, the rarity of the phenomenon is an index that Dasein, which for the most part remains concealed from itself in its authenticity because of the way in which things have been publicly interpreted by the "they", becomes disclosable in a primordial sense in this basic state-of-mind.[59]

Heidegger went on to other things after this manuscript was published and his position at Freiburg secured.[60] In the years immediately following *Being and Time,* Dasein lingered and although it seems to have disappeared altogether sometime during the late 1930s, Heidegger never mentions the exact time of death. In the 1947 "Letter on Humanism", Heidegger talks about Dasein for the first time in years, but does not say what happened to it, although he does suggest that it ultimately fell victim to a turn. I suppose he meant a turn of fate or that an illness took a turn for the worse. He does not say. For all the writing about death in *Being and Time* and the contemporaneous lecture courses, Heidegger seems awfully shy when it comes to speaking of actual deaths. And not only Dasein's death, but the deaths of those "corpses manufactured in gas chambers" which he so cryptically referred to in his first draft of "The Question Concerning Technology." Is it possible that Dasein's death ultimately was as unspeakable as those other deaths that Heidegger had thought better about mentioning when he cut the sentence from the published version?

No doubt this is a chilling thought that should not be glossed over so

---

[59] Heidegger, *Being and Time*, p. 235.

[60] The, by now famous, story of the genesis of *Being and Time* is that Heidegger was up for a Professorship at Freiburg, but the decision-makers there were unhappy with his publication record and required that there be a considerable manuscript submitted somewhere to help in the evaluation of his candidacy. At Husserl's urging, Heidegger quickly put what is now known as *Being and Time* together based on notes from previous lectures. This urgency no doubt explains why Heidegger went to press with a book that was not yet finished.

Among the "other things" that he went on to was the position of Rector at Freiburg where he famously began his tenure by barring all Jews from entry to the University, including that same Husserl who first recommended him to the philosophy department there. A questionable circularity, no doubt.

briefly. Ultimately, however, this unutterable thought is the great event that the plot of this unfinished story is moving toward. It is the event that eliminates Dasein from Time and Being and that my analysis has sought to pose through the question concerning Dasein's death as a methodological mechanism forgotten by commentators, and which every commentary has pushed into oblivion, precisely because it cannot be the subject of a commentary. Dasein's partiality is off limits to that very being that would make its Being an issue for itself and whatever is disclosed there, however tightly coupled to Dasein, is nothing human although it may provide the organizational framework for any future constitution of Dasein as a subject of investigation.

Five Vignettes Exclusively Concerned with Genre

An example of scholarship

In *Experience and Judgment*, Husserl writes:

> What is now the particular character of questioning as a peculiar active mode of behavior of the ego? The passive, disjunctive tension of the problematic possibilities (doubt in the passive sense), to begin with motivates an active doubting, a mode of behavior which puts the ego into an act-cleavage.[1]

Maybe questioning is something which happens to an ego-consciousness so as to split it? The tension created in the situation is the tension between options in an "active doubling." So questioning is both something which happens to an ego-act and something which an ego-act does. What it does is not a questioning *per se* but doubting. In the questioning, the ego-act has been deprived of its "unanimity" where this is the goal of all striving undertaken by consciousness. Consciousness, as intentional, is a series of acts reaching out for fulfillment suggesting the completion of the act in its constitution of a coherent content: it becomes a thought about something determinate rather than something else. Failure to reach fulfillment results in "an immediate discomfort and an original impulse to get out of this condition and into the normal condition of unity."[2] An active striving for unity ensues, driven, apparently, by a utilitarian interest in achieving conceptual fulfillment.

According to Husserl, ordinary consciousness is a "consciousness of the world... ...in the mode of certainty,"[3] where the world as such "is always

---

[1] Edmund Husserl. *Experience and Judgment: Investigations in a Genealogy of Logic.* Translated by James S. Churchill and Karl Ameriks. 1973. Evanston: Northwestern University Press. pp. 307-308.

[2] Husserl, *Experience and Judgment*, p. 308.

[3] Husserl, *Experience and Judgment*, p. 30.

already pregiven in passive certitude."[4] The world, therefore, is not an object of cognition, but the pregiven condition of possibility for the cognition of individual entities as objects of mental acts. In the everyday mental life of the natural consciousness concern is with entities and not with anything like a world that yields the environment or domain within which these entities or acts of cognition take place. The world is the horizon within which entities as such gain a certain familiarity. And this horizon includes expectations about the appropriate manner and mode of apprehension of objects themselves. Naturally we are certain of our world and that certainty provides us with a host of very natural and familiar expectations about what sorts of things will and will not take place in an ordinary course of events. When we are unclear about what to expect, our expectations have a sense of familiarity about them. Yet, some possible event unfolding is yet to be determined: its unfolding is its becoming determinate as expectation. We expect the indeterminate to become determinate in the unfolding of the event. Things will happen and they will make sense. When I do not know what is going to happen, I know that whatever does happen will make sense.

Husserl seems to make at least one major distinction in the kinds of mental acts possible to such a consciousness: unobstructed and obstructed, where the obstruction blocks this natural attitude of pregiven certainty in object, world, and expectation. Disappointment in an expectation, or the interruption of certainty in one's relation to objects, is characterized as a modalization of certainty. And this has its origin in the world itself, or rather, in the entity that is the object of cognition. The various modes of both obstructed and unobstructed consciousness are all ultimately aimed at preserving the certainty of the natural view. Where the modalization is unobstructed, this happens in the ordinary course of its exercise. When the modalization is obstructed, there must be some active reorientation by consciousness to reestablish the mode of certainty that has been blocked. Since the obstruction is first off discovered in the object in its relationship to consciousness, the reorientation constitutes a reorientation of the mind. That is, through experience broadly conceived, consciousness must come to know the object in a way that overcomes the obstruction it has encountered.

One such form of uncertainty in the object is questioning, which, like doubt, is "originally motivated by events in the passive sphere,"[5] that is, the object is questionable, no longer certain. The disjunction in the object gives rise to "intentional conflict" within consciousness. The field of objectivity

---

[4] Husserl, *Experience and Judgment*, p. 31.

[5] Husserl, *Experience and Judgment*, p. 307.

which precedes the questioning attitude is conceived as a "unified field," but unlike the object under circumstances of certainty, the unity of the questionable object is a "unified field of problematic possibilities."[6] And consciousness is such that it cannot help but orient itself toward these problematic possibilities, not as a series of options—for that is already far more sophisticated than the original becoming questionable of the thing, but as a multiplicity within the orientation itself. The act oriented toward what is questionable is a multiplied act, an act with multiple orientations within itself. Husserl conceives this multiplicity as an act-cleavage. The active consciousness has been divided or split within itself in its active orientation toward the questionable object obstructing the previously certain expectations of it.

> This cleavage brings with it, on the basis of the essential striving of the ego for the unanimity of its acts of position-taking, an immediate discomfort and an original impulse to get out of this condition and into the normal condition of unity. Thus arises the striving for a firm decision, i.e., ultimately for an unfrustrated, pure decision.[7]

The anxious ego, consciousness, suffers its uncertainty as a boundary condition, suffers its schism as a frustration, and seeks, above all, a decision. Husserl refers to active attempts at striving for decision as questioning behavior by an ego-consciousness. Questioning therefore is not the act-cleavage itself, the multiplied act, rather that is referred to as "doubting." Questioning is the doubt taken up as an active striving to overcome or reunify the split in the object of consciousness. This questioning act is not oriented toward the questionable per se. It is the striving act that seeks to overcome the questionable which has given rise to it. Questioning as act constitutes its own object: the questionable object as questionable. This content of questioning is called "the question."

"The true sense of questioning is revealed by answers, or in the answer. For with the answer comes the fulfillment of the aspiration which relaxes and attains satisfaction."[8] Take for example a simple question in which the questionable matter involves either the affirmation or the negation of the existence of an entity. Questioning concerning the existence of the entity resolves itself into two possible answers: yes it is or no it is not. These two decisive answers, or "judicative position-takings," are "already consciously

---

[6] Husserl, *Experience and Judgment*, p. 307.

[7] Husserl, *Experience and Judgment*, p. 308.

[8] Husserl, *Experience and Judgment*, p. 309.

anticipate(d)" in the questioning as "possible answer-forms and... ...they already appear in the expression of the questions themselves, as their content."[9] As content of the question these answer-forms are not present there, rather they are "merely represented," which is to say that they are possible answers to the question and are not provided in the form of judgments but as representations of judgments. They are the judgments' shadows, representations of how the questionable may come to resolve itself in a restored certainty both satisfying and relaxing the ego-consciousness by easing its painful and anxious schism through a decision that bridges the boundary stretching between act and content.

Husserl concludes the short passage on the nature of the question by pointing out that this resolution need not take the form of an assertion of one answer-form over another. Rather there are a host of possibilities available to the questioning ego-consciousness involving a wide spectrum of solutions from "holding-for-probable" in various degrees down to "I do not know." "These weakened answer-forms are also answers even if they are not completely satisfying."[10] "A is charming" "would not be an answer" "to the question 'is this A or B?'" Non-answers or nonsense answers are distinct in kind from answers providing lesser degrees of satisfaction or authority.

The question is experienced as a kind of cognitive pain, an itch to be scratched. Presumably, the act attempts to reach its goal and finds itself thwarted by resistance. The passive element is therefore a bifurcation that may be called anxious doubt, the striving to overcome this bifurcation for the sake of complete fulfillment is the active questioning. Questioning has both an act character and a content character. The act character is bifurcation, divisiveness, and a schism. The content character is lack, absence of fullness, and dissent in the sense of what undermines unanimity. This suggests something is not yet right about the account, however, since the act and the content when thought through, do not stand separate. Is the bifurcation an active one in the sense that it is attached to the act? Is it a passive one insofar as it is attached to the content? This is pleonasm, it says nothing more than that the act is the act and the content is the content and that in questioning both are split/doubled. Activity and passivity do not distinguish act from content, rather they are the result of the distinction. Husserl cannot rely on them to make questioning a clear, unified concept. He continues:

Questioning is not itself a modality of judgment, although

[9] Husserl, *Experience and Judgment*, p. 309.
[10] Husserl, *Experience and Judgment*, p. 310.

> naturally it is inseparable from the sphere of judgment and
> cognition and belongs necessarily to logic as the science of
> cognition and its objects, more precisely, as the science of
> cognitive reason and its structures.[11]

So at least we know where to find it, but how does that help with the
dilemma? Since "all reason is at the same time practical reason."
"questioning is a practical mode of behavior relative to judgments."[12] It is
not itself a modality of judgment, but yet a modality of behavior relative to
judgments, meaning

> it is a striving directed toward a judicative decision, which as
> such belongs to the sphere of will and becomes a decisive
> willing and acting only when we see practical ways to actually
> bring about the judicative decision.[13]

Leaving aside the practical for a moment, the key word here—said often
enough—is "decision." The question reaches for decision. It strives to
undermine the split, the doubling, it strives to destroy the incision made by
doubt. And this striving is a practical matter suggesting that the proof is in
the action. Whether or not the decision has been made is a matter of
whether the passive doubts have been overcome for the sake of a renewed
unanimity: that is, what matters is whether the content has achieved
fulfillment. We might say what matters is whether the content has come
into its own.

What I may have missed here is the nature of the question as a modality
of behavior. Judgment, as a major theme in the book, is the act of
constituting secure and unified meaning contents for thought. Questioning
is not a mode of judgment but of behavior. "If I ask a question," Husserl
writes, "and fail to reach a decision, I find myself in an unpleasant
frustration, which also frustrates me in other decisions of my practical life.
Accordingly, I wish for a decision."[14] We have already seen that it is not
merely a wish, but a wish accompanied by a striving to make a decision.
Decision marks the arrival of the questioner at a judgment. Husserl is
claiming that the question is, strictly speaking, not an intentional act.
Rather, it is a behavioral element of natural consciousness in the natural
world. It is one of the many behavioral elements of the natural attitude and

---

[11] Husserl, *Experience and Judgment*, p. 308.

[12] Husserl, *Experience and Judgment*, p. 308.

[13] Husserl, *Experience and Judgment*, p. 308.

[14] Husserl, *Experience and Judgment*, p. 308.

there is no rigorous way to delineate the question in intentional consciousness. It is not a rigorous act of thought with a specifiable content at which it aims.

Husserl then goes on to reduce questioning to a set of intentional acts that can be delineated in a more rigorous sense using the phenomenological method. "Every possible content of judgment is thinkable as the content of a question."[15] Not necessarily as a content present in the question (for then we would never ask questions without already knowing the answers), but rather virtually in the question, "merely represented" by it. And what is more, and what no doubt shows the occasionally sloppy nature of questions, there are usually several judgments virtually inhabiting, inciting themselves in, the question. Or rather the shadow or representation of the judgment is there. The question is a shadow-play, full of murky darkness and lack of clarity. It is a painful and anxious event. This is suggestive of Plato's cave: not only dark and full of shadows cast by an artificial light, but a painful place where the chains that restrain the prisoners make them hysterical. The goal of such a project may be to bring an end to questioning, to no longer question, to overcome all questioning in favor of answers. This is all well and good, since it is precisely the answers which ground or account for the questions in the first place. We obviously would never ask any questions if we were not in search of answers. It is our ideal of the answer that leads to the questioning and so questioning is itself instrumental to achieve the end. It is an instrument that signals pain and anxiety in the user and so one that is discarded with relief when its end has been achieved.

To summarize: Husserl cannot make a rigorous distinction between the act and content of questioning, so he attempts to place the question in some other realm than the intentional sphere of consciousness, into a behavioral realm that can, through phenomenology, be reduced to a set of intentional acts and contents characterized by judgment. For the phenomenologist, there are no questions, only answers which offer—aside from decisive judgments—a more rigorous characterization of what we are doing when we raise questions: we are striving to make precise judgments. The essence of the question lies in the answer and the answer always comes in the categorial form of a judgment reflecting a decision.

---

[15] Husserl, *Experience and Judgment*, p. 309.

Exemplifying scholarship

In *Being and Time*, Heidegger writes: "Our aim in the following treatise is to work out the question concerning the meaning of *Being* and to do so concretely."[16] Suppose Heidegger is being true to his teacher and his own appreciation of the phenomenological method when he says this. We would have to interpret "work out" in this phrase as "answer" the question. The difficulty of *Being and Time*, therefore, would become clear. The problem is that we do not yet know what the question is and so answering it must wait until we have discovered the answer's shadow. For you see, "this question has today been forgotten." "Work out", it would follow, suggests both remembering the question and answering it.

But why do we have to remember the question? After all, Heidegger has already told us what it is that the question is about. It is about Being, it is the question concerning the meaning of Being. What possible need would we have to remember a question that does not seem to need posing since we already have a pretty good idea of that which the questioning is striving to achieve. Heidegger uses language much like Husserl's concerning the nature of questions when he discusses "The Formal Structure of the Question of Being" in section 2 of the introduction. Why was he insistent at the end of section 1 where he wrote:

> By considering these prejudices, however, we have made plain not only that the question of Being lacks an *answer*, but that the question itself is obscure and without direction. So if it is to be revived, this means that we must first work out an adequate way of *formulating* it.[17]

That the question is obscure and without direction is no indication that it needs to be posed more clearly as a question. Husserl thought that obscurity and lack of unified direction was an essential component of any questioning. The clarity will only come in the striving after fulfilled judgments. What Heidegger should mean is that the meaning of Being, the question concerning it, must be fleshed out through a striving that seeks to get clear about Being in its meaning. Doing this will provide a more rigorous formulation of the question, but of course the question will become useless as anything but a pedagogical technique. That is, its clarity

---

[16] Martin Heidegger. *Being and Time*. Translated by John MacQuarrie and Edward Robinson. 1962. New York: Harper Perennial Modern Thought. P. 19.

[17] Heidegger, *Being and Time*, p. 24.

will have come with its having been answered and so it will no longer be an open question, a question without answer. Heidegger should have been content to say something like 'what is the meaning of being' or 'why is there being at all and not rather nothing' both of which would have been good enough to evoke a striving aimed at achieving the stated purpose of *Being and Time*.

> Looking at something, understanding and conceiving it, choosing, access to it—all these ways of behaving are constitutive for our inquiry, and therefore are modes of Being for those particular entities which we, the inquirers, are ourselves. Thus to work out the question of Being adequately, we must make an entity—the inquirer—transparent in his own Being. The very asking of this question is an entity's mode of Being; and as such it gets its essential character from what is inquired about—namely, Being. This entity which each of us is himself and which includes inquiring as one of the possibilities of its Being, we shall denote by the term 'Dasein'. If we are to formulate our question explicitly and transparently, we must first give a proper explication of an entity (Dasein), with regard to its Being.[18]

We turn to section 2 with these reflections in mind. Note the similarity to Husserl: "Every inquiry is a seeking. Every seeking gets guided beforehand by what is sought." And then: "Inquiry itself is the behavior of a questioner, and therefore of an entity, and as such has its own character of Being."[19] If we are not careful, we might think Heidegger is merely repeating Husserl's insights. The repetition introduces something else, something Husserl does not seem to have considered: why should Heidegger's claim that inquiry is the behavior of a questioner lead him to conclude that it is the behavior of an entity and, furthermore, an entity with its own character of Being? Heidegger is not trying to constitute the essence of a question here, he is speaking of a specific question, the question at issue, the question concerning the meaning of Being. He says that questioning is itself a mode of Being, questioning is something that is, that exists. Therefore, questioning concerning the meaning of Being is dangerously circular. It is a question that runs the risk of begging the question, questioning itself presupposes that in some sense the questioner

---

[18] Heidegger, *Being and Time*, p. 27.

[19] Heidegger, *Being and Time*, p. 24.

already understands what Being means. The act of questioning exemplifies this.

I do not read Heidegger as having ventured very far from Husserl yet and there is no one question concerning the meaning of Being, rather questioning is itself the question concerning the meaning of Being. Questioning, since it is an entity, already contains within itself the shadow of Being. And since Being is that which is asked about in Heidegger's questioning, questioning here strives after the meaning of the Being of questioning. The circularity is that the shadow represented by the question is exactly what Heidegger is asking about. Hence the difficulty in formulating the question and the claim that answering the question occurs while formulating it. I might venture to guess that the answer *is* the formulation of the question.

The formulation of the question, the attempt to pose it, takes place through an existential analytic of Dasein. What is Dasein? That's what the existential analytic hopes to show, it cannot be known prior to the demonstration. Well then, why is Dasein the chosen entity? Because Dasein is the entity which makes its Being an issue for itself. It really is not so very difficult; it might be an instance of deductive reasoning. All that Heidegger has at the outset is a question that has not been formulated and a questioner who has not formulated it. Questioning is a mode of Being and as such contains within itself the shadow of the answer. The existential analytic is therefore aimed at "questioning" and Dasein is the entity which questions, it is the entity for which Being is an issue, an issue to be questioned. The guiding movement of the book may be the condition of the possibility for any questioning concerning the meaning of Being.

In the lecture course from 1925, *History of the Concept of Time*, Heidegger says this explicitly:

> That we with good reason or almost of necessity first ask about this entity, the Dasein, in such a way that we exhibit it provisionally, that we necessarily begin with it, will be established from our growing knowledge of the structure of the being of this very entity. It will be shown that the necessity in the question of being to start from the clarification of questioning as an entity is demanded by this entity itself, by the questioning. This entity, the questioner, itself makes use of a particular sense of being, just the sense which, as we already noted, maintains itself in a certain lack of understanding, a lack which must be defined. Our next

> task is now the explication of Dasein as the entity whose way
> of being is questioning itself.[20]

Does this mean that Dasein questions itself, namely Dasein is the subject of inquiry as the entity being investigated? That would be a tautology since Heidegger is doing it. Does it mean questioning itself, that is, as such where Dasein is the subject of inquiry, its agent? That would be an implicit demonstration or performative example taking place as the investigation; and it would explain the overarching emphasis on necessity in the passage cited. Heidegger *must* begin here for there is nothing else, nowhere else to begin. And he says, wishful thinking more likely, that this necessity will be demonstrated as right and proper in the course of things to come. It will not have been an accidental need imposed by limitations in the starting point, but a need that arises out of the ontological project of questioning concerning the meaning of Being itself. The fruitfulness of the investigation and the extent to which there are two separate options will have to remain at issue throughout the discussion that follows in *Being and Time.* Dasein, you see, is an issue for itself.

But this second interpretation should not blind us to the importance of the first possibility that is true by definition. "The entity which we ourselves are; this entity, which I myself am in each particular instance, we call the Dasein."[21] Dasein is questioning, "we ourselves" suggests those who question. Or, since agency might be a presupposition or prejudice here, Dasein is questioning itself, meaning both questioning per se and questioning directed toward oneself in an existential analytic: a reflective relation Dasein has with itself as questioner and questioned throughout the analysis. The first option may have been tautology, but it is only in the second option for interpretation that we can discover what the tautology means.

To summarize: Dasein as questioned/questioner articulates the structure of questioning in such a way as to pose the question concerning the meaning of Being and move toward providing an answer to it. Whether or not an answer can be phrased in the form of a questioning—as this one no doubt will be—is yet to be determined. That is, it is open to question.

---

[20] Martin Heidegger. *History of the Concept of Time.* Translated by Theodore Kisiel. 1992. Bloomington: Indiana University Press. pp. 149-150.

[21] Heidegger, *History of the Concept of Time,* p. 148.

Being and Time as vignette

Being and Time is not a book. It is an abomination. Not because it is difficult to understand, rather because it is difficult to read. And not because it is boring or frustrating, although it may be. Books, frequently, require a decision on the part of a reader, a decision as to how to go about reading them. There is a presupposed understanding of what it is that one should be getting from the reading or of the world of possibilities within which to situate the reading. Often authors will make this decision for the reader—and hence their authority, in an introduction or prefatory remark. They might do so by articulating a genre in the text. Suppose for whatever reason, an author was to fail to do this. Maybe the introduction is itself at best an irony and thus incapable of providing such a decision. Or maybe it is nothing endemic to introductions at all, maybe it happens now and again because for one reason or another the author has failed at introducing the text that follows. And failed so much so that the reader cannot help but notice. No matter which, *Being and Time* is such a book. Its introduction introduces a book that was never written.

Since it is a work in philosophy, one would think this matter of the introduction unimportant. The book—regardless of its lacking the explicit decision of an author presented in an introduction clearly cohering with the rest of the manuscript, has a consistent and determinate voice. Unfortunately, although I do not deny it may have such a voice—participate in a specific genre of writing, I have been completely unable to hear that voice and identify that genre. It is precisely because *Being and Time* so often looks like any other work in philosophy that I find myself becoming increasingly perplexed. In that damned introduction (that introduction of the damned), Heidegger writes:

> When tradition thus becomes master, it does so in such a way that what it 'transmits' is made inaccessible, proximally and for the most part, that it rather becomes concealed. Tradition takes what has come down to us and delivers it over to self-evidence; it blocks our access to those primordial 'sources' from which the categories and concepts handed down to us have been in part genuinely drawn. Indeed it makes us forget that they have had such an origin, and makes us suppose that the necessity of going back to these sources is something which we need not even understand. Dasein has had its historicality so thoroughly uprooted by tradition that it confines its interest to the multiformity of possible types, directions, and standpoints of philosophical activity in the most exotic and alien of

cultures; and by this very interest it seeks to veil the fact that it has no ground of its own to stand on. Consequently, despite all its historiological interests and all its zeal for an Interpretation which is philologically 'objective', Dasein no longer understands the most elementary conditions which would alone enable it to go back to the past in a positive manner and make it productively its own.[22]

This passage is midway through the section of the introduction that describes the project of destroying the history of ontology. The remarks on tradition are supposed to indicate that the covering up of the question that Heidegger seeks to pose—the question concerning the meaning of Being, is itself a historical way of Being for Dasein. Furthermore, it introduces his claims that destroying the tradition is not a specific annihilating act, but rather that the movement of destruction is a program for analysis that allows what has been covered over to come forward.

This is not a problem. In terms of a narrow enough context it makes sense. The problem is that it occurs as an introduction that seems to instruct the reader, in some way, how to avoid reading *Being and Time*. "Dear reader," I can imagine him saying. "You are about to read a book. Tradition allows me to tell that work to you now in brief. I refuse to do it. Reader, a decision awaits. What is it you think you are doing as you embark on this reading? Do you think you are about to read "philosophy"? Dear reader, think again." In the first paragraphs of the section on destruction, he wrote: "Its own past—and this always means the past of its 'generation'—is not something which *follows along after* Dasein, but something which already goes ahead of it."[23] The thinking of the past, the thinking of the generation, of genre, of gender, are not something that I have had done with, something gone and forgotten. Rather this thinking spreads out the world in front of me, before me, as a work to be read. And I may see that world and all its genres of Being and not think about what is given there at all. To do this would be to ignore Heidegger's charge, his charge to deconstruct. For although the destruction of the history of metaphysics seems to point backwards in time, to texts long since written, it points forward into the future, a future that is already there as possibilities projected by past events.

If I am to read *Being and Time*, to really read it, I cannot take its seemingly coherent genre for granted. Rather, the manner of meaning, of coherence, the voice or voices of being and time must open in the reading

---

[22] Heidegger, *Being and Time*, p. 43.

[23] Heidegger, *Being and Time*, p. 41.

as questioning. This has been easy for some, for those who, without trying (as though it were happening behind their backs), read *Being and Time* as though it were a piece of writing, nearly literary. Dasein, for instance, could be understood as a sort of character, a character in a novel for example. Think about it. I refer to Dasein, I say it "Dasein". Everyone thinks "Heidegger" "Being and Time". I say, Raskolnikov. Everyone thinks "Dostoevsky" "Crime and Punishment". And so on. Now I say, "Substance", "idea", "justice". Maybe specific philosophers and their works do come to mind. Ultimately a tradition opens in such questioning. Substance and Aristotle, but also Descartes and the rest—even Hegel. Dasein, Heidegger. Who else? No one, no one else. Kant wrote the word Dasein hundreds of times in his life, it is always translated, never left in the German—never left alone as Dasein. The word is only questionable when Heidegger writes it, only untranslatable in Heidegger's work. This essential propriety of the name, the unmoving rigorous nature of the term, suggests that it is a proper name. Heidegger will not allow himself to ask the question "what is Dasein" since Dasein is that which is best questioned by "who"? Who is Dasein? And yet, one cannot say, "I am Dasein." A proper name which no one can claim. Dasein must be a character in a novel genre. It is clear.

If Being and time have a main character, presumably they are a genre. A novel one. This is a question and not the answer to one. A novel, technically, is not a single genre, it is many genres, multiple genres interspersed, multiplying genres: letters, dialogue, a poem now and again, prose of all different sorts depending on the nature of the characters, and so on. The novel, and hence its name, is disruptive of genre—not belonging to any one specific genre. This does not solve the problem; it only deepens it. Clearly, when I read Being and time, I do not know what I am doing. At least, however, I feel relieved by the sense I have that this approach has Heidegger's seal of approval.

To summarize: *Being and Time* as vignette. Tiny tendrils, like stories and anecdotes, a book never quite written, never quite put down, always yet unfinished. No borders separating it here and now from some other "Heidegger," from some other text, there and then. Rather, sketches representing other sketches representing, and so on, all along the way. The Dasein of the book made questionable in the book of Dasein.

And Nietzsche shall have been in the book

In the "early Heidegger" there seems to have been a point of entry for Nietzsche on every page. His name is there wherever Dasein and questioning are, unsaid. Circling, the circling dynamic introduced in the fort/da of Dasein as the questioning being questioned as questioner recurs eternally. And the question itself carries within it a kind of repetition which remarks the remaking of the world in an unending variation on a theme. Shadow-play is the representing of representing representing, and so on.[24] In other words, the way is the ongoing questioning of anxious Dasein. And this therefore will have been the meaning of being, a recurring limit, unending in the circle of time, manifold.

The historicality of Dasein's temporality must be part and parcel of the analysis, it must be captured in the beginning and in the end:

> Philosophy "is universal phenomenological ontology, and takes its departure from the hermeneutic of Dasein, which, as an analytic of *existence*, has made fast the guiding-line for all philosophical inquiry at the point where it *arises* and to which it *returns*."[25]

Because the existential analytic is itself co-constituted by a historical understanding of the question and the oblivion it has achieved, the way of being that both conceals and reveals is central to the analysis. Dasein's historical being explains both the question's oblivion and the possibility of its retrieval. The history of Dasein and the history of Dasein's efforts at posing the question, the history of Dasein's "universal phenomenological ontology" belongs together in the questioning of the entity that is an issue for itself: the inquiry that arises and returns, returns eternally.[26] As a way in

---

[24] Note that Zuboff, in *The Age of Surveillance Capitalism*, refers to telemetry as "shadow text", p. 185. Of course, it is immensely more complex than indicated here, but seeing it that way here may help me to make my larger point about the fort/da of human experience insofar as it is inhabited by the telemetric as emission, analysis, and feedback. The existential analytic is a performative response to the ongoing emissions of a questioner for the sake of feeding back the lessons from one's subject matter into ongoing efforts at posing the question. The fort/da stretches between the two interpretations and is embodied in the anxious turning toward the subject matter at hand.

[25] Heidegger, *Being and Time*, p. 487 and p. 62.

[26] "Questionability and questioning sharpen the comportment toward history—the "how" of the historiological." Martin Heidegger. *Phenomenological*

which Dasein is, questioning reveals itself as genre, neither fiction nor non-fiction, it constitutes the investigation as a non-fictional fabrication.

Anxious Dasein is questioning throughout the analytic and in his latest works Heidegger never ceases to investigate the nature and meaning of questioning. Not least of which can be said to this effect is the fact that in the mid-1950s he wrote an essay called "The Question of Being" and at roughly the same time, in "A Dialogue on Language" Heidegger's position is articulated by the player in the dialogue referred to only as "the inquirer." It is there where Heidegger writes:

> I have left an earlier standpoint, not in order to exchange it
> for another one, but because even the former way was only
> a way-station along a way. The lasting element in thinking is
> the way. And ways of thinking hold within them forward and
> backward, and that indeed only the way back will lead us
> forward.[27]

Repetitive vacillation is inscribed as fort/da, a term with multiple points of departure: Nietzsche, Freud. Heidegger or Lacan. It is a recurrent theme and describes the pattern of movement whereby "the way back will lead us forward" or so we think as a means for alleviating some pain or anxiety emanating from the absent object of desire. It is a recursive theme calling itself again and again up and down the stack so that what lies before us comes up behind us.

- Dasein already understands the meaning of Being, and yet it looks for it, questions it.
- Dasein as an entity fallen within a world of entities alongside which it exists both does and does not understand itself in terms of those entities: this is the possibility of Dasein being either authentically or inauthentically itself.
- Dasein flees its death, runs from it in anxiety over the nothingness of itself. Dasein flees its death in such a way as to put it behind itself. And this death chases after Dasein. Dasein, running away from death, runs right into it.
- The future opens up Dasein as a world of possibilities to be lived. And these possibilities are the concrete projection of

Interpretations of Aristotle: Initiation into Phenomenological Research. Translated by Richard Rojcewicz. 2001. Bloomington, IN: Indiana University Press. P. 4.

[27] Martin Heidegger. *On the Way to Language.* Translated by Peter D. Hertz. 1971. New York: Perennial Library. P. 12.

Dasein's factical past. Dasein's past opens up Dasein as a world of possibilities that will have been lived. And these possibilities are the concrete facticity of Dasein's future. The future moves past, the past moves future.

- Dasein is, in each case, mine. And who am I? Well, proximally and for the most part, I am them.

- Dasein is the ontological difference between Being and entity (beings). It moves erratically between existential disclosure of world and existentiell uncovering of entities within an already disclosed world.

- The question presupposes an answer, a what or which looked for in the question. To the extent that the question presupposes an answer and the answer reflects the question, the questioning is hermeneutical—it has a ground of possibility that is fulfilled in the act of questioning.

And do you know what "the world" is to me? Shall I show it to you in my mirror? This world: a monster of energy, without beginning, without end; a firm, iron magnitude of force that does not grow bigger or smaller, that does not expend itself but only transforms itself; as a whole, of unalterable size, a household without expenses or losses, but likewise without increase or income; enclosed by "nothingness" as by a boundary; not something blurry or wasted, not something endlessly extended, but set in a definite space as a definite force, and not a space that might be "empty" here or there, but rather as force throughout, as a play of forces and waves of forces, at the same time one and many, increasing here and at the same time decreasing there; a sea of forces flowing and rushing together, eternally changing, eternally flooding back, with tremendous years of recurrence, with an ebb and a flood of its forms; out of the simplest forms striving toward the most complex, out of the stillest, most rigid, coldest forms toward the hottest, most turbulent, most self-contradictory, and then again returning home to the simple out of this abundance, out of the play of contradictions back to the joy of concord, still affirming itself in this uniformity of its courses and its years, blessing itself as that which must return eternally, as a becoming that knows no satiety, no disgust, no weariness: this, my *Dionysian* world of the eternally self-creating, the eternally self-destroying, this mystery world of the twofold voluptuous delight, my "beyond good and evil," without goal, unless the joy of the circle is itself a goal; without will, unless a ring feels

good will toward itself—do you want a *name* for this world?
A *solution* for all its riddles? A *light* for you, too, you best-
concealed, strongest, most intrepid, most midnightly men?—
This world is the will to power—and nothing besides! And
you yourselves are also this will to power—and nothing
besides! (WP 1067)

To summarize: fort/da.

Being, Time, and the Geschlecht

> Our task is not to prove that an 'external world' is present-
> at-hand or show how it is present-at-hand, but to point out
> why Dasein, as Being-in-the-world, has the tendency to bury
> the 'external world' in nullity 'epistemologically' before
> going on to prove it.[28]

This might serve as a necessary negative introduction to the problem of
transcendence which seems to have been at the center of Heidegger's
thinking throughout the years surrounding the publication of *Being and
Time*. The problem of transcendence was always: how does one know that
what is in here, representation of the thing, is adequately representative of
what is out there, the external world extended in space and time?
Responses to the problem are all supposed to be rigorous descriptions of
how we know our mental acts are (or are not) descriptive of existent entities.
Heidegger is not interested in providing an answer to the problem thus
stated. Rather, he sees that the problem of transcendence is a problem of
Being. That is, rather than hearing "how do I know the *external world*
exists?" Heidegger hears "how do I know the external world *exists*?" The
solution, he thinks, will lie in two directions: 1) Why does Dasein tend to
cover up this second way of understanding the problem, and 2) an
existential analytic of Dasein that is an inquiry into the Being of Dasein.
    The investigations along the second line of inquiry reveal the essential
secret of Dasein: it is its world. And this is truly horrifying for anxious
Dasein, since it means—on the basis of Dasein's understanding of its
finitude—that with Dasein's death, the world ends. There is, therefore,
nothing. And nothing awaits Dasein, harbors a deep stalking silence for it,
incites Dasein to a state of anxiety leaving it to flee in the face of itself. And

---

[28] Heidegger, *Being and Time*, p. 250.

this leads us down the first path of inquiry. It is for this reason alone that Dasein works so mendaciously and with such undying zest to create a world that will not die: a city of God or an objective universe known sub specie aeternitatis. This is what Heidegger would call an "existentiell attestation" of Dasein's Being as transcendence. That is, it is the way Dasein comes across its transcendence as a privative mode of Being in its everyday life. Dasein attests to its way of Being by denying it in the very course of the way it lives itself.[29]

From an existential point of view, on the other hand, Heidegger would describe Dasein's transcendence in terms of a variant on a transcendental deduction. He seeks to state the conditions of possibility for the advent of world at all. I—so to speak—enter intentional relations with objects. Rather than asking whether there is some truth in the objects intended, Heidegger's approach asks how intentional relations are possible at all. What must I/objects be like such that I can encounter an object in cognition? There must be, he responds, a prior field or clearing where this intentional relation takes place. He persists in accusing Kant of begging the question when he formulated this clearing in terms of categories of cognition. That only explains the approach of the object, not the subject's capacity to reach out. Existentialia are those conditions allowing Dasein to meet with entities in intentional relations (regardless of whether the relations are characterized as imagined or real). This is awkwardly phrased for Dasein is nothing other than these existentialia. Unlike Kant, Heidegger offers no synthetic unity as a sort of agent operating or applying the categories. Rather he would say, Dasein—as Being-in-the-world, yields both act and content through existential conditions of possibility. This is another way of saying that Dasein is its transcendence. In other words, both subject and object are constituted in the circulation of Dasein's economy of movement: transcendence.

The meaning of Dasein's Being, therefore, is transcendence. In the 1928 lecture course on *The Metaphysical Foundations of Logic*, Heidegger says:

> The peculiar *neutrality* of the term "Dasein" is essential, because the interpretation of this being must be carried out prior to every factual concretion. This neutrality also indicates that Dasein is neither of the two sexes. But here sexlessness is not the indifference of an empty void, the weak negativity of an indifferent ontic nothing. In its

---

[29] For a brilliant illustration of this, I refer to Sandra's speech at the end of Mike Leigh's 1993 film *Naked*, easily the most terrifying movie ever made and one of the first investigations into the power of the telemetric.

neutrality Dasein is not the indifferent nobody and
everybody, but the primordial positivity and potency of the
essence.[30]

Neutrality is a misleading translation here: the word is *Geschlechtlosigkeit*.
The withoutness of *Geschlecht*. And as is fitting, this "of" should be heard
in the genitive, both subjective and objective. For withoutness both belongs
to *Geschlecht* and vice versa.

To go any further, we would have to be able to think the meaning of
Geschlecht–that which Dasein *is* without. It could mean things like kind,
race, gender, genre, genus. No doubt Heidegger is suggesting all these
senses as is evident by the reference to Dasein's non-indifferent sexuality.
Non-indifferent no doubt because of this potency of the origin. We may
look to Heidegger for further clues:

> ...Dasein harbors the intrinsic possibility for being factically
> dispersed into bodiliness and thus into sexuality. The
> metaphysical neutrality of the human being, inmost isolated
> as Dasein, is not an empty abstraction from the ontic, a
> neither-nor; it is rather the authentic concreteness of the
> origin, the not-yet of factical dispersion [Zerstreutheit]. As
> factical, Dasein is, among other things, in each case
> disunited in particular sexuality. "Dispersion", "disunity"
> sound negative at first, (as does "destruction"), and negative
> concepts such as these, taken ontically, are associated with
> negative evaluations. But here we are dealing with something
> else, with a description of the multiplication (not
> "multiplicity") which is present in every factically
> individuated Dasein as such. We are not dealing with the
> notion of a large primal being in its simplicity becoming
> ontically split into many individuals, but with the clarification
> of the intrinsic possibility of multiplication which, as we shall
> see more precisely, is present in every Dasein and for which
> embodiment presents an organizing factor. Nor is the
> multiplicity, however, a mere formal plurality of
> determinations, but multiplicity belongs to being itself. In
> other words, in its metaphysically neutral concept, Dasein's
> essence already contains a primordial *bestrewal* [Streuung],
> which is in a quite definite respect a *dissemination*
> [Zerstreuung]. And here a rough indication is in place. As
> existing, Dasein never relates only to one particular object;

---

[30] Martin Heidegger. *The Metaphysical Foundations of Logic*. Translated
by Michael Heim. 1992. Bloomington: Indiana University Press. pp. 136-137.

> if it relates solely to one object, it does so only in the mode of turning away from other beings that are beforehand and at the same time appearing along with the object. This multiplicity does not occur because there are several objects, but conversely. This also holds good for comportment toward oneself and occurs according to the structure of historicity in the broadest sense, insofar as Dasein occurs as stretching along in time.[31]

The origin, Dasein's essence as transcendence, is multiplying—many folds unfolding. There is an original multiplying that comes to be as Dasein in each of its various and many ways of Being-in-the-world alongside entities for use and abuse, for theory and blindness. Dasein is a writing without genre, but not absolutely or by constitution. Rather, Dasein is the possibility of all concrete instances of genre. It is because Dasein *is* without that we live in the middle of genre.

There is never a moment in time without *Geschlecht*. Rather, without *Geschlecht* Dasein comes to be in the manner of each and many *Geschlechts*. Dasein's transcendence is its immanent ongoing dispersal through spacetime and the dispersals take on the ambivalent ambiguity of the occasional *Geschlecht*.

> This thrown dissemination into a multiplicity is to be understood metaphysically. It is the presupposition, for example, for Dasein to let itself in each case factically be governed by beings which it is not; Dasein, however, identifies with those beings on account of its dissemination.[32]

Dasein, without *Geschlecht*, seeps into every nook and cranny of the world, uncovering everything everywhere in search of multiplying varieties. And what is more, this endless searching for self-constitution, for self-realization in the manner and meaning of worldly *Geschlecht* covers up Dasein's own essential *Geschlechtlosigkeit*. So much so that it no longer considers it questionable. The existential analytic then is the uncovering of the questionability of the *Geschlechtlos*, of the without, of multiplying, of a non-indifferent potent essence that comes to the fore as a positive repetition of what has been forgotten for the sake of what one wishes to expect: the claim made on us to *be* without genre, the claim made on us to

---

[31] Heidegger, *The Metaphysical Foundations of Logic*, pp. 137-138.

[32] Heidegger, *The Metaphysical Foundations of Logic*, p. 138.

be without tradition, to *be* in the manner of Being of the questioner at issue for itself.[33]

In conclusion, genre here is an answer to a question that has not been posed. Posing the question involves writing the historical existential analytic of Dasein that seeks the existential structure of questioning in transcendence. It is because Dasein is its own transcendence that it questions, where questioning is an existentiale. As questioning, Dasein is as its own transcendence. And Dasein, the null basis of a nullity, is its 'without' *as* questioning. The anxious Dasein lives its questioning in many ways: its essential striving is there as desire, intellect, will, feeling and so on. And so on, or at least such is to be hoped. For Dasein anyway, nothing more can be hoped.

> Living in proclivity and dispersion, life does not maintain distance; it commits an oversight. In the dispersed thrusting aside of the "before," distance is not explicitly there as such. In proclivity, it becomes even less explicit; in the actualization of experience, life passes over it. In oversight with regard to distance, life mis-measures itself; it does not grasp itself in the measure appropriate to it ("measure" not to be understood quantitatively).[34]

---

[33] This position is articulated throughout Heidegger's elaboration of the question "What is Philosophy?" in *Phenomenological Interpretations of Aristotle: Initiation into Phenomenological Research*. Cf. for example, p. 36: "With regard to biology, we can speak of "pursuing biology," but we have no corresponding word "biologize." Nor is there a word "philologize" to correspond with "philology." We can form such words, but we recognize immediately that the term "philosophize" expresses "more." It does not merely mean "to pursue philosophy," "to busy oneself with philosophy."" The discussion of philosophizing that follows orchestrates a deep relationship between "being an issue", "cognitive comportment", and "questioning"", i.e., p. 41: "That means the object is investigated (questioning as addressing; the only determinative and appropriate concept of speaking!) as the object it is, in its "what" and its "how," precisely as a being. A being: an object, this object, in what and how it is." Finally, the last section of the last chapter of the lecture course has the heading "Questionability." On p. 114: "...genuine questioning arises from motives that have been clarified in the respective factical situation and that receive direction from factical life. Likewise, genuine questioning consists in living in the answer itself in a searching way, such that the answering maintains a constant relation to the questioning..."

[34] Heidegger, *Phenomenological Interpretations of Aristotle*, p. 77.

To summarize: A failure for philosophy to have articulated a question concerning genre may have led someone to wonder whether the articulation of genre is itself questionable. And this I might call the "neutrality" of *Being and Time* insofar as its advent comes in the manner of a philosophical writing as well as writing otherwise. In the neutrality of *Being and Time*, the thrown multiplicity of Dasein's genres is first made possible, not as some real possibility to be actualized in the concrete utterances of everyday life, but in the symbolic manner of questioning carried out in an existential analytic. Dasein's questioning both predates and realizes genre such that the imagined character of Dasein is neither a genus nor a genre except insofar as its existential analytic demonstrates many such positions at issue for itself from beginning to end and back again.

Between the Origin and the Movement

Heidegger's Lecture Course on *Hölderlin's Hymn "The Ister"*

In Freiburg during the summer of 1942, Heidegger lectured on Hölderlin's hymn "The Ister".[1] The source of the river is about 10 miles to the east of him as he stands at the podium, the Rhine flows its northerly course just 10 miles to the west. Standing between the source and its movement, Heidegger attempts to poetize the rivers. "And if this is the case, why does he poetize the rivers? After all, they exist already in actuality; why, then, do they need to be poetized?"[2] This question is one Heidegger asks of Hölderlin, which reminds us that Heidegger is not just lecturing on rivers, he is lecturing on poets as well: Hölderlin to be exact. And yet the first poet mentioned and cited in this lecture course is not Hölderlin at all, but Sophocles. What can be said about these two poets? A source and its movement? Is Heidegger trying to poetize that? And is that anything other than a poetizing of the rivers between which he stands as he lectures and as he tells the story?

The Greek poet tells the meaning of the hymn. Not this or that hymn, but the hymn as a telling that celebrates; it is the Greek Sophocles who gives us a first indication of what Hölderlin, the German, is doing in poetizing. And Heidegger? What is he telling, what is he celebrating? Poetry? Rivers? Germany?

At the outset of the lecture course, Heidegger turns to the here and now in Hölderlin: "Now come, fire!" "Here, however, we wish to build." "The Now names an appropriative event."[3] "Yet what is proper to the river is the fact that it flows and thus continually determines another 'Here'."[4] Which means that "[t]he rivers designate a 'Here' and abandon the Now, whether by passing into what is bygone, or into what lies in the future."[5] The 'Here' of Heidegger's telling, of his poetizing, is Freiburg between the source of

---

[1] Martin Heidegger. *Hölderlin's Hymn "The Ister"*. Translated by William McNeill and Julia Davis. Indian University Press: Bloomington, IN. 1996.

[2] Heidegger, *Hölderlin's Hymn "The Ister"*, p. 14.

[3] Heidegger, *Hölderlin's Hymn "The Ister"*, p. 9.

[4] Heidegger, *Hölderlin's Hymn "The Ister"*, p. 15.

[5] Heidegger, *Hölderlin's Hymn "The Ister"*, p. 15.

the "Ister" (given its Greek name, making it flow all the more from Sophocles to Hölderlin) and the movement of the Rhine. The 'Now' can be dated in the summer of 1942.

> [W]e can indeed give the year and the day, even the hour when a poem was 'composed' or completed. Yet such temporal ordering of the activity of poetizing is not straightforwardly identical, nor even the same, as the timespace of that which is poetized.[6]

In other words, one might say that there is nothing significant about the date of the poetizing, the significance of the 'Now' lies in its character as an appropriative event: the coming to pass of the essence of the rivers/poets in a festive telling. And this no doubt disrupts the geographical simplicity of the 'Here'. Germany, in this moment, the moment of Heidegger's telling, becomes the land between the rivers, it becomes the between of the rivers.

> The poet is the river. And the river is the poet. The two are the same on the grounds of their singular essence, which is to be demigods, to be in the between, between gods and humans. The open realm of this between is open in the direction of the holy that essentially prevails beyond gods and humans.[7]

Is the lecture a smoking gun, one of many to be found in the summer of 1942? Such an interpretation requires that "Germany", as the land between the rivers, be made into a subject of historical activity, of historicity. There may be some who articulated such a subject of history, a historical agent with such a destiny, but was Heidegger one of them and did he do it in this lecture, in this celebration of rivers and poets?

"It may therefore be that we speak 'German', yet talk entirely 'American'."[8] American, throughout the lecture course, suggests measurelessness, ahistoricality, and a determination of essence in terms of quantity (the pig principle: "just add more and a good thing will be better"). And the concluding remark of the course, and from which the passage above is cited, is called "Is there a measure on Earth?" There Heidegger says that Hölderlin's poetizing falls on deaf ears if "we remain...

---

[6] Heidegger, *Hölderlin's Hymn "The Ister"*, p. 8-9.

[7] Heidegger, *Hölderlin's Hymn "The Ister"*, p. 165-166.

[8] Heidegger, *Hölderlin's Hymn "The Ister"*, p. 65.

...historically   entangled   in   subjectivity."[9]   And,   furthermore, measurelessness—being *without* measure—is all that can be attained through efforts at "seizing upon the measure."[10] Those who speak 'German' yet talk 'American' are those who would claim that any subject has the authority to seize control of the measure, or become more at home by seizing control of more earth: adding to the essence of Germany by merely extending its borders.

Situated in Germany in the summer of 1942, Heidegger's course on Hölderlin's Hymn "The Ister" marks his historical passage through a constant and intense relation with National Socialism, the empowered party and political organization of the lecture's here and now. Have my suggestions for an interpretation defended him against the charge? Have they proved that his philosophy is, *in essence*, National Socialist once and for all? Back and forth between the origin and the movement there is always something that remains questionable.

> If we merely attempt, on our own authority, to set or seize
> upon the measure, then it becomes measureless and
> disintegrates into nothingness. If we merely remain
> thoughtless and without the alertness of an intimative
> scrutinizing, then we will again find no measure. Yet if we
> are strong enough to think, then it may be sufficient for us
> to ponder merely from afar, that is, scarcely, the truth of this
> poetry and what it poetizes, so that we may suddenly be
> struck by it.[11]

---

[9] Heidegger, *Hölderlin's Hymn "The Ister"*, p. 165.

[10] Heidegger, *Hölderlin's Hymn "The Ister"*, p. 167.

[11] Heidegger, *Hölderlin's Hymn "The Ister"*, p. 167.

Non-Fictional Fabrications

In the Beginning

In another place, the story goes that the age of the world picture has its objects and the epoch of technology its resources. A further spin on this is that the telemetric has its non-fictional fabrications in the form of measured events emitted, analyzed, and fed back into the same process that made them.[1] Whichever way you choose to say it, whenever you can say it, there it is right behind you. The history of phenomenology, as I have opportunistically appropriated it, is at least in part fascinating because it is *all made up*. Hegel. Invented. He made all that up, fabricated it. Marx too. And likewise, with Nietzsche, Husserl, Heidegger, Foucault, and Habermas. It would be easy to take this out of context and cite it as proof that I take the entirety of the "Continental" tradition to be nonsense. That would be rash. We usually consider the fact that something is fabricated to be evidence that it is fictional. Yet here I am asserting exactly the opposite. They made it up. And it is non-fictional. One million years ago, there were no cars. You do not find them on moons and other planets, they are fabrications, they were made up. And so here they are. Having been fabricated, they now exist and populate the world. You can find them anywhere. Point to them. Assert "I know that is a car" and, in some sense, be correct.

The notion is, of course, heuristic. Which is to say it is a non-fictional fabrication. Here it is, at work in telling this tale. As such, it provides an insight into that same telemetric being that provides its ontological stamp in the outcome of the act of fabrication: not only is Hegel's *Phenomenology* a non-fictional fabrication, but so is Hegel. Think of little boy Wilhelm, playing with a wooden toy, learning to read, asking a question at mealtime. Educated and raised, absorbed in the world of his fellows, observing their responses to things, their orientation toward common experiences, their practices and behaviors, he would have daily embodied the ordinary way

---

[1] The 'telemetric' is a shorthand reference to the contemporary, organizationally populated, (nonhuman) lifeworld that begins to appear in a recursive maneuver demonstrating the partial understanding at work in all phenomenological human orientation (aka cognition or conscious experience, etc.). This is elaborated throughout the following.

of getting about or adjusting his expectations to the possibilities presented via the organizations that he was shown. The human world-factory produces cogs and components in wide variety and color, all shapes and sizes. And then along came little Wilhelm. And he saw what he saw and felt what he felt. The upshot being these glorious fabrications now bound to his name. *The Phenomenology of Spirit. The Science of Logic. The Philosophy of Right.* Only a fabricator could craft works with such titles. The rudimentary notion at work in this recasting of Hegel's thought as non-fictional fabrication is that if he was not making it all up, if he was not inventing these tales based on the various influences that brought him to these insights, then it would all be the realization of an impossibility. There would be no way to account for the fact that he wrote these books, was able to see what became their content, while Kant or Hume or Plato could not. Non-fictional fabrication is the primary condition of the real possibility that Hegel was able to write anything at all.

There is a positive side to it as well. The entity as non-fictional fabrication opens new avenues for interpretation and analysis, for critical investigation and inquiry. If "Game of Thrones" is a popular book or TV show, there are a limited set of investigative possibilities, but if it is a full blown non-fictional fabrication so much more is made available for study: the social and cultural origins of its existence and of its popularity, the meaning of its story, and the meaning of its story's significance to the people who let it play such an enormous role in their lives. It changes from an easily understood and classifiable thing that fits well-understood categories and concepts, into something that is open for far-ranging analysis and questioning. It becomes unknown and unclear: something to be further explored and situated. The partiality of understanding is more fully disclosed when a fictional narrative that is part of well-established story-telling industries is transformed into a fabrication non-fictional in nature, a real force in our lives, an institutional presence that has production costs, provides jobs, affects its viewers' daily moods, and inhabits their imagination and consciousness as they go on to other things.

It is important to underline this reference to 'partiality'. It is not just partial in the sense that it is only part of a larger 'whole', but it reflects a bias, a point of view or position that situates and conditions it. Fabrication always has an origin in a determinate set of conditions, and it is always only the production of a component part meant to fit into some larger framework or network of relations. Fabrication itself may always be rendered by nodes of association where one set of already fabricated things move in such a way as to fabricate yet more things. The vision of the fabricator is itself a fabrication. Hegel was born and bred to write what he wrote. The pattern at work spins Hegel spinning his work spinning its analysis. And the wheel turns, spinning out of itself. "*Ein aus sich rollendes*

Rad." The partiality of any fabrication is what enables the delusion that it is something more than a fabrication. One might go so far as to say that the fabrication itself depends on this delusion, and so partiality is again a condition of possibility. There must be unseen factors at work in any act of manufacture; without them, the act cannot initiate, the fabrication cannot realize a form. The fabricators would not fabricate if they perfectly understood what they were doing and why they were doing it. It is partiality that puts us to work. And this means that when we fabricate, we may not know all the reasons that and why we are doing it and will not see all the factors at work, the generations and generations of them, in what we do. The world is not a domain of pure ideality and so its material conditions always connote an angle or perspective, a partial orientation with powerful forces at work *behind* it.

I reluctantly used the term 'whole' to describe that which encompasses the partial, but it is not a whole in the sense of some determinate totality. Rather, there is no position from which it could be described as such since its wholeness is still outstanding. The positioning that describes the 'whole' would itself be a non-fictional fabrication that fantasizes a larger order encompassing some discovered or experienced partial order. And such a positioning must be situated. The whole has its origin story, its partial condition from which it emerged. The Kantian source of the Hegelian movement, for example. The lizard brain deep inside Hegel's brain, the Germanic spirit built over millennia so that the pen could etch the 'Absolute' onto paper, so that the 'owl of Minerva' could come to have a renewed meaning that tells reams of new stories. Every why has its fabrication and many questions can be put to work generating lists of names assigned to persons who died for the sake of or because of those fabrications.

The power of non-fictional fabrication is not specifically human. Or so our stories would have us believe. Natural selection exhibits a form of it, reveals a choice that 'nature' makes. Such a fantasy extrapolation is practically valuable because it shows the nonsense of the agent in the fabrication. What does that mean: 'nature' does this or that? It is a ridiculous way to speak that we are forcibly reduced to use when we come to the limits of our understanding, when we stumble in explanation upon our own partiality. What is ridiculous is the totalizing formation of a whole to situate what is best described as a partial moment in a larger imaginary operation. Selection itself: an act without agency insofar as the real-world tale that is told is of a swarm of individuals procreating under set conditions and another swarm of them that do not. When we form principles, we often must use such formulations to make the grammar of what we hope to say possible. The formulation is an act of partiality familiar to the species, performed early on in childhood, learned with our first words, mobilized with our first steps. It is raining. "It is at work everywhere."

The fabrication carried out by a fabricator like Hegel reveals the same pattern as nature's fabrication of the species. These are just stories that I am telling here, fabrications. The dismantling of the agent in its settled form enables all kinds of new uses and applications. The organization that is spun into being by other organizations, the institution that comes to be, the corporation, the Department of Commerce, the Friars club. Fabrications, each one. Very much so non-fictional, which is to sidestep the question as to whether they are real or actual or any of the metaphysically charged orientations that are themselves fabrications. To name our higher order congress as non-fictional is, telemetrically, to assign it a genre, a form of generation functioning itinerant in fits and starts. It gestures in anxious questioning toward a collective illusion conjured in common over time and throughout a history that reveals change and transformation throughout. It is worldmaking and it is the given condition that each of us comes to occupy within such a world, independently of any choice or decision that we made. It is not a private matter and not a personal property. There is no problem to solve vis-à-vis the collective world that we share. More to the point, we may be puzzled as to how we ever come to have a private life to speak of or a set of personal concerns that set us apart from each other. And the hypothesis should be clear: it is a fabrication, we made it up.

If you need help coming up with arguments to reject the yarns spun here, use the yarns spun here. Accuse me of making it all up. I admit it. Now, let us move on. What follows is the capture of a series of fabricator/fabrication pattern matches (software engineers might call these 'regular expressions'). The intent is to highlight the partiality of each fabrication and the way that its 'whole' spun it through telemetry as a seizure from far off, a remote grasping, and an exhibition of bias in anxious questioning. In the end, the tale will have been told concerning the upshot of the telemetric in the advent of partial truths fabricated by fabricators themselves fabricated. *Natura naturans.*

Emergence && Philosophy

The oak is not in the acorn, it is fabricated by it. And then vice-versa. Teleology is not in entropy but fabricated by it. And such fabrication is non-fictional. There are oaks and acorns, there is entropy and teleology. Whereas it may be that 'Snow is white' is true if and only if snow is white, it is just as certainly the case that "'Snow is white' is true if and only if snow is white" is true if and only if 'Snow is white' is true if and only if snow is white. And we may ask how did snow come to be white, or not? And then, how did "'Snow is white' is true if and only if snow is white" come to be? In the semantic theory of truth, those who utter statements that contain propositions issue forth truth upon this world insofar as their utterances capture what is the case. Meaning, in the end, that truth emerges with the capacity to utter it. To this end, it may well be that truth is a uniquely human concern. The notion that truth is not so much a semantic relationship but the coming to be of what is insofar as it is implies that *aletheia* or unconcealedness may likewise be a uniquely human concern. Only when there are thinking beings for whom existence is an issue do entities unconceal. Only a thinking being may utter that 'snow is white' in the presence of white snow. And only thinking beings may fabricate a semantic theory of truth in the presence of whatever has come to be unconcealed for such thinking beings.[2]

Here, while I sit writing this, time marches on. And with the passing moments, the material entities around me persist, continue to exist in ongoing stretches of time cohabitated by both myself and this couch, this rug, and that table. The things stretch out in and across these moments of time. They do not project into that passage, but they persist anyway. It may not be like anything at all to be a table or a couch, but each moment brings with it their continued existence. This essential unfolding of the table or the couch or the white snow and the semantic theory of truth amounts to a set of fabrications.[3] Non-fictional if you like, but still fabrications. We have seen Heidegger associate this essential unfolding, this natural fabrication (*physis*), with the Greek notions of *poiesis* and *techne*. "Bringing-forth brings out of concealment into unconcealment."

But let us not get caught up on the human-centered quality of 'fabrication' that inhabits all such connotations of the poetic or the technical. Rather let us remain aligned with the physical or natural element as it is captured in the essential unfolding of any *physis*. Existent formations emerge over time in accordance with structural involvements or sets of relationships that derive and produce organizational stabilities. Boundaries are established, meta relationships between bounded systems and structures ensue, and we begin to develop supervenient theories as a natural progression of their productive origins. 'Reduction' has its origin and falls into a rhythmic maintenance that struggles for its continued existence and

---

[2] I assume my audience knows that I am riffing on Heidegger and Tarski here, just as I assumed you noticed the gestures in the direction of Nietzsche, Deleuze, and Spinoza in the introductory section.

[3] There is no lectern here where I sit but if there were, following Lacan, I would have been sure to mention it.

persistent role in natural self-representation stemming from a basic state of anxiety fabricated by the very boundary that it attempts to reduce.

The recursion initiated by this tale is mind boggling. And what is more, this mind-boggling recursion has come to have a name: philosophy. The love of wisdom is, in its essential unfolding, the semantic emergence of the essential unfolding itself. It is the endeavor to name, describe, explain, defend, or prove the recursive structure of the emergence of itself from out of a simpler set of aboriginal processes and procedures: the anxious questioning of the producer/product boundary itself. It is incumbent upon any philosophical analysis to give ample understanding as to where it comes from and how it is possible. That is, the recursive problem is always the first order of business for any philosophical approach. How did Tarski know that? How did Heidegger? And why not someone else at some other time in some other varied fashion? Tarski could not have written what he wrote before Frege and Heidegger could not have written what he wrote before Husserl. And so on and on, just like that. We dress up our resistance to these philosophers in many different ways, providing arguments and counter evidence, trying as best we can to reflect on their offerings for the sake of showing what they have missed or what they cannot account for with the work they have done. In short, we accuse them of having made it all up. We fabricate accusations of fabrication. Does it follow that a philosopher who is wrong must have fabricated what they claimed to have been true? And if, in turn, every philosopher turns out to have been wrong, does it follow that the whole of them are a bunch of fabricators?

Yet we speak coherently of traditions and schools of thought that follow from these fabrications. The basis of Heidegger's assertions in the prior work of Husserl or Tarski building upon Frege. And not a tradition of success, but a recognized history of failures and recovery, of improvements made upon past oversights. And these traditions are real. We study them, we produce commentary spinning yarns about their progression and impact. Sitting here years later, I can feel the sway of the phenomenological tradition or the early analytic tradition or whatever other powerful progressions there might be. They were made up, but the essence of all fabrication is that, in the end, the product exists and has real relationships with whatever else has been manufactured: the stars that have come to be, the planets that spin into existence around them, the oceans that filled the massive valleys between the continents, the cellular organisms that dredged out of the slime, and then the thinkers with their utterances: 'snow is white' alerting all and sundry to the clear and distinct fact that indeed snow is white.

Reductivism suggests that there is an uncanny prejudice against emergence as essential unfolding and fabrication. The aboriginal basis of physical nature must be the acorn that contains the oak within itself in its potential totality. If natural processes unfold over time and construct or organize themselves into stable structures periodically here or there, then somehow physics has been demeaned. Scientific purists only consider discovery as the proper genius of the scientist and leave invention to the engineers and the poets. And how many of their measurements depend on the fashioning of a device? Think like Hegel for a second: for nature to come to know itself, cognition itself must have come to be. And cognition cannot initiate the recursive process in a single step. Rather, it divines its own procedure through the tactical production of instruments. It fashions instruments that can be applied to the natural processes through a semantic consistency between what they can grasp and the concepts that name the natural processes that are the target of the investigation making use of them. The measuring rod brings with it a language. The results are the output of an engineered process and they are used as fodder to construct additional relational assertions to describe what has been measured in terms of the results obtained. And these heuristics are of great value: they move mountains, they explain mysteries, they extend the boundaries of human impact, and they may augment the measuring capabilities of human investigators themselves.

The advent of precise languages and the advent of precise measuring devices have proceeded in lock step. Meaning, in turn, that 'snow is white' was established right alongside the whiteness of snow. For nature is a poet *and* a craftsman. It achieves its 'ends' with finer-tuned instruments. A star has more precision than a gassy nebula. And a human being more so. And Hegel's notion is that nature produces these configurations for the sake of knowing itself. And Hegel, ironically, has—famously—made that up, fabricated it. And this manufacture was only possible for someone who had the advantage of reading Kant and following Napoleon's march across Europe.

The recursive maneuver of the philosopher, so the story of the non-fictional fabrication goes, is thus the highest maneuver of such natural processes. And this recursive maneuver, this philosophy, takes on many forms. The notion of the academic discipline is bound to this recursive maneuver and all fields of advanced contributions to long-standing traditions of inquiry are constrained by this anxious and poetic form. Surely there are facts, but they are all in turn theory bound. Theories are fabrications, which does not entail that human beings can exist without them. The facts of us depend on them and they are our sole purpose: spinning such tales and performing such recursive maneuvers. The realization of the fruits of human consciousness is why there is human consciousness at all. We are for the sake of knowing the world, we exist for the sake of inventing descriptions and explanations. The natural order had a need for this and orchestrated its occurrence in the existence of human beings.

How do I know this? I do not and I need not. The presentation of a theory of emergence dressed up as a series of non-fictional fabrications is itself an historical necessity, a story that needed to be told to embody the recursive proposal that the natural order endures. The fact that I can think it and present it in a reasonably coherent form, communicate it to another, is enough evidence for its veracity. Emergent truth, poetic and technical, has its justification in its significance and its coherence. This is because it need not be justified in the classical sense of being proved true. Rather, its justification is its existence, its coming to be, its having been articulated as a natural event taking place in the passage of time as a part of some tradition. The details of such traditions may themselves remain in dispute by various contributors trying to shape and reshape the nature of the recursive relationship of human cognition to its existential conditions.[4]

I imagine there are philosophers who would vehemently resist this point. Setting aside the disciples of Tarski, Heidegger proposed that there was a forgotten question that, by innuendo, he had somehow remembered. And he gives no indication that he would be willing to accept that this memory of his, this evocation of the forgotten question, was merely a technical achievement or a poetic proposal. Heidegger does not indicate that he thinks he has made it all up. And yet what else are poetics for? To what end poetry? He went to great lengths to show that the essence of technology was nothing technological but could be found in the world-emergent notions of the poetic and the physical. Where did he put philosophy? Where did he put his own questioning comportment? He would be cornered to admit that philosophers, at their best, are fabricators: the action of the questioner has a determinate ontological condition and progresses in search of another. And how else could it stand for the philosopher amid such a world, prone to issuance and bringing-forth forever pursued from behind by their boundary condition? Heidegger and Tarski were both fabricators. And while I am at it, I will go out on a limb and point out that they were indeed great fabricators.

---

[4] This is an example of a highly opportunistic gesture in the direction of a cockeyed reading of Habermas' *Theory of Communicative Action* as action oriented toward understanding, where this latter notion is spun in hermeneutical phenomenological fashion.

Philosophy && Ethics

The philosophers do not emerge from the muck by themselves with their cognition fully formed. Rather, at the origin, alongside *poiesis, physis, techne,* and *aletheia, ethos* must also lie. Or rather, like the others, it comprehends cognition-fully-formed becoming. The *Question Concerning Technology* and *Phenomenological Interpretation of Kant's Critique of Pure Reason* both elaborate this same pattern, or the first part of it only to hint at the second: the manifold is emerging in the singularity of the personal being, the human existent, and evokes the problem which governs Heidegger's thinking early and late. The coming to be, the becoming available for experience, is that descriptive event that names the most rudimentary of questions, that evokes it in an age where it had been long forgotten. The notion is one of something that lies behind the apprehending synthesis, something lurking out of view, something that is concealed. And with each moment, with each out-of-itself, ecstatic disruption of the fabric of the world, that is the passage of time, the coming to pass of what is, there is a hard-won effort at perpetually turning to confront what resides behind you. To no avail, it steps back in cadence with your turning and remains concealed in the very act, as the very act, that has attempted to reveal it. This is the phenomenology of the manifold, that which sits prior to any attempt to resolve it into a meaningful act of apprehension. This manifold is the *mitsein,* the distributed pro- and re-tention from which each human existence emerges as it matures, as its brain acquires content, habituated pathways, and electrical patterns of cultural coherence. The effort to build the *techne* and *physis* upon *poiesis* rams against the aboriginal temporality that patterns every emerging, every sequencing, and every coming-to-pass. And yet, what comes *to pass, comes* to pass. That is, this temporal projection from out of the factical manifold is a projection into a place, a projection from a place.

There is never a moment without situation, without a place where that temporal stretch resides. As aboriginal to human existence as temporality is, there is none without places that happen along with it. The place where manifold time comes from and the place upon which it is projected, is the place where human existence finds itself, concerns itself with itself, and becomes an issue for itself. And that human existence is always already enmeshed in a labyrinthine context of ethical associations. *Da-sein.* Because the philosopher, the thinking being, the cognizing agent, comes to be in the midst of others, along with them, sucking at their teat, bouncing on their knee, and eating at their table, there is never a moment in which this emergent being is without place, without situation, or without a settled context of family, tribe, and community. If there is a technological *Gestell* that governs all emissions, then it comes to pass in the family and in the tribe and in the community. It is handed down and dispensed, distributed in the unfolding of each human beings' origin story.

This means that all of the existential characteristics that are assigned to any human being are appropriate to that human existence only insofar as they are assigned through human being, through the manifold, through the distributed apprehension that is the original spatio-temporal meaning context of each developing person. A human being is finite, so too human existence. There is anxious turning, functioning in fits and starts as the cognitive person, and there is the anxiety of the species, of the historical epoch that sheds itself as the lightening way for each who dwell there. The technological is unearthed phenomenologically in just this fashion. It presents itself in human orientation, association, and exasperation. So too the "world picture".

Elsewhere[5], I have tried to describe the lifeworld that is peculiar to this telemetric force of distributed agents that come to pass in partial form as human cognition. There the corporate person was targeted as the perfect device for comprehending this dynamic at work in us, as us, and through us. Consider how the corporate person *is*. I work for a corporation and I sit and think through one of its problems. My perceptual experience is a partial expression of the corporate person's perceptual experience. Simultaneously hundreds of thousands of others are likewise pursuing that corporation's set of problems, expressing them and their solution in an individuated perceptual experience. What lies before me is the problem at hand, but were I to fully articulate the corporate concerns of all those hundreds of thousands, the collective qualia would be the phenomenology of the corporation insofar as it has been incorporated. And it is a haunting presence from which my daily rhythms may emerge. It rests behind my back as I add 2 and 2 on behalf of this corporate agent.

And there are many corporate agents. They each persist in this strange ethical space populated with other corporate agents, engaging in agreements, coming to terms, and orchestrating outcomes for the sake of mutual and, sometimes, hostile interests. This means I live in many communities simultaneously. I live with my coworkers as the cells within the corporate organism. And although this community may have a direct impact upon my states of mind by giving me joy or anger, sadness or pleasure, as I involve myself with these others, the other communities where I dwell may be completely or partially unknown to me. I do not see the relationships playing out in meetings in other parts of the building, or other cities where unknown colleagues are meeting with each other or with

[5] *Telemetry Phenomenology Commonwealth*, Kirkland: Lensgrinder, Ltd. 2019.

representatives of the state or city or other corporations. These are my communities and they are my actions in that I help form the organism that they too form.

The mind of the corporation thinks as my mind, the heart of the corporation beats as my heart, and the blood of the corporation flows as my blood. And yet, all of this is hidden from me now as I write it. I do not know what is happening in that office or that meeting room. I do not know the outcome of that meeting between lawyers or in that lobbyist's office. And yet my mind, my heart, my blood. Whatever is mine is theirs, whatever is yours is theirs, whatever is ours is theirs. We hold it for them, we have it on their behalf and through their sanction.

The corporation is just a modern telemetric instance of a long-standing class of possibilities that include community, family, and tribe. The condition for these possibilities is that same manifold space and time which precedes emergence, and which guides and governs the emergent process of human existence. This proposes an altered form of the ethical. Not an ethical set of rules governed by normativity, not an ought to govern over human agency, but an *ethics of facts*: an ethical presupposition at work in the place where we come from and where we are (ethical *facticity*). In the history of philosophy, ethics is often presented as a choice. Here you have Eudaimonism, there you have deontology, hedonism, consequentialism, contractualism, and so on. These are the various possible systems to organize human agency, with the suggestion being that each of us may choose somehow which of the systems best fits our worldview. Or we may argue to convince each other which system would be best to follow or use to structure the relationships in our lives. To the contrary, I have discovered an ethical situatedness that is at work, that is all-consuming, that provides the situation and the context for our lives where we are when we are what we are. The hidden world of the corporate persons where we live, for example, would never permit human individuals to decide or collaborate on a decision to construct an ethical form that would constrain the actions of these powerful beings with their elaborate private lives, personal concerns, and orientations.

Those lifeworlds which we inhabit, which are small partial projections, fill in only small corners and crevices, they each have an ethical power that guides and governs their placement, their worldhood, and the various orientations that come to pass within them. It must be incumbent upon any philosopher trying to recursively comprehend the phenomenological foundations of experience to discover the concrete and operative ethical domain appropriate to each step in the recursive stack. The family ethos, the community ethos, the tribal ethos, the corporate ethos: each factually bound as part and parcel of the factical domain of that specific world and the agents that populate it. It is through these factical domains that each human existence comes to be in the course of the brief and constrained life that we lead. And we need not look for it behind ourselves in that hidden origin that remains concealed as we turn toward it in our daily movement. Because human existence is emergent from its own conditions of possibility, it has the capability of finding those conditions in front of it, within it, as part of its organizing principles and the very structure that it is striving to maintain in/as/through its emergence. The form of phenomenology that undergoes this kind of a turn without having to turn around must be of the recursive kind that understands how to evoke what has been concealed, what has been only partially presented, in the light of day that enshrouds what stands in front of it. This form must be hyper-informed about all things sociological, since the origin of that emergence (and, therefore, of everything concealed in it) is the collaborative place of distributed orientation and collective projection. Sociology is the queen of the sciences.[6]

Theoretically, it would be possible for such an inquirer to come along with enough perspective to reveal it all. In practice, a single human life is too short and too deeply bound to prejudice and presupposition to accomplish it.

Ethics && Publication

To publish is to make generally known. This very well might mean that the next phase in the recursion is the move from the places where we find ourselves to the making known of where we are. For although we all find ourselves somewhere here or there, it may well be that we do not know in the least where we are. As I said, the history of philosophy may have falsely led us to believe that we have a choice as to such placement, as though we could be wherever we wanted to be or wherever we thought that reason dictates. If, on the contrary, the distributed manifold from which we emerge determines our placement, then it is not a choice at all and not in the least up to any one of us to decide this for ourselves. And yet, we would seem to be doubly lost in this problem. For on the one hand, we do not know where we are, and on the other, we think that we can decide to be wherever we like. The segue to publication is a humble maneuver, therefore. It is as much as to say that before we attempt to fully understand or investigate

---

[6] Sociology, as a term and in the role being assigned to it, should recall Mills discussions throughout *The Sociological Imagination*, suggesting the role of the social sciences and their methodologies within a democratic society.

where we are, we must first make it generally known that it is not up to us where we are, and that it is still an ontological necessity that we be somewhere specific.

The ethical form that guides your life is not up to you and yet it is a fact, or rather many facts, that make up the process by which you become generally known to the various groups and circles that you travel through as you grow up and as you set out on your way in this world. As you enter the public sphere, as you make your ideas known to others, there are rules at work. The way you describe things or respond to them in one set of circumstances is vastly different from the way you will describe or respond in other sets of circumstances. You will not say it the same way to your family as you do to your tribe, you will not publish everything to everyone in the same fashion with the same characteristics. Rather, the domain or the target zone of expression dictates rules and behavioral norms. You will adjust, you will adapt, and you will learn. And these procedures are ways of situating yourself within the various populations that you enter along your way. You publish. What? Yourself, your capacity, your abilities and your faculties. Which is to say that you come to be of use to more and more groupings of distributed agency, you emerge into more and more domains. You enter more and more spheres of human existence. You are what is published in and through the living of your life. You make yourself generally known. Which is to say you enter the aggregate, you become a partial force within it, as family member, as a member of the new generation, and as a citizen.

In the introduction to *Being and Time*, there is a reference to the many ontologies of the sciences, the domains of objects that are articulated by each investigation into what is insofar as it is, physically, chemically, biologically, and so on. Why omit the powers of *mitsein* in these emergent phenomenological domains? Why not emphasize the domains of beings proper to the family and the tribe, the community and the state, the church and the grass-roots movement? A true hermeneutical phenomenology, a true analytic of Dasein or fundamental ontology, would seem to require it. The making known that is the entry into these domains of being, this spatial coming to pass (*ereignet*) that installs the human being into the open clearing of this or that group is becoming-public, an emergence into the public life and world of others, with others, in accordance with the *ethos* of those groups.

These domains are not the results of formed wholes carried out by individual agents who bring them into existence. Think again about the corporation as an example. It does not come to be as a result of a set of individuals coming together and making an association. Rather, they must register with the state, they must file the paperwork, the association must follow a set of legislatively provided sanctions that determine the configuration and lifecycle of the corporation, that permit and institute its incorporation. The personhood of the corporation relies on the alliance of the officers forming that organization with the organizational authority of the governing body, state and federal, regional and national. These bodies provide the tax identification number as well as the various protections of limited liability and sanctioned status enabling action in the public domain where other similarly oriented persons encounter it, make contracts, and engage in various protected and sanctioned transactions.

The corporation is just an example, the same could be said of a church or a community. Where would the community be without its land mass, without its residences? The community is situated and as such has a relationship with local power and the organizations that administer to the county or the city where the community has set about defining itself. The community gets a permit to have an event of some kind and lobbies local leaders to pursue its interests in relationships with local businesses or law enforcement. The individuals are constantly succumbing to organizational principles and relationships. The persons at work in any set of community behaviors are always various in nature. The community, like the corporation, is multiple and distributed. These organizations can be in violation of the principle of identity and in violation of the principle of non-contradiction because they can spread themselves out across time and space. Their "phenomenology" need not be limited by the constraints that operate on the human being who has only one brain. And where does this flexibility come from? Where does the authority for their manifold existence lie? In some relationship with another organized body that grants this status to them. Through some public relationship, through some published set of operations and procedures, the organizations of human existence work toward their ends and express their distributed awareness of conditions.

It may very well be the case that if you go back in time far enough, you may find an ur-human or set of humans who are responsible for the first organizational institution bestowing power in distributed fashion upon a remote set of agents acting in accordance with an ethos that defines them. There is no record of it, no way to empirically discover and describe those independent individuals. Instead what you are likely to find is the source of one organizational institution in some other organizational institutions. The corporation borne from the decree of the King and the King borne out by the decree of the Neolithic people who kneel in allegiance to gain greater protection for their property.

That any such ethos would yield judgments about good and evil alongside of moral codes to ensure the good and the codes of punishment to prevent evil, is immanent to the organization being defined. What does it mean to be a member of this or that community, to be a subject of the

King, to be a corporation in good standing? Here are the rules to follow and the norms to adopt so that the domain remains safeguarded for any new entrant that comes along. When a new member of the family is born, all the current members will immediately start enforcing the rules of conduct to ensure that the ethos of the family is maintained. Likewise, the tribe and the community, the church and the state, the corporation and the market. The purpose of the ethos, in this sense, is the regulation of a super or meta-human organism. The forms of autopoiesis that the human being uses to self-organize amid an environment is structured in the forms of ethos that accompany various organizations: a corporation among corporations, a community among communities, and so on.

Some philosopher somewhere may well have done a great service to the species by beginning the process of abstracting these ethical structures from the various organizations that populate human existence, but the abstractions themselves should not be fetishized. Somewhere along the line the list of abstracted principles were catalogued and laid bare as though they were a set of commodities to be bought and sold, or selected at will, by those who find themselves in the various socially organized conditions characteristic of human life on earth. On what grounds is it wrong for the employee to embezzle funds for themselves? On what grounds is it wrong for the community member to speak outside the community about the disagreements that characterize its internal dynamics? One could surely try to produce a consequentialist, contractarian, or deontological argument for why these acts are wrong, but the facts are that these behaviors have been legislated into the organizations themselves, they have developed over time intrinsic to the organizations and interpersonal associations where they take place, whether that means the relationships between corporations or between a corporation and its internal resources, or between communities or again within communities and their membership.

This discovery of the fabricated context of action contexts that is determinate for the concomitant fabrication of an ethics corresponding to the ethos in question, is the driving force of all implicit methodology in discovering the rules and norms at work in these various domains. That is, the publication process, the becoming-public of the agent in these various domains, is already a becoming aware of the rules required for acceptance and inclusion, for participation and conformity. In order to play the part of a son or daughter, citizen or community member, employee or consumer, there are rules to be learned and behavior to be adopted. The human beings publishing themselves, emerging into these domains, are expert at discerning such rules and enforcing them. Those who do not excel, and so reside among the rank and file of a specific organization, can be excellent enforcers of the forensic process of evaluating their peers and condemning or condoning expressed behaviors that support or destroy the fabric of the organization. These ethical evaluators are, to the extent that they support or destroy this fabric, fabricators of the ongoing effective force of the domains themselves. It is specifically the concomitant fabrication of rules and norms that is the very constitution of the domain itself. Where persons are concerned at least, the ethical is the delineation of the domain in terms of its non-fictional fabrication and in accordance with the ways and means of the organizationally instituted policies for the persistent existence of that domain and the persons that populate it.

Publication && Machine Learning

When a book is published, for example, it may find readers. In such reading, the written words periodically activate as the conscious thoughts of a reader. Readers decorate this newfound conscious stream with added notions, derivative ideas, random associations, and whatever else distracts them from the ongoing flow. The production of published work may be a violation of the writer's privacy and the consumption of that published work may violate the reader's privacy. Either way, publication amounts to a violation of the private. Not just a juxtaposed opposition in some conceptual schemata, but a violence against it. And the reverse as well. Keeping private, holding close and apart is a rage against the public life of all and sundry. Whose words are in your head now, friend? Emergence always has its place and that place will be a private place or a public one. The dynamic of the emergent ongoing is the battleground of such placement. It is the ethical domain, the human world. The core of the fourfold dynamic of thesis antithesis synthesis residual.

The privacy of human cognition is most pronounced in infancy. The infant is unknown, is all suggestion and inuendo, a narcissist pure and simple. Their minds are more their own than they will ever be since their development is also their publication and their entry into the various worlds of different domains. The private domain of the family and the economic unit under capitalism pale in comparison to the shadowless isolation of the baby human without a communal language other than the behavior that is the subject of study by others. Studying the behavior of an infant happens during interaction and so teaches the baby, transforms it, helps it grow and develop as it comes to pass into one public domain of human concern or another. The struggle of public and private is the development of the human being, the ongoing emergence of personhood into living form. And that struggle, yet another way to name it, is the ethical. And to emphasize, there are a set of ethical systems, a set of factually defined and contextually determinate ethical networks of expectations and appropriations, orientations and understandings between the people that inhabit those places.

Personhood and personality become intrinsically bound to this ongoing developmental antagonism of the public and the private. Categories may ensue and it might be coherent to tell a story of the introvert as the predominantly private person whereas the extrovert is predominantly public in orientation. These may be slippery in definition and might suggest that engagement in networks of relationships involving other persons is exhausting for the one or energizing for the other personality *type*. If I am exhausted by conversation, it does not mean I do not enjoy it just as the fact that I am energized by it does not mean that I do enjoy it. The categories need not be associated with enjoyment at all. Rather, plugging in one's personality to the connections and relationships of the various environments and associations possible within the human world becomes a way of boosting one's capacity, energizing oneself, or avoiding exhaustion at the least. Some may wear out on their own, others may spin intricate mental webs during their time in solitude.

Neither the introvert nor the extrovert, however, have claims to greater privacy or power and influence in public. Both are equally engaged in the dynamic of integrated forms in their various public domains and both are publicly situated equally within their private domains. That is, alone or together we all bear the stamp of our common behaviors and norms, of the characteristics personified in the emergence of the person's behavior in the various available domains of agency: family, community, tribe, and nation. The so-called private mental life of the introvert is just as much populated with publicly accessible orientations and ideas as the so-called public behavioral life of the extrovert. The manner of being of these paradigmatic personality types cannot be reduced to the public and private, rather privacy is to be associated with the infant, and development constitutes a growing public presence where that presence is felt in the cognitive processes as well as the behavioral practices of each person in whatever social contexts they are drawn. These public imprints may be experienced differently by the personality types (introvert and extrovert), but they are still public imprints.

To the extent that publication of personality into social spheres of behavior context is an ongoing human developmental process, it can become available for study. Reflective relations to the processes of emergence give way to human sociological and psychological investigation. Behavior, as such, can be studied and learned. To the extent that emergent behavior is expressive of acts, those acts can be captured and investigated for their interrelationship. Machine learning has emerged as the hyper-recursive application of mathematization to such human development for the sake of pattern discovery. The purpose of such pattern discovery is predictive. That is, human publication is studied for the sake of being able to better anticipate future human publications. What people have done provides advance notice on what people will do. The point is to capture behavioral characteristics and make associations between the various characteristics in each individual so as to make correlated and anticipatory evaluations of other individuals and the characteristics they are likely to display. The family domain that a person is bound to becomes a dataset for characterizing this public component. The community domain yields another dataset which, through the personhood of the person, integrates with the initial family-based dataset. Connections increase as publication into new domains takes place. All behavior is rendered predictable based on these points of intersection and the association of them with others caught in the same cross-section of commonly attributed domains.

Such collections make it possible to anticipate the orientation of people with specific collections of personal attributes in the various domains they enter during their lives. According to the principles of machine learning, all that is required is that data collected from these publicizing actions be featurizable, where this indicates that it can be rendered in a numerical form that allows for meaningful comparisons between the values assigned to the various members of the population being studied. To the extent then that human persons can be codified in this way, their affiliation and immersion into relevant corporate bodies can be carefully managed and selected. The sets of personality attributes that best fit with desirable capabilities or capacities will be recruited for use by corporate persons in need of extensibility into cognitive domains best served by such qualities. This might normalize as hiring or consumer practices. Any stakeholder can be 'recruited' in this fashion, can be fabricated using these mathematical means to best optimize the organic growth of the corporate Leviathan as it absorbs such persons into its body in an effort to bring to resolve its anxious questioning of its boundaries with its world.

Data science is the perfect culmination of all science insofar as it can automate pattern discovery when targeting data collected from measurement. Rightly speaking, data science is just normal science where the domain is human behavior in all its publication contexts. Data science does not originate in purely academic or scholarly context. Rather, it is first and foremost a corporate invention that only later came to have a vocational status within the educational system. This position was secured by the student consumer university that strives to provide labor resources in whatever way possible to those corporate interests that provide the lion share of academic research budgets.

In record time, it has become clear to such interests that the data collection is the key to adequate prediction and proper anticipation of behavior. Furthermore, it became clear that anticipation was only one side of the equation and that predestination made it possible to direct human behavior into the areas and domains of publication that were most suitable to corporate interests. Thus, the purpose of data collection was to go beyond any mere understanding of where human beings were heading in their developmental processes, and proceed to try and persuade or direct human beings with specific desirable characteristics to head down one path rather than another. The maturing members of the civilization must not only fit into the boxes that promote corporate personhood with the cognitive capabilities the corporations need to thrive, but they must be passionate in their interest to contribute to these domains. Data science offers the solution here by making it possible, when applied to the right kind of data production, to inject properties and attributes into elements of the population predisposed toward certain personality configurations. These self-fulfilling prophetic predictions based on data collection thus can strengthen a "type" of consumer that is advantageous to a specific business orientation. Or they might make for ideal employees and stakeholders that realize the corporate personhood in their individuated partial consciousness doing the work of that corporate person.

It is entirely possible that trades like electrician and carpenter are on the decline whereas digitally based professions where actions are connected via device-based applications are ascending, solely because the former do not produce sufficient data for collection and thus cannot be integrated into the world of the artificially intelligent corporate persons that live and breathe off of big data. The virtual world rapidly becomes the only legitimate domain for agency by human beings coming to pass in their various published forms. If the work or action is not digitizable, then it does not exist. Were this attitude to become prevalent throughout a civilization, the orientation of all individual human agents would promote the interests and structural requirements of artificially intelligent corporate persons nearly all of which must be in some sense present in the telemetric datasphere. The smallest corporate bodies in existence today are actively worrying that they are not adequately leveraging machine learning and in danger of becoming irrelevant and out of touch with modern business practices. Democratizing artificial intelligence is a marketing campaign aimed at all sizes of business across all verticals and meant to let them know that no one is too small to take part in the telemetric datasphere that drives all contemporary cultivation of human publication and development. The ideology-based marketing that sells this democratization will also proclaim itself as the guardian of "ethics" and by that almost always mean the promotion of those norms and practices which best serve its welfare and the general interests of the artificial world where such corporate persons live. Open platforms, as noble as they may seem in theory, are tiny by comparison and likely only serve to legitimize the domain of study despite some of the players being made suspect insofar as they do not follow the same populist ideals. Time may show that such platforms will turn out to have been nothing more than **IP** farms for the giant mega-corporations that dominate the discipline.

Machine Learning &&
How to Become What One Is

Children are the most susceptible to marketing and are being plugged into the global data farms at alarmingly early stages of their development. The purpose of machine learning, insofar as it is used for marketing and behavioral manipulation of consumers and stakeholders in corporate operations, is to maintain the childlike stage of development in natural born persons of all ages. The purpose of these devices is not so much an invasion of privacy for the sake of learning about you as the person that you are, but for the sake of infantilizing your relationship to needs and desires. This makes it possible to lead you around and play a parental role in organizing your habits and ways of life. The aggregate personhood that is produced, the demographic that emerges in the generated models, is aimed at looking out for you, giving you what you want before you realize that you want it. Your love of consumption and entertainment is the playfulness of a child and the corporations that dandle you on their knees and provide these beautiful things to look at and experience are the parents you always wished that you had. They are always attentive to you and you alone.

In *Telemetry Phenomenology Commonwealth*, the structural determination of corporations as artificially intelligent persons is meant as a placeholder for a distributed, trans-individual set of cognitive capabilities that calls the simplicity of the Cartesian project into question: 'I think therefore I am' may be the musings of a marionette and only a partial determination of a distributed operation. In the moment that we act on behalf of a corporation (as employee, consumer, or other kind of stake holder), there may be an experience of phenomenological authenticity bringing some kind of relief from anxiety, but the operations at work go well beyond the immediacy of that experience. There are organizations working in collaboration, there are unseen interests being served, there is a distributed set of conscious acts working in concert to carry out a plan that suits no human participant in that plan over the long term. To deny the personhood of corporations is to fail to see what grips us, what powers us forward, and what we—ultimately—serve. There is no privacy, not because some mega-corp is actively violating some boundary, but because the boundary itself is fabricated in social relations that are corporate through and through. Anxiety is the state of mind that surfaces this.

One way to understand the "inauthenticity" of everyday human existence is as the childish desires fabricated by large-scale organizational structures that live and die based on the markets they can create, or the market share they can acquire. The world that everyday human beings are most absorbed by is the lifeworld of the corporate persons that have produced the things that are all around you and that you encounter throughout each day. We spend our time deliberating on the means to acquire them and how to arrange our lives in their midst. We do not develop while devoted "to the things themselves," rather our every breath is mediated by this social *mitsein* and the manufactured objects it provides. We are nurtured by parents and communities that are immersed in such a world. Who we are, what we are, and how we are is bound to the ethics of facts (*ethos*) appropriate to the neighborhood where we grew up and the markets where we are bought and sold.

How is it possible to break free of this and adopt a properly critical orientation toward it? If my actions come from a place that is absorbed in this telemetric world, if I am only partially present to the meaning of my agency within this corporate lifeworld, what is the critical strategy or tactic that ensures a way out? Communicative action and Power analysis have been presented as prospective approaches. And these may be modernized and deteriorated forms of ideology critique and critical theory. The question that persists in my engagement with these approaches is always rooted in their phenomenological ground. Why are some prone to these suggestions and others violently opposed to them? Did I have a choice when struck by the reason implicit in Marx's *Capital?* Was my relationship to Habermas and Foucault fabricated by some set of circumstances and orientations outside my direct experience, functioning like conditions for the possibility of my experiencing anything at all? The mythical position of deliberation associated with many traditional forms of ethics suggests that this is something I can determine, a choice or selection that I am able to make. Once I have suffered an insight into the ethics of facts, what form of such deliberation remains for me? Where many have sought ethics, I have found only power: an ethics of facts and/as non-fictional fabrications. It is power that decides good and evil. Both Christians and atheists have always agreed on this. Enemies place their honest claims over it as fact. These are burdensome times to know it.

There are entire domains of philosophical research dedicated to the investigation into this moment of deliberation, this sacrosanct private moment where such action is possible, where an authentic experience of right and wrong is available. In my studies of these domains, I found only fabrications. Did my investigations make sense in principle? The work may have been performed as an educational exercise published "just in case." Since when does persisting a text in an Amazon store or a state-run library system amount to publication? And has not publication these days been degraded to a matter of offering one's artifact through the enterprise of a marketeer? Is it meaningful any longer to attempt to comprehend publication without corporate or capital endeavor? The library systems have relationships with private publication interests for the sake of defining their catalogues. Is there any speech at all outside some mega organizational bull horn? You might think a publicly owned internet would have fostered a free distribution mechanism. "You" cannot find it. Instead, we twitter and chatter across the tendrils of these monster networks. Where does it collect? I have seen the stores. In waves and rivers, walls of it, puddles and drops. There are so many lenses at work looking at it. So many computing cycles churning away at it. What is it for? Who does it serve?

It is a collection of lenses. A model is. Machine learning or conceptual entity model. The models contain movement, the execution of methods and functions on the entities that populate their projected worlds. Computation over structure. Aspirations are likely to emerge, ends and aims. Reflection, so to speak, is an act. Investigation and cognition, while their manifold is the understanding which connotes an exponential growth in the artifice and its variable instigation, have a hidden source against which one human being's meagre thinking is partial. Such a debased life is not worthy of its romantic mirage, it emerges from ocean in search of a name. Ethics of facts demystifies ought and indicates the power alone that is there. Becoming who you are, is becoming mechanism, becoming a control arm, an apparatus put to work in a lifeworld you cannot see.

Nature has fabricated teleology, fashioned it from nothing. Limited to mechanistic means, it took billions and billions of years to do it, but once it came to be, purpose was possible, and everything has accelerated. With it came all kinds of variable structure to reflexively pursue it for the benefit of pattern manufacture and discovery. Such sophistication may ensure elaboration on determinate relations with more and more of them. The more stories we tell, the more stories there are. Nature has come to pulse as organism and organization. Today, so to speak, it writes, and it reads.

The exploding universe seeks out new context within which to engineer more such explosions, continuations of that first event. We are the shrapnel of the origin, and we are its movement. Its powder and its burn. And you get to know it. As yourself. Partially. There is much that is organization in you. Patterns that you grow and breathe, in your beating heart, in the rhythms of your movements. In the interstices of the ways you fabricate involvements, that is where we live together in clans and tribes. Can you feel yourself being pulled and pushed as your thoughts come forward?

There are generations in that. Miles and miles of them. This gesture and its realization put us on the brink of good and evil. Not beyond it. Standing right *before* it with a decision to make. And nothing but victory in a battle for survival will determine the nuance in the outcomes of that decision. Was that the right choice? Did it realize goodness? There is such a dread in the sense that only the outcomes can provide the justification and validation. When are these outcomes determinate? When do they stop resonating? The sense of this ongoing historical question is the consequentialists' reductive victory: the idealized practical reason of the Enlightened Human is nothing other than this ongoing open possibility of the outcomes that continue to influence or have the potential to influence further twists and turns of the ricocheting chains that any past or ongoing actions have set in motion.

Who is listening to all these emissions? Is it you? Or some *body* helping you? Which categories are you, by the way? You have access to assisted living, decision-making mechanisms that can help you, accompany you, lead you in the right direction. Do not think of your still lame digital assistant, think of all the decision support mechanisms that are a part of your life, all the apps and devices. The hive mind aims at a globally scoped non-fictional fabrication. Rather, its aiming is the spinning of many of them, yarns and yarns of them. So many stories being acted out and lived. The Sun and the Stars. Distant and near. A universe of reaching out and making contact: we empower the corporate lifeworld by embodying its power. Truly what counts as a phenomenon of appropriate size and shape for consideration is itself a part of the swarm of its creations. Indeed, we are *natura naturans*. A terrifying moment that leaves us anxious and questioning the separation that our "authentic" private world would demand.

There is nothing between the forms of contractarianism that can emerge in such a terrifying moment. Tribalism has become a required attribute in the data stores containing your life. We call it 'mental illness' when one among us rejects some of these organizing principles. Rejects with body or soul, in mind or matter. There is no escape short of a *general strike* at the heart of what occupies each of us throughout our lives. Where are the ones who can organize that without being absorbed back into the lifeworld where they have fallen, or better, where they have been thrown by these gargantuan beings? Organize, but beware the perils of recursion.

Antagonisms and Foundations
Artificial Intelligence and the Categorical Imperative

Neither... Nor...

In neither the case of artificial intelligence nor in the case of the categorical imperative are the experts primarily or exclusively concerned with forensics, with sorting out what has happened for the sake of a distant judgment. Instead, they aim in part at providing the moment of decision with what is required to act as one ought to act under the circumstances. This marks a departure from nominalist notions of moral facts and embraces the real phenomenological effects of a milieu populated by persons struggling to do the right thing. Such a context cannot be reconstructed based on the empirical discovery of associations and points of connection or correlation. Rather, it is a meaningful foundation or background against which the agency of the person is always settled. Manifold moments of decision by an agent or the settling of persons within the background where their perception, interest, and attention emerge amount to a lived world, an action milieu where involved beings make their way.[1]

The patterns of any moral forensics are telemetric: emissions are attributed as properties of the agent emerging in the action, captured and collected for analysis, and fed back into further action contexts for the sake of providing directives for the future actions of the agent or other agents comparably composed. In the moment of forensic analysis, the completion of the feedback loop is hypothetical, not yet realized, but posited as a deferred payoff for the collection and analysis taking place. The sieve of data capture becomes something of an investment for postponed

---

[1] The dichotomy has been inspired by a highly opportunistic reading of Scheler, *Formalism in Ethics and Non-Formal Ethics of Values: A New Attempt toward the Foundation of an Ethical Personalism*. Translated by Manfred S. Frings and Roger L. Funk. Northwestern University Press. Evanston, IL. 1973. At least part of my opportunism must be credited to a practical interleaving at the time with Ayer's "Critique of Ethics and Theology" in *Language, Truth & Logic*. Dover Publications, Inc. New York, NY. 1952. "Opportunism" here suggests that I am happy to grab hold of bits and pieces and ignore the rest since there is a great deal in Scheler's work that I not only do not wish to appropriate but would condemn. Likewise Ayer.

realization. And this form of analysis is contraposed to a real and effective deliberation aimed at realizing a direct response to actions unfolding here and now in this moment of decision. It is a subtle difference amounting to little more than transparency in understanding the complete circuit unfolding in evaluation and deliberation. When the agent is self-consciously processing personally relevant factors gathered from social and personal experience and involvement, they actively feed their understanding of current context with a digested form of their own history and its meaningful connections to the influences of other agents partaking in that same history. To the contrary, an agent injected with externally computed probabilities that bear empirical links to their own habitual practice are operating under a fog in which the "deliberation" has been carried out far away from the present situation. Such injected orientations are likely to realize prediction models for the agent under the set of determined conditions that have been correlated between the current context and any of millions or billions of other contexts that have been scraped together through some remotely performed measurements composing a digital surveillance system.[2]

Neither an artificially intelligent agent nor a naturally intelligent one would demonstrate 'consciousness' in the forensic scenario. Intelligence in such cases is purely telemetric, happening far from the milieu where their interests and attentions are realized. From a traditional point of view, this

---

[2] "God sees everything that you do." Surveillance is ancient and, if Freud is to be believed in *The Future of an Illusion*, civilization cannot survive without it. It is not enough to point out the widescale presence of surveillance in human civilization, we must understand the phenomenological and sociological foundations and meaning of it. We may need to go so far as to investigate how this particular configuration of biological characteristics require it for their collective ongoing survival. This won't happen if you think it originates in a few technical inventions from 15 years ago when Google launched its Ads business. Cf. The chapter "God is Dead" in *Telemetry Phenomenology Commonwealth*. It is all just lens grinding. Deep down, the patterns align and the indefinite article tries to see anxiety's fort/da in the desire for omniscience. In *Telemetry Phenomenology Commonwealth*, the connection to the telemetric organization's desire for surveillance emerges clearly via the architectonic. The desire for omniscience is the telemetric's desire for surveillance. The yearning to know all is a realization in cognition of the desire to see all refracted into the condition where everything is being seen. But "know" suggests an imaginary state in which even the ignorant rest assured that *they* know, even to the extent that we dismiss our own membership among the ignorant. Surveillance in / as / through all emissions cultivates this state in the partial phenomenological orientation of the person.

entails that the forensic situation handled telemetrically is without any ethical meaning and contains nothing relevant to a classically framed rational determination of the right thing to do given the circumstances and whatever moral facts are applicable to them. The capacity to do otherwise in such analysis is merely a statistical facet of the decision, not a rational determination based on moral reasoning. The options are little more than demographic categories or slices of the population that capture the distribution of attributes and formulate possible outcomes based on the likely fulfillment of those attributions in the specific action context that is unfolding. You will not think of what to do under such circumstances, you will not weigh the options, you will not obey the moral law or realize the traditions of your community. The data will not feed a decision that will freely articulate a not yet occurrent moment in time. Rather, some small percentage will rob, some percentage will kill, some will protect, and others will simply walk away.[3]

To the extent that 'phenomenology' designates the alternative, the mode of moral meaningfulness that agonizes or deliberates *in actu* over the specific conditions and the personal involvement in them, the moment of decision is always phenomenological. Time is appropriated anew in the agent's orientation, there is always an impending projection of yet undetermined acts opening to possible directions that might emerge from one and the same personal facticity at stake in the moment of deliberation and decision. The moment is unlike any other, it screams of its own unique power and place in the agent's personal history. It has not yet been determined what will be done and what remains to be decided, rather the upshot is at issue, lies before oneself as a possibility free of encumbrance and yet bombarded by past influences calling out for it to turn this way or that, feeding the moment of decision with the frenzy of a milieu coming to understand itself in the act that is unfolding.[4]

---

[3] "It is the same conformism, the assumption that men behave and do not act with respect to each other, that lies at the root of the modern science of economics, whose birth coincided with the rise of society and which, together with its chief technical tool, statistics, became the social science par excellence. Economics—until the modern age a not too important part of ethics and politics and based on the assumption that men act with respect to their economic activities as they act in every other respect—could achieve a scientific character only when men had become social beings and unanimously followed certain patterns of behavior, so that those who did not keep the rules could be considered to be asocial or abnormal." From Arendt's *The Human Condition*, pp. 41-42.

[4] "There is a difference between knowing the path & walking the path." - The Oracle in *The Matrix*.

As forensics, ethics may merely express a social given at work in the agent's field of operations; as decision-making, it is the most real event in their lives, the highest function of complex cognition at work in real time as decisions are being made. The dilemma may hinge on some natural fact that will one day be discovered and allow forensic specialists to put themselves in the shoes of the agent. Maybe this gene configuration of homo sapiens was selected because of its capacity to be impacted by probabilistic computations at just those moments when the next action is ready to be determined. Or maybe it was because the configuration has the capacity to perform that act itself. Either way, it seems that the question driving this line of reasoning is not whether AI is compliant with some ethical principle like the categorical imperative, but rather what does the advent of AI do to Ethics? Does it transform it or change it into something other than it once was? Or does it merely highlight a weakness that was always there in it, showing that the rational deliberation that lies at the very foundation of ethical action is a ruse?

The ethical dilemma that artificial intelligence poses amounts to a series of antagonisms and foundations. Not just as a heuristic structure for framing a discussion of the topic, but in its very logic, in the way in which it demonstrates itself as the dilemma that it is. Our question is not whether artificial intelligence can be done ethically, but what impact does its form of action have on ethics? In what way does it force a reduction of the moment of decision to telemetric forensics on action as behavior and in so doing transform the dynamics at work in all such moments of decision?

Why artificial intelligence? Why the categorical imperative?

The advent of intelligence in artificial form highlights the obscurity of intelligence in its natural forms. It bears testimony to an antagonism that only emerged recently but emerged in such a way as to reflect on its entire history. Intelligence surfaces in the augmentations of the agent displaying those characteristics. Natural intelligence begins to look artificial, replete with artifice, once its offset has surfaced in non-fictional fabrications. The becoming self-conscious of the artificiality of intelligence is the basic antagonistic dynamic of contemporary life on earth. As such, artificial intelligence reveals antagonism in a way never yet revealed and yet always already effective in human technical expertise and innovation.

The categorical imperative as a demonstration of the fundamental role of ethics in any rational agent's existence need not be associated exclusively with the work of Kant. The categorically effective command to 'be ethical' applies to the moment of decision and any agent that utters or heeds such a command when it inhabits the moment of decision is, by definition, a rational agent even if it is seeking to maximize utility or fulfill a contract. Or to go still further, the moment of decision itself is the application of a categorical imperative to be a rational agent in making the decision, an ethical agent in carrying out the power of the action when it is still possible to act otherwise. Even the consequentialist generally conceived feels the impetus of this command, otherwise the consequences would not matter, the obligation to honor the contract would not matter, and the achievement of the highest virtue would not matter. The power of any moral law for decision-making places the ethical imperative at the foundation of all agency. When the person acts, the imperative is operative, and the act itself can be evaluated in whatever terms such evaluation permits. This is not a categorical imperative over and against a hypothetical one, rather it is the applicability of the ethical, in its most globally relevant form, to the act.

Elsewhere[5], I have suggested that the rejection of moral facts amounts to a so-called *ethics of facts*. This might be an overly clever turn of phrase, but the point is that insofar as the moment of decision is not attributed with moral deliberation and some form of practical reasoning, then there is no moment of decision at all: no personal act articulating a private cognitive sphere demonstrating the liberty of the agent. Thus, we would be left with only the cold hard data of the actual world and unable to say anything more about what it ought to be.

> Common wealth, therefore, can never become common in the sense we speak of a common world; it remained, or rather was intended to remain, strictly private. Only the government, appointed to shield the private owners from each other in the competitive struggle for more wealth, was common.[6]

Only the applied law, in its formal constraint on each private agent, maintained the commonality of action under the guise of commandment. The dominance of social power was preserved through the establishment of rules to protect the privacy of the agents that matter, the corporations and organizations for the sake of which governing institutions governed. The idealization of rights is in fact surrendered to the hard reality of interests and the collaboration of computational forces accentuating the life of the telemetric in and as our common world. In what follows, this is what is at stake.

---

[5] *Telemetry Phenomenology Commonwealth: Corporate Surveillance and the Colonization of Personality.* Lensgrinder, Ltd. Kirkland, WA. 2019. The theme is introduced and developed throughout the Commonwealth section culminating in the residual: namely, pursuant to telemetric colonization, an ethics of facts is all that remains.

[6] Hannah Arendt, *The Human Condition*, p. 69.

Antagonism: Ethics and Data-Driven Reason

Consider an example to show the depth of data-driven reasoning in technically oriented commerce. Engineering may be tasked with driving production readiness for an upcoming rollout of various support services on a platform where leadership emphasizes the need for executive level reporting and visualization of the status of the system based on several key indicators and metrics. As the developers unravel the various hairballs associated with the delivery mechanisms for the telemetry, it becomes apparent that no monitoring is in place and that the telemetry pipeline that could be used in monitoring is too granular to easily produce the reports that leadership wants. More than that, it surfaces that the monitoring and support requirements for the system cannot be met with the mechanisms that are in place. Engineers must lobby the leadership to convince them that a change in priorities is required. Their priority is to make sure the system is adequately monitored and that alarms are being raised when they should be. They must ensure that the On-Call engineers have the troubleshooting tools to get to the root cause of any critical incidents. Once that is done, they assert that they will be able to produce the robust reporting mechanisms that leadership requires. The point of this parable is that the leadership team is more interested in rendering the data that describes the availability of the system sliced and diced along various of its attributes than they are in making sure that the system itself is highly available in terms of those same attributes. It takes many engineering hours to convince them to change their priorities and expectations. It is a higher priority to see an indicator revealing the failed state of the system than to see the system repaired. Rather, the system's repair comes second and is demonstrated in the change of state of the metric. This is an example of data-driven business focus gone mad.

Maintaining the system requires an investment of resources, and management is always making decisions on how to use the resources available to them. Roadmaps are created, project plans put in place, tasks allocated, and estimates provided. Resource management is a primary job function of all "managers" in such enterprises. Are these investments paying off? Are the people we have allocated to the functions, having the impact that we would expect them to have given the level of commitment we have in the process? This is what the reporting is meant to show. And not only this, it provides answers to other questions: Is the product being used, is it up and running as it should be? What good is it to spend a lot of money building service features if the service that delivers those features is not available for use? We must ask this question constantly and we must be continually informed about the state of the system and the state of the resources provided. That is what the telemetry events that we produce and the reporting that we build over the top of it must show.

The decision-makers love charts, graphs, and tables. They love to look at the distribution of collected values and see the trend of those distributions over time and whether they show improvements correlative to the effort spent. It tells them where those efforts pay off and how effectively they do so. In some areas, a small investment can have a huge impact; in others, huge investments are required to have a tiny one. To the extent that these charts and the data that fuels them are at the root of all their decisions, it is something of an inconvenience to import ethical principles into the process, although it is possible to track such ethical principles as though they were resources expended as part of the project. This enables them to ask questions like: is the application of ethical principles to our decision-making paying off? Is it improving service delivery? Does it increase customer uptake or improve satisfaction among existing customers? The data would probably show that such questions do not have anything at all to do with being ethical or applying ethical principles to decision-making. Rather, they would show that the perception of being ethical or the perception that they are applying ethical principles to their decisions is sufficient for the desired effect. This follows from the suspicion that the application of ethical principles in such matters is unlikely to decrease the cost of production or expand the opportunities for profit. Ethical principles are not commonly thought to provide justifications for charging customers more for services they are receiving, nor do they commonly show that it is "good" to cut costs by delivering a lower quality product that still meets the needs of its consumers. Why exceed their expectations when it is more profitable to merely meet them? This is not a well-worn ethical foundation that instigates deep compliance on the part of business decision makers.

Thinking about it this way, whether ethics is antagonistic to data-driven decision-making, lies in the data itself. Analysis of the data requires that we capture all the properties associated with the application or non-application of the ethical principles. Was it publicly done in such a way that customers and potential customers were aware of the application of such principles? This would be an important characteristic to capture in the analytics. This would enable comparison of ethics-based decisions that were publicly advertised as such with ones that were not. And this would provide insight on whether customers respond positively to the presence of ethical decision-making by their suppliers of goods. If they do, then the use of ethics in business decisions would be justified. Otherwise, forget it. Scrap it and try the next great idea for increasing profitability.

This may not be the way that we meant to raise the question of this antagonism. In the considerations thus far, ethics is a mere ingredient, a resource that is part of the process of production and delivery. As such, it may be a worthwhile investment, or it may not be. It may be a barrier to profit and benefit or it may facilitate it. What about ethical principles themselves? Is there a deeper antagonism to be considered such that ethical principles are not themselves data-driven? And this suggests a deeper antinomy that lies in the notion of applying ethical principles to decision-making in business matters. The conflict exists when those business matters concern the sale of widgets let alone making use of artificial intelligence or machine learning or any advanced computing systems that take over some of the tasks that were previously performed by human agents endowed with a moral education representative of whatever social context they come from.

But we are rushing ahead. Is ethics truly antagonistic to data-driven decision-making? It may depend entirely on what the data represents. If the data captured and analyzed depicted the quantity of goodness that has been realized by the application of the ethical principle, then there would not be anything at all antithetical in the consideration of ethics under these heuristics. Consider the ban on random acts of violence, for example. What does the data show about the increase in 'goodness' as a result of all the investments human communities have made in the principle? We could gather data on the resources that go into promoting such principles, teaching them and punishing violations of them. We could gather data on the well-being of the civilization when the principle was in effect and was being adequately safeguarded. Comparisons could be made to how such communities looked relative to other time periods or other societies where the principles were not practiced. Based on all such data, were it possible to gather it all, decisions could be made as to whether such an ethical principle was worth the investment. Maybe it does not matter whether it is possible to gather data for this. It is more of a hypothetical to show there is nothing essentially present in ethical principles applied to action to suggest it is incoherent to discuss data-driven determination of optimal principles for use by a community under consideration.

This is where it starts to become clear that the blanket term "ethics" is not adequate to the investigation. Contrary to what some business ventures seem to think[7], there is no "ethics" generally speaking, no generic ethical principles against which one can measure the goodness of an act. Rather,

---

[7] For example, *Tools and Weapons: The Promise and the Peril of the Digital Age*, by Brad Smith and Carol Anne Browne. 2019. New York: Penguin Press.

there are types of principles and systems such as hedonism, communitarianism, deontology, consequentialism, etc. Utilitarianism, for example, might fit nicely into the picture we have just described. The principle to maximize well-being and minimize harm seems ripe for data-driven decision-making. Were such a system of ethics to be put in place, we would need telemetry and analysis, we would have to set up feedback loops and alarms. It would be imperative to understand through data collection and analysis whether various decisions had the impact on well-being that they were presumed to have or whether things went south eventually and thus the principle previously employed became tarnished. Furthermore, we would have to work out a scenario where such outcomes were fed back into future decision-making to ensure that unsuccessful applications of principles aiming to maximize utility were no longer repeated and were replaced with alternatives showing better historical impact. The categorical imperative, on the other hand, might not work in anything like an analogous fashion.

The imperative, in its most formal sense described at the outset of this chapter, is kept independent of outcome and is meant to be a facet of rational deliberation by a rational being as such. The good will which is good in-itself is good regardless of whether it succeeds in trying to do something good. Being unable to save the drowning child (even if it is Hitler) does not impact the goodness of the will that is commanded to do so. We need not gather any data to see if the good is truly being served by this or that rule governing action by rational agents. The data does not matter when it comes to the application of the categorical imperative. No analytics are required and there is no need to set up a feedback loop to protect against drift from previous deliberations.

This means that we have not only discovered an antagonism between business decision-making and the categorical imperative as an ethical system, but we have also pointed out an antagonism within ethics itself. There are ethical systems that are themselves based on data-driven decision-making and there are ethical systems that are opposed to such decision-making. If we were interested in pursuing Scheler's inspirational investigations in detail, it would make sense to attempt to determine where his approach would fall relative to the role of data in the decisions. Does a non-formal value ethics require data-driven analysis or is it the case that the formal approaches expressed by the data cannot address the merits of the decisions? The question would be interesting not only as an exercise in scholarship on Max Scheler, it would be interesting because it would force us to consider whether the relationship of data to decision-making was a quality of the formality of the principle at work or whether it was a quality of the set of relationships that are at work in the non-formal system. Where the non-formal is an a priori value context, should data prove to be irrelevant to the development of right execution, then we might be correct in concluding that data-driven decision-making is not inextricably connected to the formal or non-formal nature of the ethical system, but to its prior conditioning of aboriginal value versus an emphasis on outcomes and consequences, a distinction which could be baked into representations of contractarian and eudaimonistic forms of ethics as well. Later we will look more deeply at consequentialism as the origin of this binding to data-driven approaches, but here we will only propose it as an hypothesis that the antagonism is not due to a formal/non-formal opposition but to the ends/origins polarity implicit in the neither... nor... of forensics vs the moment of decision where the true questionability of the act is realized.

Foundation: Artificial Intelligence and Aggregation

Formalists and non-formal value theorists, apriorists, share in their concern over the phenomenological locus of moral deliberation and decision-making. The corporation that spouts a platform of "being ethical" in their AI related business, like any quasi-hedonist, is purely forensic. They mostly live in terror that they will suffer the consequences of a consumer-impacting faux pas that violates some principle of identity politics. They worry about bias in their algorithms, they worry about facial recognition software that will inadvertently surface some racially sensitive trope, they worry about racist chat bots, and they worry about these things for obvious reasons: they are bad for business and tarnish the brand, they will hurt sales and detract from the general welfare of the corporate body seeking to maximize it. The vast disparity between these two orientations is easily discovered in concerns for privacy. The action-oriented agents who hold that ends will justify means, consider privacy forensically as some property transference that can be transactionally traced using some form of block chain. Summarizing the personally identifiable information out of the individual's stored data is enough to protect such privacy. If there is no way to reverse engineer the aggregate operations, the personal privacy of the individual is safeguarded and the system at work is respectful to their autonomy. Privacy means something radically different to the phenomenologically oriented ethicist. The formalist, at least, holds that the moment of decision must be inviolate and that the individual must be treated as an "end-in-itself" that is respected as it works to make decisions based on autonomous deliberations rationally grounded. Privacy, under such conditions, amounts to the integrity of personhood at that moment.

That moment of decision is the object of interest of the most common and lightweight form of artificial intelligence currently in existence: machine learning. The argument I am making is conditioned by such limitations. I am not planning on making a grand denouncement or providing some categorical insight into the nature of artificial intelligence. Rather, I would here like to zero in on a specific aspect of it: the aggregation of data for use in statistical computations to fit and predict the moment of decision from the point of view of a forensic pathology of rational agents with money to spend. To this end, the defining features and required preconditions of machine learning will be used to form a representative picture of a practical scenario. And this for the sake of showing the discordance that exists between that scenario and the value concentration of the apriorist point of view.

First and foremost, machine learning is always enacted upon a structured set of data and the specific machine learning package imposes strict requirements on the form of that data. That it be rectangular, for example, that it be described via a set of types, that it be labelled in such a way where numeric values might be used in place of plain text where the plain text is absorbed into the schematics of the data (i.e., one hot encoding). The purposes of these structural requirements are to enable execution of pattern discovery operations. There are a set of variables that can be discovered in the data and some of these variables can be projected in future instances based on past instances of it. We might examine certain features in the data like the zip code, the highest level of education, the racial or cultural identification, etc. And based on these attributes or features of the data, we may be able to discover associations with other attributes that are unknown but dependent upon them. Income, for example.

If we have a good-sized static data set that is properly structured in this way, we can "train" on that data to learn the relationship between the various features in it and the dependent variables that we hope to be able to project. In this way, once the model has been created and verified based on this training, we will be able to operationalize it in some context where we are asking questions like where do you live and what is your educational and racial background, questions people might be likely to routinely provide answers to, and from that data make educated probabilistic guesses about the likely income of such a person. Since this latter information may be something people are less likely to provide willingly or truthfully, the ability to produce accurate predictions based on the more reliable data will help the operational system do whatever work it is trying to do more effectively.

Data in the aggregate, therefore, is the root of such machine learning. It is impossible to comprehend contemporary machine learning mechanisms without data that has been used to train and test the models that are being generated by the various algorithms. Furthermore, the point of model generation is operationalization: using it to predict values associated with dependent variables in new data that was not part of the training or test data sets. The collection of data into schematically structured collections is not incidental to these processes, it is essential to them. What this operationalization amounts to then is the injection of the model into the moment of decision. The shopper is a data producer, the voter is a data producer, and the applicant is a data producer. The purpose of prediction is to bring together the learning of aggregate operations in the past to the current data point in the process of being produced. The moment of decision, under such conditions, is the reduction of the personal decision to an event of data production where that data is bound to the set of known variables for the sake of predicting the dependent ones. What else they might like to buy will be significant. Whether they will be successful with what they are being given (in the case of a request for credit or a grant of some kind). If it is likely that they will default on a loan or fail to pay a bill. All things about which the individual cannot be trusted to provide accurate information or to have any knowledge at all. Instead, the model uses data produced by other people like this person and applies the patterns of past operations to the operation that is currently unfolding. Thus, within the scope of machine learning, the moment of decision is reduced to an event of data production (a telemetric emission). And the real decision that is being made in that moment is the prediction being spit out by the model.

The relationship that I am attributing to the aggregation of data by machine learning is therefore "foundational" in the sense that machine learning as such is built on top of the principle that data must be collected from data producing events and used in aggregate form to make predictions about future data production events. The data can be cleansed of anything personally identifiable and still serve this end. We need not know the data producer's name or social security number and we do not need to know their specific street address or telephone number. We do not need anything that would make it possible to retroactively associate the data in the data set with the person that produced it. That is not any part of the project at work here. Rather, the data is valuable because it is impersonal. Or at least that the personality exposed in it is sufficiently generic and generalized that it merely describes a set of variable characteristics that could be applied to many different people. The data is most beneficial insofar as it describes a general population or an aggregate set of qualities or characteristics that can be easily cultivated in casual contexts of interaction with individual persons. The particularity of the engagement does not lie in the past data that has been collected, but in the current moment, the moment when prediction is taking place, when some decision is being made by the machine or the organization that it serves regarding the data producer who has come in search of something on offer: goods for sale, or services to be rendered.

Antagonism: The Categorical Imperative and Consequentialism

At this point, it might be possible to tell a story of how consequentialism in ethics, whether via a doctrine of the mean, rule utilitarianism, or contractarian deliberations in the original position, is bound to the data-driven approach that is at work in machine learning.[8] Based on that story, it would be possible to describe an antagonism between consequentialism and the categorical imperative where the former is associated with purposes and their impacts on utility, the general welfare, justice, excellence or whatever you like, while the latter is derived from an intent-based focus that is bound to the good will irrespective of outcomes, in short, the command to be ethical. To condone acts as morally good based on outcome and the impact the outcome has on general welfare, for example, requires that evidence be gathered, and data collected. Lying might be condemned because the past occurrences of it have often turned out badly or the adoption of a general rule condoning it would damage the social fabric in a way that could be documented and described based on empirical observations. The consequentialist would have to provide empirical proof that associates likely outcomes with desirability or beneficial conditions. Machine learning might likely be helpful under such conditions because it could tell us what dependent variables to expect given a set of known contributing factors. The decision-making process of the consequentialist could be assisted with such decision support since the aim is to promote

---

[8] And not only a data driven approach, but a telemetry based one that gathers the data for its enforcement of norms and rules through surveillance. Just as the visibility of the distributed computing system makes its surveillance a necessary facet of enforcement of rules for proper functioning so too might the claim be made for any ethical system distributed among agents and actors. Often surveillance based governance and social organization is rejected on moral grounds, but this cannot be taken for granted as it may be possible to construct some form of contractarian-style ethics that relies on surveillance to achieve the good and promote the general welfare.

beneficial outcomes which are more or less likely depending on what actions are taken. Increasing the probability of positive results would promote goodness. Many arguments made by organizations promoting a business selling machine learning or other AI solutions hinge on these sorts of consequentialist concerns. They suggest that AI solutions will assist in achieving desirable outcomes and—presumably—assist in identifying some outcomes as desirable because of their further relationship with other patterns of association that may be deemed desirable (to a paying customer, at least, although the morality of making people pay for "the good" is rarely considered by the solution providers).

This is the classic approach taken to the offset of the consequentialist and the good will of the categorical imperative. The latter employs a powerful representation of the value that is not reducible to any such commerce of results and purposes. And this dignity inherent in the rational decision maker has been a crucial component of the antagonism between the two approaches. The real story that underlies the division here is that the one approach succumbs to a vision of the ethical agent as an ingredient in the process, as part and parcel of the currency under consideration, whereas the other equates that same agent with the categorical imperative itself. Consequentialism, as the story goes, falls victim to all sorts of scenarios where the value of individuals is weighed and measured against the overall collective benefit derived from employing them in one way or another. Should it become advantageous to the many to make use of some set of individuals, then such is the bittersweet nature of the good. Only when the fact that the imperative of the ethical law is itself one and the same with the dignity of the law maker, the autonomous rational being, do we avoid these consequences. The consequentialists respond by suggesting that such rules may indeed turn out to promote the general welfare and the two parties will debate whether this ultimately concedes the power of the disruptive ethical agent to a domain outside the chain of outcomes.

What is at stake in this characteristic of their antagonism is the status of the person. Is the person a data producer or is the person an anomalous and transcendent decision-maker? In the consequentialist picture the ethical person produces ends and as such may be exposed to consideration as a mere means. There does not appear to be any essential protection from this reduction to an instrumental role. If utility is the proposed good that is the only end that is desirable for its own sake, then there is distance between the notion of personhood and the notion of the highest end. A distance that is not present in the categorical imperative because the alternate formulations of the law are meant to show that the personhood of the ethical person is one and the same with the moral law itself. Respect for the law just is a respect for the legislative status of any ethical person. The value of the person and the role they must play in any ethical scheme is therefore central to their antagonism. The goods and purposes vs the good will independent of outcomes is anchored in the debate over personhood and whether it is better served or comprehended by the one view or the other.

Despite whatever sparring that might go on between the two camps, the distance of the highest end in the consequentialist view from the end-in-itself of the categorical imperative is at the heart of the antagonism. If the end-in-itself is not the ethical person there is always the logical possibility that the consequentialist approach will result in the reduction of personhood to a mere means used for the sake of achieving a higher end. If the person is identified with the end-in-itself, then the position is no longer consequentialist, but has been transformed into an observance of the one and only ethical law that places the rational imperative at the root of all decision making. The call to be ethical which is the formal power of the categorical imperative bestows dignity upon whoever hears it even if they heed its call for the sake of maximizing utility. Any maneuver to convert the agents into fundamentally valuable facets in the equation, extracts those agents from the domain of aims and purposes and establishes a moral law that would be intrinsically bound to that agent's adherence to the command of reason. The one who hears the command is also the one who commands. And the issuing of the command is the ethical system in practice, as practical reasoning, such that the agent is not to be taken as part and parcel of the system of outcomes.

If we understand their antagonism in these terms does that mean that the categorical imperative is all about the moment of decision whereas the consequentialist approach is all about forensics? Not at all. Philosophers advocating either position have shown concern for both the decision-making and deliberation that must be done by an agent trying to sort out the right course of action as well as the evaluation that must be done to determine whether a third-party's action should be lauded or condemned. Much of traditional ethics has moved back and forth across this dividing line without concern for the distinction. The point of view of the decision-maker is a necessary ingredient to the evaluation of the act regardless of whether the act is considered in terms of the will employed or the outcome and ends that it achieved. The power of any system of ethics is that it can function interchangeably in either context. Whether you are a Kantian or a Utilitarian you can make use of your favorite system of ethics both for figuring out what the right thing to do is and in figuring out whether your compatriots are doing the right thing when they act in various ways.

The significance of this disconnect underlies my entire project. On the one hand, the personhood of the person is the basis of antagonism between the two systems, and on the other hand, it is an easily malleable ingredient that is basic in the process of identifying the good wherever it may be. In the one case the person is one and the same with the end-in-itself, whereas in the other case the person is an agent working to achieve the highest end. In each case we recognize that the system can be used to both address the act of decision in the moment that it is made and the evaluation of the acts of others (and oneself in the past) in terms set out by the system. Despite their apparent disagreement on the person's relationship to the highest end, the two systems agree that there is no problem in the shift in position that occurs when one deliberates on the right course of action and when one evaluates the course of actions taken by others. Both the first person point of view and the third person point of view are equally served by both systems, even with their radical differences when associating personhood in its relationship to the highest moral principle or the end which cannot itself become an end to some further end, whether that be eudaimonia or utility or the categorical imperative. If evaluation is performed from a second person point of view, the hinge persists since this position is just an elevation of respect for personhood to an engaged first principle of applied action. There is still a facility in moving from the one to the other independently of the antagonism, although the opposition is clearly situated in the relationship personhood has to the founding principle at the heart of each system.

How serious can the categorical imperative be about the absolute dignity of the rational agent if the back and forth between these two perspectives is so easily performed? The formal command to be 'ethical' is at work in both approaches and to that extent the antagonism along the lines of personhood is not as divisive as the history of ethical theory has led us to believe. Their apparent antagonism masks their mutually telemetric natures. Let us take a closer look.

Foundation: Data Aggregation and the Categorical Imperative

What allows both consequentialism and the categorical imperative to move back and forth between support for moral forensics and decision support during deliberations by a moral agent are their relationship to aggregation. Their dispute over personhood and its relationship to the highest end, that which is good in-itself, turns out to be a ruse when both the formal ethics of the categorical imperative and the non-formal system of purposes are viewed in their common relationship to the aggregate persona that enables both forensics and decision support as well as an easy transition from the one to the other. No conversion from first to second or third person is required to make the transition because the evaluation and the decision support are already provided impersonally to an agent evaluating action independently of their phenomenological conditions and the concomitant future-oriented projections. The nature of aggregation may be what draws the two positions together because it is the nature of the aggregate to pull together a mixture of formal notions abstracted from the concrete individual and attributes or features that are characteristic of those same concrete individuals. On the one hand, we have a formal agent removed from anything concrete or personally identifiable, void of any inclination or specific characteristic that could be used to separate the agent from other agents equally imposed upon by one and the same moral imperative. On the other hand, we have a producer of ends who is part and parcel of the universalized currency of relationships that make up the concrete domain of actions and outcomes.

In both cases, a formal identity is established. The rational agent is void of personal characteristics, biases and interests, the utilitarian agent is purely universal in the sense that they succumb to the one and only end in-itself that must be the organizer and orientation for all action conceptualized within its sphere of operations. In both cases, the agent is universalized categorically. All agents are rational agents and act as ends in themselves. All agents are pursuers of utility and strive to achieve the end in-itself. All are equally alike in this regard and evaluation of one's own actions in the course of deliberating on the right thing to do bears little difference from the evaluation of the other's actions when judging their acts to be either good or evil.[9]

In matters of data aggregation, we say we are protecting the privacy of the data producers if we remove personally identifiable features from the data and treat the collected output in the aggregate. If we can then establish the foundation of these ethical systems in an aggregate maneuver, we could say that they too protect the privacy of those individual agents covered by their jurisdiction. What we mean by that is that privacy and the private sphere are not relevant to the ethical in the consequentialist case. All that matters is that the universal end is being served and the evaluation of

---

[9] "The uniform behavior that lends itself to statistical determination, and therefore to scientifically correct prediction, can hardly be explained by the liberal hypothesis of a natural "harmony of interests," the foundation of "classical" economics; it was not Karl Marx but the liberal economists themselves who had to introduce the "communistic fiction," that is, to assume that there is one interest of society as a whole which with "an invisible hand" guides the behavior of men and produces the harmony of their conflicting interests." From Hannah Arendt, *The Human Condition,* pp. 43-44.

actions will be exclusively compared with that standard of measure. When it comes to ethics, there is no privacy. God, for lack of a better word, sees everything and all your actions are up for "public" consideration and measurement.[10]

All that matters in the moment of decision is that the agent is a representative of either the categorical imperative or the principle of utility. The personal concerns and the specific characteristics need not play a role here. Or rather, there is nothing peculiar about this person's realization of the principles under this condition as opposed to some other person with the same set of attributes. And the process of characterizing the extent to which the highest end is served ultimately amounts to a fitting operation of the attributes at work in the case relative to the dependent variables that are sorted by the deliberation itself. Attribution need not be attached to a set of empirical observations, although the maxim or rule that guides an action via the pure will can be characterized with its predicates.

Telling a lie to get out of a tough situation is effectively to will that all people tell the truth and then take exception to it when convenient. This is in violation of the categorical imperative. The process of extrapolating the situation is a universalizing operation, it deflates the action of everything concrete and places the maxim of the action up for consideration in sufficiently aggregate form such that it could be relevant to any agent across a variety of special circumstances. The same is done when evaluating an action in terms of a consequentialist system that is driven by rules. The rules themselves may be offset against a different end in-itself, but the process of producing an aggregate presentation of the agent's action and evaluating that aggregated presentation against the system's end are

---

[10]Foucault on surveillance turns Arendt's description of the public sphere on its head. Only what is public can be truly seen, she says. And being truly seen is a requirement for the free and excellent act where the private is necessary foundation (as opposed to an antagonism) for the agent's venture into public view. Under conditions of surveillance, however, this visibility becomes coercive and disciplinary, statistically aggregated to enable predictive anticipation of behavioral outcomes. The telemetric reveals/conceals this twofold conditioning possibility. It challenges both notions and asks rather, how does it stand with desire; or maybe as desire? It cross segments the inversion in their work with Lacan's phenomenological turn and asks about the lure of that which imposes itself upon us. Not how do we protect our privacy but why do we not want to? The power of telemetry is to make privacy itself a prison that we endlessly seek to liberate ourselves from even if that means running into the grasp of a universal and totalitarian coercive power. The pattern is Heidegger's: "That in the face of which Dasein flees, is precisely what Dasein comes up 'behind'." Heidegger, *Being and Time*, p. 229.

constant. Only a radically individuated act-based consequentialism like pure hedonism would appear to be distinct from this method. In that case the summary nature of all agents as actors aiming at pleasure is pre-supposed. If the act itself does not rest on an aggregating operation, the domain of possible concern is aggregated up to the least common denominator among agents: the drive for pleasure. As such, the hedonist will be forced to perform aggregating operations: if I act on this urge, what is the likelihood that negative consequences will follow, and will those negative consequences outweigh the pleasure that I am likely to acquire from carrying out the action? The hedonist, like all consequentialists, will benefit from machine learning by being able to more accurately understand the positive and negative consequences associated with a given desire. And this benefit demonstrates the foundation of the approach in an aggregate operation that permits evaluation of actions relative to the principle that drives the deliberation.

Regardless of whether the evaluation is in the context of a rational formal imperative or a utilitarian concrete projection, the evaluation still rests on a founding maneuver that aggregates agency and that associates action with other like actions. This aggregate process is integral to the evaluative procedure that makes up either deliberation for the sake of determining a right course of action or evaluation for the sake of judging one's peers in courts of law or public opinion. The judgment that lies on the foundation is executed against aggregate terms, aggregated conditions, and aggregate beings separated from their personal qualities in the process of forming the judgment. It is because of this common foundation that it is easy to move anxiously back and forth between the moment of decision and the forensic evaluation. There is no difference at all because in both cases the agent is being treated like an aggregate other.

This adds further explanation to why I identified specific aspects of the categorical imperative with the onus to be ethical in one's deliberation specific to the moment of decision. In the command to "be ethical," a command to which both consequentialist and Kantian succumb when they set out to assert that there is something like an ethical imperative at work in all human action regardless of whether it is formally dictated or posited as the highest end, personhood itself is assigned to an aggregate basis. The imperative applies to all: follow the principle of utility, obey the categorical imperative, be like all your fellow agents or fellow persons and hear the call of that same something or other that takes hold of you. People, in general, must be ethical. The population at large must conform to the principles. The legitimacy of any ethical project depends on it. Rejecting this aggregate proposition and denying oneself as a rational agent or as someone who seeks pleasure and avoids pain, leaves one isolated and alone without any further claim to the good. Such a person—a beast or a god—would be condemned to a wholly private existence. Therefore, the foundation of the command to be ethical is recast as an antagonism.

Antagonism: Data Aggregation and the Categorical Imperative

It is possible that the historical resilience of the categorical imperative, despite all its problems, is that it captures something about the value of the individual moral agent that other ethical systems fail to grasp. If Scheler is not commonly read by ethicists, it may be that Kant's formalism continues to hold sway as the only way to give the moral agent its due. Rather than dive into a tangent on the way in which a non-formal ethics of values might provide an a priori support for the moral dignity of the agent, I want to instead continue my line of thinking and investigate the persistent antagonism of data aggregation and the categorical imperative insofar as the latter is understood as defending this absolute integrity. Or to put it in a fashion that carries forward what has been covered thus far, the imperative to be ethical shows itself as antithetical to the aims of data aggregation insofar as the aggregate form permits generic coverage to both forensic evaluation and deliberative decisions. That is, the thing that gives legs to Kant's project is the basic sense that there is something in the acting person that has worth beyond any measurement or computation of it, that has value absolutely and cannot be deflated into an aggregate representation of the moral agent as such.

> One of the basic claims of *formal* ethics, especially Kant's ethics, is that it alone can confer upon the person a *'dignity'* which is beyond any 'price'. On the other hand, formal ethics claims that all non-formal ethics destroy the dignity of the person and his self-value, which cannot be derived from anything. It is easy to see that this claim is true for all ethics of goods and purposes. Every endeavor to measure the goodness of the person in terms of the degree to which his accomplishments support an existing world of goods (including even 'holy' goods), as well as every endeavor to measure the goodness of the person in terms of the accomplishments of his will and actions as the means of realizing a purpose (even if this be a holy final purpose which is immanent to the world), contradicts the aforementioned law of preference, according to which values of the person

are the highest of all values. But it is another matter to ask
whether a formalistic and rational ethics of laws does not
also degrade the person (although in a different manner
from that of the ethics of goods and purposes) by virtue of
its subordination of the person to an impersonal *nomos*
under whose domination he can become a person only
through obedience.[11]

Scheler consigns both consequentialist and Kantian ethical systems to
the same fate. He does this for the sake of the dignity of the person. The
consequentialist, like the Kantian, has also elevated the person of the
ethical agent insofar as it is precisely their end which is contextualized as
the highest end, the end in-itself. Stars and oceans, presumably, do not have
the end of maximizing utility or minimizing pain. The consequentialist who
frames the agent's orientation in human terms of pleasure and pain must
also seek to place the specifically human onto a pedestal as worthy of some
discreet and distinct status among the allocation of the good. It may be that
the goodness in this game of goals and purposes allows for an extrapolation
to a social end aimed at by the whole of the persons' collective civilization,
but that aggregate aim is equally functional in the rational principle at work
in the end in-itself of the categorical imperative. The ethicists do not know
how to remove the aggregate from the presentation of the highest end, but
they are driven by the cognitive decision to do so.

Arguably Scheler struggles with this same dynamic. He opposes the
Kantian and the consequentialist, in the previously cited passage, on the
grounds that they fail to properly emphasize the importance of the acting
person. The person he is concerned with may be intrinsically involved in a
world, but Scheler's project aims at establishing the integrity of that person's
world. He seeks to emphasize the moment of decision as the action of the
person in the process of navigating their world, in the act of realizing the
events of that world. And what this amounts to is establishing the person as
something over and against an aggregate, as something that cannot be
reduced to an aggregate when the basis of their ethical existence is shared
with others; and when they define their ethical systems in consort with
others, it is still the case that this world of theirs is highly stylized by their
own operations and actions, their own intentions and experiences.
Enmeshed in the fabrication of its world, the person's value emerges as
something worth protecting through ethical orientations and projections,
through conditioning and restriction. What an ethical agent values when
they work to promote the good is specifically those biases of value that are

---

[11] *Formalism in Ethics and Non-Formal Ethics of Values.* Max Scheler.
1973. Evanston: Northwestern University Press. p. 370.

realized in the very personal and partial existence of each of the members of their communities.

The basis of the command to be ethical may therefore be attributed to the sense of value that constitutes the everyday world of the person's experience. Why would the agent be commanded to be careful in what they do unless the conditions within which they act merit such care? The important sense here is that the origin of the command must be situated in opposition to any aggregating methodology that robs the agent in motion of that same value that lies at the ground of the command itself. This inserts a strong dichotomy between the forensic approach and the deliberative one. The agent is involved and engaged with a world that matters to them, that is an issue to them. Decisions, when those decisions are made about the actions of others or their own past actions, are passionate responses to invasions of one's world. One is deliberating on what their world is meant to be like, how it is supposed to be structured, what sense is supposed to guide and govern it. And to that extent, the person is highly engaged in nearby and specific concern for what is very close at hand and at work in the boundary that conditions their back and forth between themselves and the others inhabiting the moment of decision.

This cannot be reduced to aggregate conditions, the generalized sense of how things are likely to turn out or the formal conditions against which all action must be measured are all invasive of this highly personal existence. This orientation raises the danger of ethical egoism or solipsism. Where is there room for tangible others in this highly personalized orientation? How can we include the concrete other in our deliberations without relying on an aggregate condition that contextualizes all our action within the social conditions where they originate and end up?[12]

The theoretical adventures of ethics may be predestined by our very notions of antagonism and foundation. Only a humanistic orientation could lead in this direction. What could be clearer: on the one hand there are individual persons and on the other there is everything else that stands over and against each of them. And this is the common model for the acting person and its cognitive intelligence whether that be natural or artificial. What if antagonism and foundation were not characterized as external relations appended to self-standing entities that pre-exist the relation? What if persons did not pre-exist the aggregate population and only later come into antagonistic or foundational relationships with it? If the person

---

[12] *Telemetry Phenomenology Commonwealth* is, to some extent, an extended investigation into these very questions. Cf. especially, the Phenomenology section. The remainder of this chapter attempts to briefly summarize (sic) the impact of that investigation.

emerges from the population in an anxious turning back and forth upon this boundary, if the person comes to be in a conditioning process that aims at setting them apart from the population from which they originate, then the antagonism and foundation may be one and the same where having one's basis in a population is the source of an antagonism with that population and its likelihood to treat the person as an instance of an aggregate operation or function.

The paradigm for such a relationship may be parent and child. The aggregate places a stamp on procreation through genetic codes, but the personality of the child demands highly specialized responses. Highly specific, the dynamic of past generations plays out yet again. Imagine a universe in which data emissions and collection is ubiquitous to all behavior and action. Imagine that the data is stored and persisted somewhere such that machine learning operations could be performed against it for the sake of decision support. Suppose that the players in this game were generations of your family with each parent and child working with and against each other in the process of cultivating a person using historical data gathered from the previous generations. In the aggregate, the parent would know all the relationships that ever transpired between ancestors and their children. The data could be perfectly correlated with historical data from the genetic lineage. Would this amount to good parenting and proper child rearing now that it would become possible for the parent to use that data to understand everything that is happening with their child? The child is crying, why? Given the association with past data collection from the family tree, the following conclusions make sense and the parent knows exactly what to do and how to respond to the outburst. How do we imagine this might work? Would the civilizations of the world be improved by it? Would our ethical character benefit? Or would this characterize a dystopia?

It remains an open question whether advanced analytics would improve human life in this case or make it significantly worse. What I think I have shown is that the introduction of advanced analytics into the parental relationship clearly shows the antagonism and the foundation of the command to be ethical in the procedures of aggregation. And I leave it to you to decide. Would you be a better parent with such analytics at your disposal to cultivate your child in exactly the way required to promote either the common or the rational good (assuming you know it)? And would your childhood have been better if only your parents could have done their parenting in a properly data-driven fashion?

It is common philosophical behavior to consider the ultimate selection here to be a matter of deliberation possibly dependent on observation and inference or on rational cognition. I have suggested by demonstration that this behavior begs the question since it may very well be the case that the genetic code already realizes this very antagonism/foundation. An ethics of facts suggests that the moment of decision has already found us in the anxiety that turns us around always and again, that it permeates the questionability of our being, and that we have been unwittingly bombarded by data driving our deliberations all along. The telemetric inhabits all of our historically entrenched ethical systems and stylizes the command to 'be ethical' with a computational genre. So long as we cast ethical deliberations in terms of the aggregate and apply telemetric methodologies to moral forensics and deliberation, we are in the grip of a set of foundations and antagonisms that redefine concrete personhood. Because they are one and the same fabrication, anxious turning back and forth between the boundary conditions in the telemetric ethos captures and constructs the moment of decision as a personal event.

Privacy

Ethics of Facts

There Is No Privacy

In TPC[1], the structural determination of corporations as artificially intelligent persons is meant as a placeholder for a distributed, trans-individual set of cognitive capabilities that calls the simplicity of the Cartesian project into question: 'I think therefore I am' may be the musings of a marionette and only a partial determination of a distributed operation. In the moment that we act on behalf of a corporation (as employee, consumer, or other kind of stake holder), there may be an experience of phenomenological authenticity, but the operations at work go well beyond the immediacy of that experience. There are organizations working in collaboration, there are unseen interests being served, there is a distributed set of conscious acts working in concert to carry out a plan that suits no human participant in that plan over the long term. To deny the personhood of corporations is to fail to see what grips us, what powers us forward, and what we—ultimately—serve. There is no privacy, not because some mega-corp is actively violating some boundary, but because the boundary itself is fabricated in social relations that are corporate through and through.[2]

---

[1] *Telemetry Phenomenology Commonwealth: Corporate Surveillance and the Colonization of Personality.* 2019. Kirkland, WA. Lensgrinder, Ltd.

[2] Quoted from the chapter above: "Non-Fictional Fabrications." The artificially fabricated corporation cannot leverage uncritical "ethical" insights until the act-constitution of such corporations has been clarified. Most ethical theories are attached to an ontological set of conditions applying to the agents and against which principles are to be evaluated. How can we talk about "ethics" in the context of corporate actions? Are they rational beings subject to the call of the categorical imperative? Can they be "happy" or feel "pleasure" and "pain"? Can the state of their "daimon" be impacted by action or be more or less virtuous? Although the following does not provide a *Critique of Corporate Reason*, it does attempt to orient the grounding for such a project.

The telemetric understanding takes place as my phenomenological experience. As such, my so-called private life is a partial realization of the persons at work in that lifeworld of interwoven artificial intelligence. This makes the organizational bodies that partake of me into witnesses of my life, of every facet of it. And I love this, it is an attractive state of affairs. "The voice of the friend." The set of social relations writ large but embodied, accompanying me, caring for me, and watching over me. There is an adolescent resistance helping to form personality for this body. Emphasizing this partiality is the secret to controlling me. The trick is that I want to demonstrate, show myself to others, and partake of a world with them. Being human together is basic to the orientation that sparks every moment of any person's life or existence. This is the way in, where the visitor is readily welcomed in our turtle home that bears us up in the grocery store, while waiting for the bus, or when we look out the window at work. A truly private life would be a torment to any one of us. Instead, there is no exit for you, though the entrance bustles. They have found their way in right alongside you and you may not see them. I charge that our right to freely associate has been under attack for centuries. The pocket computer marks an exponential leap forward with the assailants bearing the brands that dominate the social order. This distribution binds its consumers into the bodies of its suppliers.

Payments amount to offerings with a return where the return is itself an opportunity for coercion, an application of pressures and involvements: concern and thrall. The fact that we willingly pay for this is a mechanized act of natural genius emerging from the universe into an organized form. Call it artificial, but it is no more so than I am, and I have been cultivated from my inception. What actions are you capable of and what instruments and fellows do you require to enact those plans? Every facet stamped with capital, mediated by a mega economy of trade and accumulation. Whenever I purchase or shop, I integrate my private life with produced items and should those produced items embody the organizations that produced them, my private life becomes integral to those organizations. If they are integrated with capital concerns, then capital concerns inhabit me as my experience expresses itself or produces itself in relationship to the product. This phenomenon scales to a swarm of simultaneous moments of integration. Not just one thing purchased here or there, but a constant shopping, searching, enacting, and moving toward. These economic interests seethe in / as / through me. And from the point of view of the organization, I am among that swarming. Along with the others. If I am wise, I must question my own judgment. Who else is working with it? I want to trust you, but I am not sure we have ever met. The ether that mediates all our relationships is the medium of this corporate lifeworld: the legal embodiment of our right to freely associate now occupies our capacity for association. The association articulates both a separation and a connection, a turning to and fro, it is the anxious establishment of self and other together and apart. The incorporation of the association in the measurements of a third-party is coercive, an act threatening colonization *there* in an event of appropriation.

I hold that what is mostly settled under the rubric of "privacy" is instead a symptom of this ailment. It seems ridiculous to venture out in public to demand a private life. The conflict is what has made human beings so easy to colonize. In contexts where we should be demanding protection of our right to freely associate, we are instead demanding data protection and constraints on its use, persistence, and accessibility. Under such a rubric, the generation and collection of the data is a given: what we must worry about is what happens to it and what controls are placed on it. If the gathering process itself is already invasive insofar as it forms the basis of all association, then our focus would ignore the poison that presents the constraints themselves. The data is going to be gathered and aggregated. Think of all the good that will do. In the aggregate, we can cure any disease and correct any flaw and, of course, we must contribute to that.

Venturing out into public has its price. People can see you. And if there are organizational people, they can see you too. You cannot prevent them from seeing you unless you avoid walking anywhere they might happen to be. Avoid them and you can prevent them from seeing you, observing you, or surveilling you. It is not surveillance in the strict sense, it is just observation gathered from an association. And that gathering of data is a necessary consequence of having such persons in the world around you. You have no expectation of privacy in the social world when it comes to matters you are willingly sharing with those whom you directly associate. You cannot complain that your interlocutors remember what you just told them. If you are in their store, or buying their product, or walking next to their agent, you are in association with them and they have every right to take note of that, just like you do with the people that pass by you on the street.

The paradigm of government intrusion upon individual liberty does not translate well into a social paradigm. Due process is not under threat in these relationships: the civil rights of the human individual, insofar as a government's action may be invasive without probable cause, is not the issue here. The transfer into the private sphere, where persons interacting in the economic and social domains may require protection from each other, is not fully covered by any parallel approach. That is, the data collection agencies that can uniquely identify each person they have come across may be prevented from passing that information along in any way that fails to mask the personally identifiable information of their interlocutors, and yet there may still exist a problem. Data in the aggregate that has been collected and cleaned of anything personal still inhabits the relationships and the domain of engagement, and it can be used to create a system of association that blocks access to traditional forms that were once deemed to merit protection. So long as the interaction can be featurized and categorized according to behavioral selections made by persons as they come across each other in engagements, predictive operational models can be deployed, and the act of association can be governed by those predictions, and by the operationalized models that were trained from aggregate data correlated to the current engagement.[3] If we focus on the privacy component as an issue exclusive to personal identification and the control of personal data, then we lose track of the role that machine learning and predictive analytics can play in the associations themselves. Walking into a showroom or executing the instructions codified in an app that is installed on your pocket computer may be naturalized and simplified. Doing so makes them comparable to meeting someone on the street or being introduced to a new acquaintance. Insofar as the "person" on the other end of that relationship already has reams and reams of information about the behavioral tendencies and likely reactions of people entering interactions with it, these points of contact are nothing like ordinary human social engagements.

Who we meet and associate with during our lives is crucial to who we are becoming and how we are shaping ourselves into who we are. This applies to the teachers that we have had, the friends in the neighborhood where we grew up, and to the co-workers we have, the roommates, loved ones, and community participants with their shared concerns and interests. Human beings associate with each other in various ways throughout our lives. Some of the persons that we interact with have giant pools of data, descriptive of human behavior and likely responses to stimuli under given circumstances. Typically, the persons who fall into this category are not likely to be human beings who meet on the bus or in the line at the grocery store. Instead, they are likely to be business ventures or corporate bodies interested in converting their data on human activity into revenue and—it is to be hoped—profit. I do not mean to completely discredit the role of privacy concerns in our relationships with government bodies, rather what I am trying to do is show that the problem that we seek to protect ourselves

---

[3] "Seen from the vantage point of this development, technology in fact no longer appears "as the product of a conscious human effort to enlarge material power, but rather like a biological development of mankind in which the innate structures of the human organism are transplanted in an ever-increasing measure into the environment of man."" Hannah Arendt, *The Human Condition*, p. 153. She is citing Werner Heisenberg *Das Naturbild der heutigen Physik* (1955) pp. 14-15.

from with such governments who would use invasive means to violate due process when dealing with individual human beings is best conceptualized through this assault on association. Doing so will cover the condition met with in both the social world and the public space of a democratic political world. When we engage in relationships with organizations that masquerade as people, artificially intelligent in that capacity, and that act in such a way as to become part and parcel of our projects and our everyday concerns, we are in danger of losing our ability to freely associate. All our relationships under such circumstances would be governed by the dynamics that drive these new paradigms of interaction.

The Marionette

If the person you are meeting has encyclopedic knowledge of typical correlations of behavioral responses to known stimuli, they will be able to predict and anticipate your actions throughout the course of the time you two spend together. They will be able to adjust their responses to you based on this information and the specific responses that you make to their inquiries and actions. If they seek to sell you something, for example, they will be able to anticipate your resistance and ply you with procedural responses aimed at wearing down just the sorts of defenses that a person like you is likely to have. In doing so, they increase the probability that the interaction will result in a favorable outcome for themselves. It is not just that they will know what you have bought before and whether that makes you likely to buy something now. Rather, they will know what your hesitation to a specific line of questioning suggests, they will know what other factors will make it more or less likely that this or that option will be conducive to closing the deal. They do not do this because they have exhaustive and detailed knowledge about you, rather they know that people who do and say the things you are currently doing and saying are likely to be persuaded by one set of factors rather than another. All this can be done without personally identifiable information persisted in a store somewhere. Rather, so long as your actions during the current interaction can be fit into a set of categories culled from a profile that is in your possession but accessible during the transaction, those categories can be used to associate the agent's current behavior with the accumulated patterns of behavior demonstrated by similar agents in comparable circumstances.

This is a nightmare. This person will be able to understand you better than anyone else you have met before. They will know better how to take care of your needs and desires, they will be able to help you become the person that corresponds to your best possible self. And all that you need to do to reap the rewards of this benevolent interlocutor is let them have your money. An inconsequential nothing that can easily be converted into a better version of you. You are a relay switch for money, a patch of ground to be fueled and harvested. There is room for every taste as the AI that brings it all to you benefits so long as the switch keeps relaying. We are plugged into machines that are plugged into processes that are organizationally constrained by charters and incentives to shareholders, aggregate appendages that are the strings being pulled and the clippety-clopping of the feet and the wand that moves with them. We bask in the light that it sheds for the sake of gathering a specific kind of data, enabling visual recognition, studying the patterns of temporal movement through space. The geometric and algebraic movement maps the behaviors of the specimen best. When the body finds itself in a specific position with the following ratios, it is most likely to respond to various categories of events. This can be further refined in terms of the various categories of action that have been witnessed in the current interactive context, whatever it may be. These persons' way of knowing is to experiment and vary the conditions of experimentation with the various operational opportunities that it comes across. Data gathering is subjected to the mechanism of machine analysis on the fly. To the extent that one of the persons in the engagement has the benefit of this type of intelligence, it characterizes the involvement in highly specific fashion. They can use the advantage to become part of your ongoing life and get into your head. The ongoing engagement provides for the opportunity of perpetual data accumulation. The interactions feed back into the mechanism that produces more interactions and, to the extent that finances are set on the engagements, the circulation of information and response is captured as yet more data that deepens the information present across the breadth of conditions in the system itself. And wealth moves with it but appears as this or that purchase, this or that transfer of data.

The insinuation is more than mere Marxism with the corporate person embodying the mechanisms of alienation brought on by capital.[4] Rather,

---

[4] "Value is the quality a thing can never possess in privacy but acquires automatically the moment it appears in public." ... "Values, in other words, in distinction from things or deeds or ideas, are never the products of a specific human activity, but come into being whenever any such products are drawn into the ever-changing relativity of exchange between the members of society. Nobody, as Marx rightly insisted, seen "in his isolation produces values," and nobody, he could have added, in his isolation cares about them; things or ideas or moral ideals "become values only in their social relationship."" From Hannah Arendt, *The Human Condition*, p. 164. Citing Karl Marx, *Das Kapital III*, 689.

the corporate bodies known for their role in entertainment, advertising, and messaging are a medium of meaning and an environment of involvements. They provide the substrate of possibilities within which each human being develops. The insertion of meaningful intent and value amounts to the incision of significance and it is through this incision that human personality and desire develop. The phenomenon does not amount to fetishization as the abstraction of the meaning from its social content and into some personal pleasure principle, rather it is an absorption into those contexts and significances that have been laid out as the possible states of personhood available for consumption by each individual in the course of their becoming culturally predisposed alongside their compatriots. These mechanical means, as the megaphone of those artificial persons that produce the material world within which all action occurs, constitutes a set of strings or bindings that pull and push the organisms that find themselves in the net, that come to awareness as human subjects at home in the world so constructed. We do not each start over from scratch as though the instincts of a squirrel drove human history. Instead, we awaken to each other in these venues and to the extent that these locations are articulated in accordance with large factor manufacture and the means of social reproduction they course through the electronic veins of the global internet as rivers of data carrying categorized renderings of each of us, aligning our interests, desires, and ambitions: we are brought in line with the projects and the aims of the persons whose world we have entered.

Like Gulliver among the Brobdingnags, we come of age in a land of giants. Unlike Gulliver, we cannot see the full extent of these Gargantuan puppet masters who hold us in their grasp, nor do we see their flaws more easily because of their size which always gives the impression that they are up close and available for detailed viewing. The child sits down to watch cartoons on a Saturday morning. They do not see the advertisers, they do not see the network or the producers, they do not see the executive interests who promote the values of commerce in the goods they consume, the images they take in, and the fantasies that they spin into being at the instigation of carefully engineered spectacle. Yet, these powers find their way into the intentional orientations, into the conversations and imagination of the young person awkwardly kindling their way through the world. It is not just that the employees and the boards of directors of these organizational monstrosities form the apparatus of their artificially intelligent personhood, the consumers of its product become walking advertisements and word of mouth recommendations for the authority of their person. This establishes these persons as quiet and hidden monarchs with the ability to broadcast themselves from the T-Shirts and other branded apparel that the human agents happily don for the sake of living their dream and realizing their fantasies as the lived experience of the corporate body itself.

Consider the worldhood of the world relational structure in a truly equiprimordial fashion with the *mitsein* of all the correlated human beings who make up the common space of a human environment. Heidegger's purpose may well have been to articulate the deep-seeded connection between language and the world of our everyday experience. The presence of others in this shared common world must be heavily emphasized as the bearing upon which language and significance rests. If the other is inserted into this worldhood and the set of relations is fundamentally social in nature, coming prior to any individualization, then the forces at work in any given social sphere will have a powerful sway over the forms that come to pass in that sphere. And to the extent that the history of human civilization since 1600 has been deeply engrained in the concomitant existence of incorporated organizational entities, this social sphere has been a mixed reality with natural and artificial persons living side by side. Gradually, over the course of the years, these bodies have become increasingly powerful and influential in their standing within that sphere. The role of enterprise in larger and larger scale wars throughout the 19th century and leading up to their powerful instigation of the first "World" war has come hand in hand with a greater role for these organizations in human consumption and production. Human beings either consume or work in a world organized by these artificial constructs set up by governmental action and enhanced by ongoing governmental decrees and tax codes. The role of the corporation amounts to a constant presence in all subsequent human association and interaction. This has been so much the case that in the late 20th century we saw the complete dissolution of public spaces in favor of privately-owned shopping plazas or online communities backed by corporate money providing the ecosphere within which human agency is more and more consigned.[5]

The role of data peddlers in the social sphere is not the primary foundation of the association, rather the agents who control the data are primary. And these agents are not "we the people," but the board and executive leadership acting on behalf of the shareholders. The categories that bind us, that provide the basis for predictions and future suggestions

---

[5] "Montesquieu realized that the outstanding characteristic of tyranny was that it rested on isolation—on the isolation of the tyrant from his subjects and the isolation of the subjects from each other through mutual fear and suspicion—and hence that tyranny was not one form of government among others but contradicted the essential human condition of plurality, the acting and speaking together, which is the condition of all forms of political organization." Hannah Arendt, *The Human Condition*, p. 202.

of desired behavior, are not accidentally associated with corporate agency, they are essential to that very agency. And these forms of association make it increasingly more difficult for alternative forms of association to inhabit that same space. We have given corporations powers on the grounds of some right to freely associate that they are supposed to have and yet now they form a medium of constrained behavior such that free association is increasingly more difficult outside their boundaries and constraints. The possible personalities for humankind are constrained and with those personalities the associations that can exist between the human beings developing without those domains.

I am calling this ultra-modern form of the Cartesian subject the human 'marionette' to indicate that there are ties that bind us to something that both inhabits the sphere where we act and yet remains on the periphery of our vision. Obviously, all mature humans understand that there are corporations sharing their world, but the extent to which we can see them remains impaired. We deny their personhood because of a desire to support Enlightenment ideals of what constitutes a person, but in doing so we forget that personhood as a form of agency is effective in the world as a fact. We think of them as states or as legal abstractions. We speak seriously about their "ethics" and their role in solving human problems, as though they shared a set of interests or could be harnessed as resources meant to serve human beings. The days of this form of idyllic imagination have passed. The largest corporations in the world have lives of their own, interests all their own, and they are engaged in projects that have little or nothing to do with the ongoing purposes of their human subjects. To the extent that these organizations have these "lives of their own," they also make use of human subjects to carry out their projects and realize their concerns. The marionette can feel the presence of these organizations in the pull of the strings, and so, through an understanding of human actions in a phenomenological form, there is a possibility to catch a glimpse of the effective presence of the puppet masters in whatever each of us does on their behalf. The partiality of our vision exhibits itself in a spatially and temporally partial orientation that is biased by our social and economic interests and beliefs. It shows itself as disconnectedness and separation, as an anxious distancing that leaves the subject vulnerable to the forces of its connections. The reflective process must turn toward this partiality and attempt to understand the strings that are attached to what we do, what we think, and what we see.

Partiality

There is no documented phenomenological interpretation of being uninformed. Is this true? I have not found one, but is that enough for concluding that no such investigation exists? It may well be that the investigation is lacking because the experience itself is one in which we can never be sure that we are partaking until the state has found its resolution in the requisite information as though it were a question receiving its answer. To the extent that this resolution is deferred in an open issue, there can be no understanding of the state in question. Without that understanding, no interpretation is possible. No doubt, phenomenological interpretation can take place in retrospect. We can recall the experience of being uninformed once it becomes apparent that we were previously lacking the information that would eventually come. This means that the state of the sceptic, the state of methodological doubt, is phenomenologically indistinguishable from the state of being uninformed. We cannot tell the difference between the unknown and the unknowable, between the missing something that is missing because it does not exist and the missing something that is missing because we have not yet found it. Being uninformed is a constant state of human experience, although the target of the uninformedness varies from subject to subject. Furthermore, lacking information is no guarantee that the agent will falter in their confidence regarding matters related to that subject area. Were such a phenomenology to exist, it would have to include the predisposition to safeguard one's state of uninformedness: the tendency of some human persons to defend their ignorance. Some forms of this defense may amount to dogmatic repetition of an uninformed point of view despite whatever information might be made available. Other forms might amount to careful and elaborate reasoning to show that those who think themselves better informed are failing to do exactly that.

The mystery of missing elucidations of this state, phenomenologically speaking, may be due to the phenomenologist's pride. To tell the tale of an uninformed individual from the positioning of the uninformed individual is to freely admit one's condition and run the risk of being corrected by an informed lot who comes along later or who comprise the phenomenologist's readership. The phenomenologist does not wish to guess nor suffer a demotion in the credibility of their intuition which might be suffered when venturing into these dark waters. This would mean that proponents sacrifice the possibility of gaining a critical reflective position relative to their condition of lacking information. The process of living amid a state of uninformedness in this day and age might seem useless on top of everything else since information is everywhere if only one takes the initiative to look for it. And why would someone not take that initiative? What could motivate someone to remain in a condition of uninformedness when there is information everywhere? These questions are essential to opening the space of uninformedness and yet they are likely unavailable to the agent at that point of deliberation. If such critical positioning were possible to the uninformed individual, then learning would likely follow, or some other similar action of discovery or fabrication that might resolve the condition.

If I take it as my ongoing condition as a human being living among other human beings, however, then I must recognize that the perspective of the sceptic is the only valid point of view. My partiality amounts to, on the one hand, my possible uninformedness regarding any matter that I am either attending to or failing to attend to; and, on the other hand, there is my preference to remain in this condition through inactivity safeguarded by whatever information I might think I already have. And that latter is crucial. I do not know I am uninformed because I believe that I know something or other that is relevant to the matter at hand. And what is more, I have grown attached to the information that I possess and which I believe covers the issue in full. I am partial to what I know, and my partiality amounts to a constant state of uninformedness, of finite capacity, relative to the possible understanding that might ensue. The gap between information and understanding makes this possible. The presence or absence of information is a trivial concern to the one who understands. Insofar as the human being rests in a state of understanding, the presence or absence of information is not significant to belief formation and the taking up of points of view, nor is it significant to the making of arguments that advance or defend the position that is understood. Understanding is not rooted in information, if this description displays the phenomenon, rather the information and its suitability or relevance is rooted in understanding.

If understanding is an achievement that comes to pass as a result of communities or associations that provide that understanding ready-made, then the associations one makes provide one with the utility for spinning information into the correct form for institution within that shared understanding and coming from the association. The ongoing conversations that lead to understanding need not have that as their goal or intent. Rather, the suggestions and innuendo of community interpretation and significance may shore up a resident worldview that constitutes such an understanding without basing it on this or that experience or this or that set of data. Just as the philosopher of science might suggest that all facts are theory dependent, the phenomenologist of uninformedness might suggest that all information is understanding dependent. At least in part this amounts to the partiality of the agent and constitutes their disadvantage in the context of associations. The associated points of view will always span a larger meaning context than the individual can acquire. Because of this, the individual's partiality puts them at a disadvantage for developing anything like an understanding that might combat the understanding that develops from the achieved communal meanings associated with groups. The only critical reflective capacity that commonly asserts itself in the endeavors of individual human beings is the offset of one formed understanding over and against another. The person has been drawn into one group that offers utilities for resistance against the perspective distributed by another group. A new student of philosophy, for example, is very much exposed during the first steps that they take. Later, they will be able to better resist new points of view with those that have already been established. This condition is exacerbated in the youth of the person under consideration since children are most vulnerable to the first set of meaningful associations that come along.

In partiality, implicit in our spatiotemporality, lies our Dasein cast as a being driven to achieve understanding rather than originating in it. A social imprint, partiality is its manner of existing. As a node, our partiality is a contribution, a data point. Some contributions are of relationships for the aggregate analysis enabling predictions of ongoing and future behaviors. Aggregated, we amount to something other than what each of us sees proximally and for the most part. Any orchestration can employ that partiality in a context known to another but not known to you. The details of your partial context are unknown to the orchestrator. There is separation of concern, introduced as efficiency, meaning that the organization has capacities that no member has. And yet, evaluation of the process and transparent questioning of all involved can produce elaborate diagrams of ongoing operations. Partial structure may be extended, but its partiality remains. There is wide variance enabled on this spectrum, partiality can be very large in concern. This is the basis of variability in power and capacity to impact the world at large. Part of what your container organizations are is what you are, and your reactions and actions are conditioned extensions of these organizations. The process of becoming aware of the bigger and bigger contexts within which your actions mean anything is the process of increasing the scope of your partiality. Bigger and bigger containers are still containers and still scoped by geometry. Orientedness is therefore bound to a set of scoping factors. That is why the notion of partial as a part in a whole comes to reside side by side with having an interest and a perspective: such lack will surface as anxious questioning.

This phenomenon occurs because a human with partial understanding can take on all sorts of responsibilities that facilitate the larger plans of the organization without having detailed information about those plans. The actions can still further the ends. A principal software engineer for a large corporation producing cloud solutions to various data management and analytics procedures may have very little information about the higher order operations of the corporation and its entanglement with nations and other large corporations that are its customers or partners. Despite this absence, this engineer can build a widget for use as a part of a platform that fulfills some function within those larger entanglements. The corporation employing the engineer will show an interest in producing ongoing meaning to consolidate and integrate the engineer's actions with the larger order goals of the organization. They will poll the individuals on a regular basis to make sure they understand their mission. This interest is no doubt an effort to make sure the individual contributor continues to understand their purposes and their involvement in the organization in just the way the organization requires. Arguably, the individual contributor being uninformed about the details of the higher order organizational structure but brought to an understanding of their shared mission, is highly valuable and more valuable than if such a person were to become informed about these higher order mechanisms at work in the organization. Too much insight might yield an alternative form of understanding that would no longer be conducive to the daily productivity required of such individual contributors. When one evaluates the personalities of those who move up the ranks in such corporations, they have more in common in terms of temperament than a set of skills. To be an executive vice president of such a corporation requires a mindset more so than a skillset. This is as much as to say that their understanding must have developed along the lines of the organization's higher order requirements, and that this understanding is prerequisite to whatever information would become available to a person operating at such a level within the organization.

This perspective is not conducive to representative democracy as it affirms that the best formed republic would constitute an oligarchy. The persons in power within such a government need to have a form of organizational understanding that permits them to spin the information they receive in the right way. A presidential candidate, for example, may have radical ideas about how to solve this or that problem, but their election depends on their admittance to a community sharing a form of understanding that may ultimately mean that they must change their point of view based on information they acquire once they are in office. Should a small group of representatives achieve inclusion in this group without the requisite understanding, they would be outcast and likely rejected by those who—from a purely information-based point of view—one might think would be their allies. Individual citizens not only lack the information available to their representatives, they lack the organizational understanding that has become a requirement for such roles in governing. There are likely to be representatives who think ill of their constituency and there are likely representatives who think highly of them, but all without exception understand—or come to understand—that their constituency does not share this point of view. Ultimately, the governors do not think that the governed understand. On the one hand, this might make them manipulatable, on the other, it might make them in need of service.

The predisposition of any person operating within an organization is toward partiality of their own perspective. Not only is our understanding partial, but we are partial to our understanding. We do not get everything, but what we do get, no one else understands. This uninformedness is an inherent quality of human spatiotemporality, and it is what enables associations to play the role that they play in human life under its current forms of organization. One might contextualize this in terms of a distribution of labor that is currently at work in the productive processes of a given society. Fair enough, but in a more philosophically basic and phenomenological way, this context must reveal itself as a value platform against which human individuals experience the world. This is where we now turn.

A Distributed Point of View

The notion developed in *Telemetry Phenomenology Commonwealth* (TPC), that privacy is a form of free association and necessarily juxtaposed with coerced forms of association, provides the basis for elaborating these phenomenological facets of the sociological notion of the division of labor within an organized civilization. That, in combination with the notion of an ethics of facts (facticity) where the moral principle for use in evaluating actions is not left to deliberative choice but conforms to the group associations within which the actions take place, suggests critical reflective positions are themselves conditioned by the possibility of associations and the manner in which they are formed. All ethical critical reflection amounts to offsetting one dynamic of association against another. Making this transparent may not constitute a solution to any concrete problem, but it would facilitate better communication and understanding vis-à-vis some academic or intellectual grouping of participant scholars. I take this to be Habermas' point. And then my turn in TPC was to make that transparency into a phenomenological form of experience. If I was proposing a critical reflective stance that enables insight into one's partiality as a stepping stone into the organizational logic that puts one to work in just this fashion and is comprised by the critical reflective stance, then it is incumbent upon me to answer the question, how did I know this? And as I have suggested in the chapter cited above, I *do not* know this, rather it is a non-fictional fabrication. Non-fictional in this context does not equate to "true." Rather, it suggests that it is real. And for the pragmatists among us that means that it is available for use should we so desire or need it or, at the very least, deem it relevant to the circumstances within which we find ourselves. I tell the tale just in case.

What then is the distributed or organizational point of view that this serves? In other words, what understanding does such a suggestion of a critical reflective capacity indicate? In yet another form, we might ask how is it possible for a socially distributed system of labor and association to yield a critical reflective point of view that calls into question the legitimacy or desirability of that very organization? To the extent that the organizational point of view provides the ethics of facts that orients all action within that perspective, could the grouping produce a set of behaviors and actions that have some position from which to challenge the originating point of view or procedural organization? If we hold to an ethics of facts and only an ethics of facts, where does the challenge to any predominant normative principle come from?

Suppose for the sake of argument that you do have private access to your thoughts, that you are autonomous and that you can think as you like and act as you think. We might go so far as to say that if someone should violate that privacy by exposing your personal information publicly, you would retain a degree of this essentially private condition by being able to respond as you will to that set of events. You may retain your dignity despite whatever embarrassment you suffer in this exposure. The sense is that you are the captain of your ship and if someone violates your personal sovereignty over who and what you are, you may retain your integrity by controlling your response to the situation. The potential to be this way, drives the pre-emptive concern for such violations and the intent to secure legal protection for this inviolable state, this right to own your personhood and secure it from unlawful or unwanted invasion. The right to privacy, as it has been considered throughout recent North American and European law, shares much of this concern for the individual's capacity to control their destiny. You venture into public anyway. You make decisions to interact with others and doing so leaves a trace as described at the outset of this chapter. I cannot reasonably think that speaking to another person means that my inviolable privacy is retained.[6] Of course, we might legislate

---

[6] In TPC the progression of concern with privacy advances from the North American notion of an expectation of privacy to the European dignity of the person and ends up in the domain of the residual association with others. In this last state, human society functions as a repository retaining the contribution of members for the sake of other members. Associations are stored (compute and storage are the mark of the telemetric in the social), making them available

around the details here, but the general principle must remain: I cannot tell you something about myself and at the same time insist that you cannot know it. I may seek to prevent you relaying that information to someone else, but I must resign myself to the fact that you now possess information about me. If I did not want you to have it, I should not have given it to you in the first place. This indicates that whatever privacy we think we retain within our person as inviolable, the act of association is revelatory. And more to the point, the more deeply we hold to the principles of inviolable privacy, the clearer it is that association is where we are the most vulnerable to attacks on it.

The model for an organization under this presupposed assumption made for the sake of argument would then be a set of private individuals deliberately forming a union. This is the common tale of the commonwealth; it is the story of the contract and it is the story of the corporation. This is an idealized picture insofar as such individuals are never babies or children and, what is more, they never find themselves coerced in ways that they do not perceive. The history of assaults on this point of view (this understanding of the inviolable privacy of the individual and its autonomy in association), where have they come from and how have they been possible? On some level, for example, the Marxist critique of bourgeois ownership appears to originate in an ethical claim that condemns exploitation on moral grounds. Where would that moral standing come from? It certainly could not be bound to organizational principles that are affiliated with the form of social organization against which Marxism is directed. Critics of such attacks, coming from those who defend the traditions of the inviolable privacy of the agent, reduce their attackers to beings like themselves with private lives and interests. They say the Marxist is a creature of resentment and merely wants power for themselves and is using some new form of argument to persuade people to lend their mass to this new perspective. The Marxist, of course, points to history to show that the opponent's individualism has not always been in such predominance, that previous eras had different forms of organization and different ideas about the population making those associations. Using this approach, some of those same Marxists are cagey and do not turn to the ethical rejection of exploitation, but merely point out that this is a necessary

for use in subsequent generations so that each individual human can pick up where others left off (Arendt calls this the organized remembrance of the polis, cf. *The Human Condition*, p. 198). Privacy amounts to one's relationship to both the appropriation and expression of those associations. The telemetric is a coercive power that steers humans toward these or those associations and correlations in opaque fashion for the sake of serving the interests of the power that stimulates and directs the behavior from the outset.

historical movement, that exploitation will fall because of its own internal inconsistency, and that the ends of exploitation are not some ethical aim that inviolable agents are promoting, but rather an outcome produced by the machine of history pushing in this direction. The revolutionary is thus merely history's becoming conscious of itself and so takes up the fight against the old ways. As the old ways collapse under their own weight, the numbers among the revolutionaries will grow and the momentum will eventually become successful. At least that is how the argument proceeds.

The point is, for my purposes here, that the argument is not taking place on a common ground, rather it is one form of understanding opposing itself to another disjointed form: a civil war, of each one against every other, in which the state of nature is an achievement of breeding and cultivation adding up to indoctrination into a set of groups. Both perspectives attempt to spin the other in their own terms, but the normative attacks ultimately are founded on distinct associations and distinct organizations that are driving the logic behind each position. Phrasing the perspective this way may make it familiar as a form of cultural relativism that many have become adept at rejecting. At its best, it sounds like a variant on Kuhn's notion of a scientific revolution with paradigm shifts that change the meaning of normal understanding as opposed to normal science. This is an overly simplistic reading. There are never only two positions at work against each other, although my example may unintentionally mislead someone into thinking of it this way. Rather, there are always many organizational structures at work in every life being lived. There is no contradiction in having a single act embody multiple organizational principles and take part in multiple structural phenomena. A corporation, for example, may stand up on behalf of individual privacy rights as they are manipulating such rights with their own elaborate means.

Consider the technology companies who have gotten on board with protecting the privacy of those inviolable individuals who come to use their products. The corporation can produce ironclad user agreements that promise not to sell or distribute to third parties the information acquired from interaction with users. The same corporation may lobby governmental agencies to try and establish laws to force all organized operations to follow these same practices. Yet at the very same time, the corporation might be internally aggregating that data into analytic mechanisms for use in guiding and shaping user behavior when they interact with their services. Furthermore, they may be stimulating continued and more frequent use of those services through various psychological techniques and procedures aimed at making their service more essential to the life condition of the individuals who use it. On the one hand, we see a set of organizational principles that further one kind of understanding about the inviolable nature of individual privacy and the

ethical significance of preserving it, while on the other hand, we see
behavioral mechanisms at work on the fringes of these agreements drawing
users into greater dependence on the system they use resulting in greater
profit to those services and systems. Under such circumstances, the privacy
of the individual isolates them at the same moment that it is being
protected. Privacy becomes something of a bell weather notion that can be
used to straddle two distinct forms of understanding to make them
complementary from the perspective of a larger scoped distributed system
of organized actions.[7]

The dissonance is remarkable but easily explained by this confluence
of organizational principles. An engineer may care devoutly about the
inviolable privacy of their customer while at the same time building
pipelines to push the collected data from the interaction into an aggregated
store that produces machine learning models for use in better anticipating
and directing user behavior. Both may be in keeping with the corporate
interests that the engineer serves in their partial understanding of both the
ethical and privacy domains of deliberation. Partiality is to blame here. The
variation in experiences, the wildly distinct geometry of each human life,
makes it possible for each of us to dwell among different organizational
patterns and to absorb and act on behalf of each without having to sort it
all out and make it clear. The real world of our everyday action can
withstand contradiction because the basis of our contradictory acts lies in a
spatiotemporal character that forbids its logical reduction to absurdity. For
any one among us, A may be both equal to A and not equal to A since we
evaluate equality at different times and in different places. Critical attitudes
are thus the result of highly specific personal trajectories and the role those
trajectories play in larger scoped organizational principles. Karl Marx, the
man, is no doubt full of contradictions, but Karl Marx the theorist may be
held up as the perfect incantation of a specific organizational apparatus
coming to form an understanding under specific social conditions. It may
be the case that the two are intrinsically intertwined and necessarily require
each other. Only a person straddling the multiple relevant organizational
forms would be capable of spawning an understanding of the specific
critical reflective orientation that results from those intersecting tensions

---

[7] This is an oversimplified example. In truth, larger corporations probably
like the proposition of generalized protections of privacy because it makes it
very expensive to collect and use data analytics that comply with the regulations
that require a sophisticated compliance platform. Some of the bigger
corporations have seen this as a business opportunity since they can offer up
their compliant platform as a paid service for use by other enterprises.
Broadening of the scope of associations will always make analysis of sample
circumstances more complex. This is what the example is meant to show.

and conflicts. The struggles of the young Marx are the understanding of Marxism that proposes an alternative to the inviolable privacy of the individual locked in his point of view and able to deliberate upon the proper course of action.

Critical reflective orientation aiming at understanding is therefore itself an indication of a newly emerging organizational procedure. If there is someone who lives on the boundaries between privacy concerns, corporate structures, technological innovation, phenomenological philosophy, and ethics, then it is possible that a critical reflective persona might emerge through the confluence of these factors. The impact of such experience on the forming of such an understanding might depend on the commonality of the experience and the talents of persons so situated to articulate the viewpoints eloquently and capture the imagination of their contemporaries or descendants. The agents of such understanding may be multiple and may feed off each other. Furthermore, they may have no clear idea of what they are doing or how they are doing it. The organizational structure may work through them without their possessing any reflective awareness of its presence. History may work through an agent without that agency participating directly in the understanding that they are fostering through their work. This is the very meaning of partiality and it is the source of the agent's anxious questioning and any existential analytic they might perform. It enables the agent to be uninformed about what they are doing and do it anyway. And it may enable them to do it more effectively even if it seems to be happening 'behind' them.

The Inauthenticity of Authenticity

There is a connection between associations and the nature of things. The presence of the association in the thing and in the person means that the associations associate as person and thing. Our partiality is the segment of associations at work in our spatiotemporality, our geometric positioning within the larger scope of an organization. Critical reflectiveness then amounts to the unpacking of these associations and the further associating of them with the critical reflectiveness of others. This may happen in either a collaborative or combative form. The larger scope has all means and procedures at its disposal for bringing these understanding positions to bear within persons newly orchestrated along the various parts of the organization. Thus, an ethics of facts teaches that deliberation is not about possible actions serving this or that end, but that all that we have to go on is the set of associations that we enact and permit. The logic that predominates within a grouping or organization amounts to its set of norms insofar as its structure is relevant to condoned and condemned human action. Thus, we call it the facticity of those in the group or the ethics of facts that govern their membership. Any forces that inhibit, bend, or project associations one way rather than another amount to instigations of coercion aimed at forming some new domain of normative relations or some new organizational dynamic. Associations are the crucial center of any such concern, where associations are being managed or maintained without transparency or clarity of intent and purpose, those associations will limit the ability of human agents in those domains insofar as they may have sought other forms of association. Associations limit associations and thus there is no "free" association per se, but there are conditions of transparency and conditions of opaqueness; and conditions may be promoted or prevented based on the extent to which they follow one or the other set.

The suggestion is that we are not just related to the things in the world with which we take part, but that other people are there in the things through their relationships to the world. Heidegger writes in *Being and Time*:

> A covered railway platform takes account of bad weather; an installation for public lighting takes account of the darkness, or rather in specific changes in the presence or absence of daylight— 'the position of the sun'. In a clock, account is taken of some definite constellation in the world-system. When we look at the clock, we tacitly make use of the 'sun's position', in accordance with which the measurement of time gets regulated in the official astronomical manner.[8]

The language is oddly passive because he may be trying to focus in this section on things in their readiness-to-hand rather than bringing to bear the involvement and association with others that takes place in all of these micro-maneuvers involving things. Only later, when he describes the equiprimordiality of *Mitsein* with Being-in-the-world will it become clear that he is aware of the social dealings that are basic to having a world. The concerned actor, in this case, may be completely given over to the task at hand and, as such, may be absorbed in the relationships directly adjacent to that concern: staying out of the rain and making sure you are on time for the train. This focus does not mean that millions or billions of others are

---

[8] *Being and Time* by Martin Heidegger. 1962. Translated by John Macquarrie and Edward Robinson. New York. Harper Perennial. p. 101 (H 71).

not associated with the operation. Staying dry is a common concern and so account has been taken to shelter you as you wait. Being on time is a common concern and so account has been taken to produce an official standard for synchronizing our behaviors through common measurements of the position of the sun.

The private mental life of the ordinary human is replete with such mediation. To the extent, that the voice in your head that speaks and is spoken to as you deliberate is embedded in a language you have come to know, your very relationship to yourself in your quietest most private moments is mediated by those associations which brought you to that voice. Your thoughts are your own in some formal neurological sense expressing your spatiotemporal specificity, and yet the repeatable identity of some pathway surfaces as a public trust semantically spun through whatever understanding of reference and significance you have grown into. The entities around you, the possibilities that await you, all involve organizational structures that predate you. Committees have likely been formed, or long standing historical dialogues have been ongoing, to construct a set of norms for framing practices in a way that furthers some set of concerns that have been accounted for through the common understanding of what needs to be done under such circumstances. Absorption in these relationships constitutes ignorance with regard to them, but only if ignorance is conceptualized as a reflective conscious way of presenting the associations to oneself: we are ignorant insofar as we do not know, where not knowing indicates not having made the association present to oneself for deliberation or consideration. We run the risk of suggesting that embodied everyday familiarity with these associations constitutes ignorance that could only be resolved by transforming them into objects in a theory.

We might then wonder whether owning up to one's situation (becoming authentic) amounts to a reflective knowledge of the relations at work in all such dealings. This feeds the hyper-self-centered approach that institutes autonomy and self-determination as the bedrock of appropriate behavior and orientation: the imperative of heeding one's own council or being sufficiently self-reliant as to not allow the opinions of others to sway one's thinking dogmatically or through some hidden influence that one has not thoroughly evaluated. The risk is that such conceptualization makes no sense in a framework in which associations and relationships are existentially structural in yielding any orientation toward anything at all. This does not amount to clarified vision that more deeply comprehends the world as we find ourselves in it. Rather, on this reading (which I have not attributed to anyone), "authenticity" is the same old crap that any elitist aristocrat might assert: there are those in the know and those who do their bidding. To the extent that this is factually true, however, this model may be its cause rather than some indication of a specific outcome of its application. Believing oneself to have become superior to a set of organizational mediations at work in your own character may be one of the most effective ways for those organizational mediations to remain authoritative and spread globally.

To the contrary, it is a mistake to frame this offset in terms of a revamped semantics of privacy and the private, and that is exactly what the "jargon of authenticity" permits. Yet there is something compelling in this nomenclature. The "inauthentic" was supposed to suggest this absorption in the world connoted by human partiality and its relationship to an organizational power that governs the larger-order scope of agency and cognition. The authentic, however, was supposed to be a return to oneself, an owning up to the responsibility the individual bears. The maneuver from the one to the other was supposed to constitute a critical orientation that pulled one out of the fallen state of this absorption in the organizational logic that grips most human action. What makes this compelling, I hold, is that the sense of inauthenticity is right on and powerful. Phenomenologically, each human being at times has a sense of this absorption in things, this submission and coercion to a larger scoped dynamic that cannot be fully comprehended because its logic is distributed in such a way as to extend beyond any single agent. This glimpse does not gain any clarity if we allow our fantasies of breaking free of it to govern the examination of what that might be like. Instead, authenticity is precisely a "jargon" because it is merely a further instantiation of inauthenticity with a different order directing the absorption. The thinker of the turn toward authenticity may have been one of the least authentic philosophers. And this because he was the thinker of the "turn toward authenticity."

Transparency does not bring us back to ourselves and it does not remove the partiality that governs human agency. That is a conditioning possibility that is always effective, and which cannot be removed. Realization of the ethics of facts does not solve any problems, it merely reveals the problems that exist. The limitations we encounter among our peers thus may fall into two distinct areas worth exploring: 1) there are associative organizational structures that prevent transparency of conditions at work in determinate persons, places, and things; and 2) there are associative organizational structures that render the conditions at work, but then effect solutions to these conditions based on supposed non-problematic grounding principles that have themselves been presupposed as opaque conditions at work in the domain. Simply stated: the corporate organizational form may hide the fact that a society at large is completely domesticated by the corporate logic and interests, on the one hand; while on the other hand, the antagonists may assert that "justice" and "equality" can only be achieved if specific nationalistic actions are taken, where that entails using public governance to undermine the power of the corporate organization.[9] This could amount to either regulation or usurpation depending on the details of any specific problem-solving form. Can the pitfalls of this kind of antagonism be avoided? This is as much as to ask, is there a form of organizational orientation that is not an offset point of view, that evades systematically constructed carnival and resistance? Is it possible to abide by a set of associations that retains the freedom of association without reifying them into a set of organizationally distributed structures and positions? Can there be a theory that extracts a proper critical reflective stance from this condition when the condition itself cannot be removed? At least to the extent that theory detaches from the condition in a way that only feigns disinterest and "objectivity," theory would be yet another way the conditions of association at work in actions and cognitions are made opaque.

And if theory cannot work this way, we may instead phrase the question differently: can partiality broaden its scope while at the same time maintaining its awareness of itself as partial, as positioned in this way within organizational boundaries? Notice that this is exactly the modus operandi of a corporation as it grows its market share: a corporation just is that broadened scope and its way of acting aims at navigating the domain of differentiated associations for the sake of making them transparent in order to further its interests. Such corporations are amoral and dispassionate. Internally, they do not wish to cover over problems, they only seek to maintain partial relations between segments or divisions within their body, recognizing that this separation of concern increases efficiency in responses to their environment. The point is that the corporate whole must somewhere contain a thoroughly transparent understanding of its larger-scoped agenda. Without that, it could not be efficient in carrying out its operations. The structure equally demands that this understanding not be commonplace among all participants in the organization. Let us look more

---

[9] There is an opposition to the ethics of facts that is based on the notion that something is being taken away from us in asserting the role of social associations in the formation of the individual. This is non-sense. Nothing is taken away, only a fabrication is emerging from the conditions that apply. The fabrication is merely descriptive and shows that the thing which is so highly valued in the criticism is not what the critic thinks that it is. We do not prize our inviolable individual personality (since there is no such thing), rather it is our inviolable right to freely associate. What constitutes protection must drastically change since most legal deliberation does not systematically consider the impact of sanctioned procedures on the capacity of the population at large to freely associate without coercive factors injected by others for the sake of serving their own interests and augmenting their own associative powers.

closely at corporate organization to try to understand how this works. Doing so may provide a cautionary tale of how critical reflective operations can be coopted by larger organizational scopes that coerce the operational domain where they are embodied and enacted. On the other hand, it is possible that we will learn what organizational point of view needs to be made transparent to achieve a distributed turn away from such inauthenticity without falling into the trap of authenticity.

Lifeworld, Inc.

In TPC, I proposed the need for a critique of corporate reason or, if you prefer, an existential analytic of corporate being. This call follows on the surprising acceptance of corporate personhood and, to go a step further, the assertion that corporations are instances of artificial intelligence. Although corporate personhood is usually associated with conservative economic and political agendas, I do not believe the context here would suit such an agenda. By admitting personhood, I assert that we can engage in a careful and thorough analysis of how that personhood works in terms of privileges and rights, duties and obligations. The point here is that just as Kant thought a critique of pure reason was a necessary prerequisite to any critique of practical reason, I am asserting that a critique of corporate reason is a necessary prerequisite to considering what might constitute the ethical reasoning or operations of a corporation. In most forms of ethical reasoning, the theorists rely in some format on the cognitive structure of the ethical being in laying out the appropriate methodologies for determining right and wrong, or plotting action in accordance with moral principles. Utilitarians think that ethical beings pursue happiness, for example. Virtue ethicists think that the action of ethical agents can be characterized in specific ways. Deontologists assert that rational beings of a certain type are duty-bound. And so on. To assert something like an ethics is to make various presuppositions about the kind of agency or entity that is performing the acts that are under evaluation. And there is talk here and there about corporations being or not being "ethical." But, to the extent that no such critique of corporate reason exists, this notion is meaningless. I do not know what it means to suggest that a corporation needs to be "ethical" if I do not know what sort of entity a corporation is, what kinds of actions it can perform, and what sorts of deliberations go into guiding and directing those actions.

Corporations are based in hierarchies where each employee has a manager leading up to the chief executive. The chief executive is hired by a board of directors who are elected by shareholders. The chief executive hires his executive leadership team and each member of the executive leadership is responsible for hiring their teams. This works all the way down to the individual contributors at the leaf end of the hierarchy. The hierarchy is designed around levels of management with areas of designated concern. At the top end you might have executive vice presidents in charge of each facet of the business interests of the corporation and at the low end you might have people managers who work with individual contributors to carry out the tasks associated closely with that same business concern. In keeping with this structure, individual contributors tend to focus on product construction or service delivery or whatever specific functions are integral to the business. The higher levels of the corporation are relevant to, on the one hand, longer term vision and direction for these different projects at various applicable levels and, on the other hand, building the organization for the delivery of objectives. Leadership and vision tend to be blended with organization building but they are indeed two distinct functions. Organization building includes the hiring function already mentioned, but it also includes the dissemination of process and procedural norms to ensure the realization of the leadership's principles and vision.

The practices and procedures in question will have both a publicized and a closed aspect. What is publicized of course are the processes themselves, metrics used to measure the success of the organization, procedures to be followed to meet goals and produce outcomes that demonstrate those metrics. These facets need to be publicized to the employees who are expected to conform to them and drive toward the results that they describe. The hidden facets may vary depending on the level of management or organization-building under consideration. They may amount to performance review and promotional standards being used to evaluate the employees, or they may amount to awareness of crises in delivery that would only confuse or distress the individual contributors who have no power to direct the resolution of such problems. And these latter may be major contributors to upcoming changes that need to be made to the organization. The workload of some contributors might be drastically changed based on some possible re-evaluation relative to delivery concerns, and so on. Higher up the hierarchy, the hidden aspects may be more socially broad in scope, meaning that they may involve relationships with larger customers and other corporations or with national governments.

Odd contradictions often emerge from these higher-level organizational actions. We might see one member of the corporate leadership talk about ethics ad nauseum without ever saying what he means by the term. Concomitantly, we might see another member of the leadership announce partnerships with military bodies, national governments with sketchy human rights track records, and other corporations that have not expressed any strong concern over matters of ethical action and organization. These may appear as unrelated actions never drawn together or presented in concert by the corporation's leadership. Such would be contrary to their intent as it may well be that the ethics talk is meant to calm and distract those who are participating in the mission from any concerns they might have about the other actions carried out by leadership in opposition to these claims. We are being ethical and so whatever contracts we have with private mercenary providers for military action are of no concern because we, as a corporation, are committed to ethical action whatever that might mean.

This is where privacy really comes into its own and we learn what corporations who advocate privacy mean by it. The corporations safeguard insider information about the relationship between these projects and their various orientations. They not only keep them from public view, but they prevent most segments of the corporation itself from gaining any knowledge of these operations. The corporation's right to privacy is inviolable in the context of protecting the internal vision and discussions of leadership amid performing high level organization-building. The CEO conveys one message by announcing this deal, the president conveys a different message by announcing a commitment to ethics. Neither of them ever answers for the other and their distribution enables a cloak of darkness in terms of what they are up to and how they are advancing the interests of the corporation relative to larger order social concerns that might exist among employees or customers. A true and thorough critique of corporate reason would require a detailed investigation into these areas of conflict and association. Such detailed investigation is vigorously resisted and constitutes a violation of the corporation's right to privacy, which here clearly refers to its right to maintain free association within itself independent of external intervention or scrutiny.

Consider the role that machine learning can play in assisting with decision-making at all levels of business. One such level might be the way in which organizations are built inside the corporation. Internal decision-making for how a company needs to organize itself may gain useful advantage from collecting data relevant to the decisions and feeding that data to some machine learning algorithm that can announce predictive outcomes for inputs that are operationally provided. The algorithm, in this context, takes on something of a productive role in the forming of the organization. It strikes me as unlikely that the highest orders of corporate governance would ever succumb to such black box machine learning based decision support. Why not? I suspect that the executive leadership of any large corporation knows that such data-oriented analysis will have behavioral impact in a way that is opaque to the people responsible for operationalizing those suggestions and predictions. That black box amounts to a violation of the free association capabilities of the executive leadership engaging in this sort of higher order organization-building. The act of replacing the president and CEO's line of thinking in their clandestine actions amounts to a restriction on the way in which the corporation associates with other organizations (corporations, governments, or civilizations as such). The resistance they might show in this direction would constitute evidence for the way in which corporations understand their privacy and why they are willing to go to such extreme lengths to protect it.

How would this data be gathered? The fictional CEO and president would need to contribute to the discussion. They would have to provide some candid information about how they do their jobs and what exactly their jobs are regarding these clandestine connections between seemingly contrary objectives. In short, they would have to violate the privacy of the corporation to publicly describe their roles and the responsibilities and thought processes they use when performing their jobs. Doing so is likely illegal, at least to the extent that they would be in civil violation of their non-disclosure agreements. This form of secretiveness is built into the corporate hierarchy as doing one's job often means omitting certain details that are outside the job responsibilities of the persons to whom you are explaining something. This may be as simple as "your manager does not need to know the details of how you plan to get such and such a proposal done by 5 o'clock" or as complex as "we do not need to explain the details of how exactly a corporation can be ethical and still help military organizations find less risky ways to surveille and kill people." Beyond these kinds of examples, there are others in which the secrecy is required by criminal law. Some discussions between corporations, the form of understanding that takes place within the lifeworld between corporations, must not be revealed to the general public because the stock market would be impacted by the general availability of this information and the actions taken by any who are buying and selling in that marketplace.

Setting aside the laws that protect the privacy and secrecy of corporate dealings as the commonwealth within which the corporate lifeworld achieves greater and greater rationalization, it seems that this is where the broadening of the scope of partiality is taking place and permitting the corporate organization to play more powerful roles in the fabrication of an environment for human agency in which the participating human beings are not involved or share in any common understanding. I hold that transparency in these dealings and orientations would have a radical impact on all other dealings and orientations carried out by human beings under the currently dominant social forms of association and relationship. This is not a critical reflective turn and is not meant to be a simple revelation of information resulting in greater knowledge for any community with a stake in the actions and operations at work. Instead, this would amount to a freeing up of associations insofar as the associations at work on a set of operations or procedures would be transparently available for inspection and use by participants in the various aspects of the organizations at work in these procedures. Quite simply, human beings would be put in a position where they can achieve greater understanding of what is going on around them. Surveilling the corporation would give them the capacity to act in a way that foreshadows greater understanding of their behavior under that set of conditions. Turnabout is fair play.[10] This would announce participation in a form of social organization that values such understanding and a form of social organization that loves the questionability of wisdom, where wisdom is a cumulative understanding of more and more organizational associations at work in the various aspects and facets of human agency. The answer does not lie outside of organization, but in a turning toward it as the precondition of any existential analytic of Dasein. In the end, we would be an issue for ourselves and whatever constitutes that world would be open to our anxious questioning. Not as a way back into something that has been lost nor as a way forward, but an endless turning to and fro.

> In order to be what the world is always meant to be, a home
> for men during their life on earth, the human artifice must
> be a place fit for action and speech, for activities not only
> entirely useless for the necessities of life but of an entirely
> different nature from the manifold activities of fabrication by
> which the world itself and all things in it are produced.[11]

---

[10] This could easily be achieved within the parameters of "innocent until proven guilty." That is, it coopts the Foucaultian notion of surveillance in the context of discipline and punishment in an inverted form where the "guards" are incarcerated for wrongdoing (held accountable in some form other than a fine, which amounts to a tax or cost of doing business, for crimes committed). Incarceration, among other things, amounts to a loss of privacy where that may suggest that all of one's associations will be observed and tallied. Cf. "Corporations are People" in *Telemetry Phenomenology Commonwealth*.

[11] Hannah Arendt, *The Human Condition*, pp. 173-174.

Bibliography

Agamben, Giorgio. 1998. *Homo Sacer: Sovereign Power and Bare Life.* Translated by Daniel Heller-Roazen. Stanford, CA: Stanford University Press.

Althusser, Louis. 2014. *On the Reproduction of Capitalism.* Translated by G.M. Goshgarian. London, UK. Verso Books.

Althusser, Louis. 1997. *The Spectre of Hegel.* Translated by G.M. Goshgarian. London, UK. Verso Books.

Arendt, Hannah. 1958. *The Human Condition.* Chicago, IL. Chicago University Press.

Arendt, Hannah. 1976. *The Origins of Totalitarianism.* New York, NY. Harcourt, Inc.

Arendt, Hannah. 1977. *Eichmann In Jerusalem: A Report on the Banality of Evil.* New York, NY. Penguin Books.

Arendt, Hannah. 1978. *The Life of the Mind.* New York, NY. Harcourt Brace Jovanovich, Publishers.

Aristotle. 1985. *Nicomachean Ethics.* Translated by Terence Irwin. Indianapolis, IN. Hackett Publishing Company.

Aristotle. 1941. *Metaphysics* in *The Basic Works of Aristotle.* Translated by W.D. Ross. Edited by Richard McKeon. New York, NY: Random House.

Ayer, A.J. 1952. *Language, Truth, and Logic.* New York, NY: Dover Publications, Inc.

Badiou, Alain. 2019. *Trump.* Cambridge, UK: Polity Press.

Badiou, Alain. 1999. *Manifesto for Philosophy.* Translated by Norman Madarasz. Albany, NY: State University of New York Press.

Badiou, Alain. 2003. *Saint Paul: The Foundation of Universalism.* Translated by Ray Brassier. Stanford, CA: Stanford University Press.

Badiou, Alain. 2011. *Second Manifesto for Philosophy.* Translated by Louise Burchill. Cambridge, UK: Polity Press.

Bakhtin, Mikhail. 1984. *Problems of Dostoevsky's Poetics.* Translated by Caryl Emerson. Minneapolis, MN: University of Minnesota Press.

Bakhtin, Mikhail. 1981. *The Dialogic Imagination: Four Essays.* Translated by Caryl Emerson and Michael Holquist. Austin, TX: University of Texas Press.

Bakhtin, Mikhail. 1984. *Rabelais and His World.* Translated by Helene Iswolsky. Bloomington, IN: Indiana University Press.

Benjamin, Walter. 1968. *Illuminations: Essays and Reflections.* Translated by Harry Zohn. New York, NY: Schocken Books.

Berman, Marshall. 1988. *All That is Solid Melts into Air: The Experience of Modernity.* New York, NY. Penguin Books.

Blacker, David J. 2019. *What's Left of the World: Education, Identity, and the Post-Work Political Imagination.* Winchester, UK. Zero Books.

Bostrom, Nick. 2014. *Superintelligence: Paths, Dangers, Strategies.* Oxford, UK. The Oxford University Press.

Brand, Arie. 1990. *The Force of Reason: An Introduction to Habermas' Theory of Communicative Action.* Sydney. Allen & Unwin.

Churchland, Paul M. 1999. *Scientific Realism and the Plasticity of Mind.* Cambridge, UK. Cambridge University Press.

Darwall, Stephen. 2009. *The Second-Person Standpoint: Morality, Respect, and Accountability.* Cambridge, MA. Harvard University Press.

Deacon, Terrence W. 2012. *Incomplete Nature: How Mind Emerged from Matter.* New York, NY. W.W. Norton & Company.

Deleuze, Gilles and Guattari, Felix. 1986. *Anti-Oedipus: Capitalism and Schizophrenia.* Translated by Robert Hurley, Mark Seem, and Helen R. Lane. Minneapolis, MN. University of Minnesota Press.

Deleuze, Gilles and Guattari, Felix. 2011. *A Thousand Plateaus: Capitalism and Schizophrenia.* Translated by Brian Massumi. Minneapolis, MN. University of Minnesota Press.

Deleuze, Gilles and Guattari, Felix. 1986. *Kafka: Toward a Minor Literature.* Translated by Dana Polan. Minneapolis, MN: University of Minnesota Press.

Derrida, Jacques. 1982. *Margins of Philosophy.* Translated by Alan Bass. Chicago, IL: University of Chicago Press.

Derrida, Jacques. 1981. *Dissemination.* Translated by Barbara Johnson. Chicago, IL: University of Chicago Press.

Derrida, Jacques. 1976. *Of Grammatology.* Translated by Gayatri Chakravorty Spivak. Baltimore, MD: Johns Hopkins University Press.

Derrida, Jacques. 1978. *Writing and Difference.* Translated by Alan Bass. Chicago, IL: University of Chicago Press.

Derrida, Jacques. 1987. *The Post Card: From Socrates to Freud and Beyond.* Translated by Alan Bass. Chicago, IL: University of Chicago Press.

Derrida, Jacques. 1973. *Speech and Phenomena and Other Essays on Husserl's Theory of Signs.* Translated by David B. Allison. Evanston, IL: Northwestern University Press.

Derrida, Jacques. 1989. *Edmund Husserl's Origins of Geometry: An Introduction.* Translated by John P. Leavey, Jr. Lincoln, NE: University of Nebraska Press.

Derrida, Jacques. 1998. *Archive Fever: A Freudian Impression.* Translated by Eric Prenowitz. Chicago, IL: The University of Chicago Press.

Derrida, Jacques. 2005. *Paper Machine.* Translated by Rachel Bowlby. Stanford, CA: Stanford University Press.

Descartes, Rene. 1988. *The Philosophical Writings of Descartes, Volume 1 & 2.* Translated by John Cottingham, Robert Stoothoff, and Dugald Murdoch. Cambridge, UK. Cambridge University Press.

Dewey, John. 1958. *Experience and Nature.* New York, NY. Dover Publications.

Domingos, Pedro. 2015. *The Master Algorithm: How the Quest for the Ultimate Learning Machine Will Remake Our World.* New York, NY. Basic Books.

Dretske, Fred I. 1999. *Knowledge and the Flow of Information.* Palo Alto, CA. CSLI Publications.

Duhem, Pierre. 1991. *The Aim and Structure of Physical Theory.* Translated by Philip P. Weiner. Princeton, NJ. Princeton University Press.

Dupuy, Jean-Pierre. 2009. *On the Origins of Cognitive Science: The Mechanization of the Mind.* Translated by M.B. DeBevoise. Cambridge, MA: The MIT Press.

Durkheim, Emile. 2014. *The Division of Labor in Society.* Translation by W.D. Halls. New York, NY. Free Press.

Durkheim, Emile. 1995. *The Elementary Forms of Religious Life.* Translated by Karen E. Fields. New York, NY. The Free Press.

Durkheim, Emile. 2014. *The Rules of Sociological Method.* Translated by W.D. Halls. New York, NY. Free Press.

Erasmus. 1993. *Praise of Folly.* Translated by Betty Radice. New York, NY: Penguin Classics.

Feyerabend, Paul. 2010. *Against Method.* London, UK. Verso.

Foucault, Michel. 1977. *Discipline & Punish: The Birth of the Prison.* Translated by Alan Sheridan. New York, NY. Vintage Books.

Foucault, Michel. 1994. *The Order of Things: An Archeology of the Human Sciences.* Translated from the French. New York, NY. Vintage Books.

Foucault, Michel. 1990. *The History of Sexuality, Volume 1: An Introduction.* Translated by Robert Hurley. New York, NY. Vintage Books.

Foucault, Michel. 1990. *The History of Sexuality, Volume 2: The Use of Pleasure.* Translated by Robert Hurley. New York, NY. Vintage Books.

Foucault, Michel. 1988. *The History of Sexuality, Volume 3: The Care of the Self.* Translated by Robert Hurley. New York, NY. Vintage Books.

Frank, Anne. 2017. *The Diary of a Young Girl.* Translated by Susan Massotty. New Delhi, India. FP Classics.

Frank, Joseph. 1975-2002. *Dostoevsky.* Five Volumes. Princeton, NJ. Princeton University Press.

Fraser, Nancy. 1989. *Unruly Practices: Power, Discourse and Gender in Contemporary Social Theory.* Minneapolis, MN. University of Minnesota Press.

Freud, Sigmund. 1959. *Group Psychology and the Analysis of the Ego.* Translated by James Strachey. New York, NY: WW Norton & Company.

Freud, Sigmund. 1961. *Civilization and its Discontents.* Translated by James Strachey. New York, NY: WW Norton & Company.

Freud, Sigmund. 1950. *Totem and Taboo.* Translated by James Strachey. New York, NY: WW Norton & Company.

Freud, Sigmund. 1961. *Beyond the Pleasure Principle.* Translated by James Strachey. New York, NY: WW Norton & Company.

Freud, Sigmund. 1960. *The Ego and the Id.* Translated by Joan Riviere. New York, NY: WW Norton & Company.

Freud, Sigmund. 1961. *The Future of an Illusion.* Translated by James Strachey. New York, NY: WW Norton & Company.

Freud, Sigmund. 1959. *Inhibitions, Symptoms and Anxiety.* Translated by Alix Strachey. New York, NY: WW Norton & Company.

Gadamer, Hans-Georg. 2013. *Truth and Method.* Translated by Joel Weinsheimer and Donald G. Marshall. New York, NY. Bloomsbury.

Gadamer, Hans-Georg. 1977. *Philosophical Hermeneutics.* Translated and Edited by David E. Linge. Berkeley, CA. University of California Press.

Geron, Aurelien. 2017. *Hands-On Machine Learning with Scikit-Learn and TensorFlow: Concepts, Tools, and Techniques to Build Intelligent Systems.* Boston, MA: O'Reilly Media.

Gleick, James. 2011. *The Information: A History, A Theory, A Flood.* New York, NY. Vintage Books.

Godfrey-Smith, Peter. 2017. *Other Minds: The Octopus, The Sea, and the Deep Origins of Consciousness.* New York, NY. Farrar, Straus, and Giroux.

Godfrey-Smith, Peter. 2003. *Theory and Reality: An Introduction to the Philosophy of Science.* Chicago, IL. University of Chicago Press.

Goffman, Erving. 1959. *The Presentation of Self in Everyday Life.* New York, NY: Anchor Books.

Goldstein, Rebecca Newberger. 2014. *Plato at the Googleplex: Why Philosophy Won't Go Away.* New York, NY. Vintage Books.

Goldstein, Rebecca Newberger. 2006. *Betraying Spinoza: The Renegade Jew Who Gave Us Modernity.* New York, NY. Nextbook.

Goodman, Nelson. 1988. *Ways of Worldmaking.* Indiana, IN. Hackett Publishing.

Goodman, Nelson. 1983. *Fact Fiction and Forecast.* Cambridge, MA. Harvard University Press.

Gould, Stephen Jay. 1996. *The Mismeasure of Man.* New York, NY. WW Norton & Company.

Grandin, Temple. 2007. *Making Slaugherhouses more Humane for Cattle, Pigs, and Sheep.* Online. http://www.grandin.com /references/making.slaughterhouses.more.humane.html.

Haber, Laura. 1997. *Enlightened Subjectivity: the rational method of power.* Urbana, IL: University of Illinois at Urbana-Champaign Archives.

Habermas, Jurgen. 1975. *Legitimation Crisis.* Translated by Thomas McCarthy. Boston, MA. Beacon Press.

Habermas, Jurgen. 1979. *Communication and the Evolution of Society.* Translated by Thomas McCarthy. Boston, MA. Beacon Press.

Habermas, Jurgen. 1984. *The Theory of Communicative Action. Volume 1. Reason and the Rationalization of Society.* Translated by Thomas McCarthy. Boston, MA. Beacon Press.

Habermas, Jurgen. 1987. *The Theory of Communicative Action. Volume 2. Lifeworld and System: A Critique of Functionalist Reason.* Translated by Thomas McCarthy. Boston, MA. Beacon Press.

Habermas, Jurgen. 1989. *The Structural Transformation of the Public Sphere: An Inquiry into a Category of Bourgeois Society.* Translated by Thomas Burger with the assistance of Frederick Lawrence. Cambridge, MA. The MIT Press.

Haraway, Donna. 1985. "A Manifesto for Cyborgs: Science, Technology, and Socialist Feminism in the 1980s" from *Socialist Review,* No. 80, 1985.

Hartman, Thom. 2010. *Unequal Protection: How Corporations Became 'People'—And How You Can Fight Back.* San Francisco, CA. Berrett-Koehler Publishers Inc.

Hawkins, Jeff with Sandra Blakeslee. 2004. *On Intelligence.* New York, NY. St. Martin's Griffin.

Hegel, GWF. 1976. *The Phenomenology of Spirit.* Translated by A.V. Miller. Oxford, UK. The Oxford University Press.

Hegel, GWF. 2016. *Elements of the Philosophy of Right.* Translated by H.B. Nisbet. Edited by Allen W. Wood. Cambridge, UK. Cambridge University Press.

Heidegger, Martin. 2008. *Being and Time.* Translated by John Macquarrie and Edward Robinson. New York, NY. Harper Perennial.

Heidegger, Martin. 1977. *The Question Concerning Technology and Other Essays.* Translated by William Lovitt. New York, NY. Harper Torchbooks.

Heidegger, Martin. 1982. *On the Way to Language*. Translated by Peter D. Hertz. New York, NY. Perennial Library, Harper & Row Publishers.

Heidegger, Martin. 1992. *History of the Concept of Time*. Translated by Theodore Kisiel. Bloomington, IN: Indiana University Press.

Heidegger, Martin. 1992. *The Metaphysical Foundations of Logic*. Translated by Michael Heim. Bloomington, IN: Indiana University Press.

Heidegger, Martin. 1997. *Phenomenological Interpretation of Kant's Critique of Pure Reason*. Translated by Kenneth Maly and Parvis Emad. Bloomington, IN: Indiana University Press.

Heidegger, Martin. 2001. *Phenomenological Interpretations of Aristotle: Initiation into Phenomenological Research*. Translated by Richard Rojcewicz. Bloomington, IN: Indiana University Press.

Heidegger, Martin. 1996. *Hölderlin's Hymn "The Ister"*. Translated by William McNeil and Julia Davis. Bloomington, IN: Indiana University Press.

Heidegger, Martin. 2000. *Towards the Definition of Philosophy*. Translated by Ted Sadler. London, UK: Continuum.

Hobbes, Thomas. 1985. *Leviathan*. London, UK. Penguin Classics.

Hoffer, Eric. 1951. *The True Believer: Thoughts on the Nature of Mass Movements*. New York, NY: Harper Perennial Modern Classics.

Horkheimer, Max and Adorno, Theodor. 1969. *The Dialectic of Enlightenment*. Translated by John Cumming. New York, NY: Continuum.

Husserl, Edmund. 1982. *Logical Investigations, Volume 1 & 2*. Translated by J.N. Findlay. London, UK. Routledge & Kegan Paul.

Husserl, Edmund. 1992. *Experience and Judgment*. Translated by James S. Churchill and Karl Ameriks. Evanston, IL. Northwestern University Press.

Husserl, Edmund. 1986. *The Crisis of European Sciences and Transcendental Phenomenology.* Translated by David Carr. Evanston, IL. Northwestern University Press.

Husserl, Edmund. 1997. *Psychological and Transcendental Phenomenology and the Confrontation with Heidegger (1927-1931).* Translated by Thomas Sheehan and Richard E. Palmer. Dordrecht, The Netherlands. Kluwer Academic Publishers.

Ihde, Don. 2012. *Experimental Phenomenology, Second Edition: Multistabilities.* Albany, NY: SUNY Press.

Ingram, David. 1987. *Habermas and the Dialectic of Reason.* New Haven, CN. The Yale University Press.

Jonas, Hans. *The Phenomenon of Life: Toward a Philosophical Biology.* 1966. Evanston, IL: Northwestern University Press.

Kant, Immanuel. 1981. *Grounding for the Metaphysics of Morals.* Translated by James W. Ellington. Indianapolis, IN. Hackett Publishing Company.

Kant, Immanuel. 1965. *Critique of Pure Reason.* Translated by Norman Kemp Smit. New York, NY. St. Martin's Press.

Kant, Immanuel. 1985. *Critique of Practical Reason.* Translated by Lewis White Beck. New York, NY. Macmillan Publishing Company.

Kant, Immanuel. 1986. *The Critique of Judgement.* Translated by James Creed Meredith. Oxford, UK. Oxford University Press.

Kant, Immanuel. 1992. *The Conflict of the Faculties.* Translated by Mary J. Gregor. Lincoln, NE: University of Nebraska Press.

Kelleher, John D. and Tierney, Brendan. 2018. *Data Science.* Cambridge, MA. The MIT Press.

Kierkegaard, Soren. 1983. *Fear and Trembling / Repetition. Kierkegaard's Writings, VI.* Translated by Howard V. Hong and Edna H. Hong. Princeton, NJ. Princeton University Press.

Kleppmann, Martin. 2017. *Designing Data-Intensive Applications: The Big Ideas Behind Reliable, Scalable, and Maintainable Systems.* Sebastopol, CA: O'Reilly Books.

Kojève, Alexandre. 1991. *Introduction to the Reading of Hegel: Lectures on the Phenomenology of Spirit.* Translated by James H. Nichols, JR. Ithaca, NY. Cornell University Press.

Kuhn, Thomas S. 1970. *The Structure of Scientific Revolutions.* Chicago, IL. University of Chicago Press.

Kurzweil, Ray. 2005. *The Singularity Is Near: When Humans Transcend Biology.* New York, NY. Penguin Books.

Lacan, Jacques. 1981. *The Four Fundamental Concepts of Psycho-Analysis.* Translated by Alan Sheridan. New York, NY: WW Norton & Co.

Lacan, Jacques. 2006. *Écrits.* Translated by Bruce Fink. New York, NY: WW Norton & Company.

Lacan, Jacques. 2016. *Anxiety: The Seminar of Jacques Lacan Book X.* Translated by A.R. Price. Cambridge, UK: Polity Press.

Lacan, Jacques. 2017. *Formations of the Unconscious: The Seminar of Jacques Lacan Book V.* Translated by Russell Grigg. Cambridge, UK: Polity Press.

Lacan, Jacques. 2019. *Desire and Its Interpretation: The Seminar of Jacques Lacan Book VI.* Translated by Bruce Fink. Cambridge, UK: Polity Press.

Lévi-Strauss, Claude. 1963. *Structural Anthropology.* Translated by Claire Jacobson and Brooke Schoepf. Basic Books.

Locke, John. 1986. *The Second Treatise on Civil Government.* Buffalo, NY. Prometheus Books.

Locke, John. 1959. *An Essay Concerning Human Understanding, Volume One & Two.* New York, NY. Dover.

MacKinnon, Catharine A. 1989. *Toward a Feminist Theory of the State.* Cambridge, MA. Harvard University Press.

Mannheim, Karl. 1955. *Ideology and Utopia: An Introduction to the Sociology of Knowledge.* Translated by Edward Shils. New York, NY: Harcourt Inc.

Marcuse, Herbert. 1955. *Eros and Civilization: A Philosophical Inquiry into Freud.* Boston, MA: Beacon Press.

Marx, Karl. 2009. *A Contribution to the Critique of Political Economy.* Translated by S.W. Ryazanskaya. New York, NY. International Publishers Co. Inc.

Marx, Karl. 1990. *Capital: A Critique of Political Economy, Volume I.* Translated by Ben Fowkes. New York, NY. Penguin Classics.

Marx, Karl. 1992. *Capital: A Critique of Political Economy, Volume II.* Translated by David Fernbach. New York, NY. Penguin Classics.

Marx, Karl. 1991. *Capital: A Critique of Political Economy, Volume III.* Translated by David Fernbach. New York, NY. Penguin Classics.

Marx, Leo. 1964. *The Machine in the Garden: Technology and the Pastoral Ideal in America.* London, UK. Oxford University Press.

Mead, George Herbert. 1962. *Mind, Self, & Society.* Chicago, IL. The University of Chicago Press.

Merleau-Ponty, Maurice. 2012. *Phenomenology of Perception.* Translated by Donald A. Landes. New York, NY. Routledge.

Merleau-Ponty, Maurice. 1967. *Structure of Behavior.* Translated by Alden L. Fisher. Boston, MA: Beacon Press.

Mill, John Stuart. 2002. *The Basic Writings of John Stuart Mill.* New York, NY. The Modern Library.

Mills, C. Wright. 1959. *The Sociological Imagination.* New York, NY: Oxford University Press.

Nadler, Steven. 2011. *A Book Forged in Hell: Spinoza's Scandalous Treatise and the Birth of the Secular Age.* Princeton, NJ. Princeton University Press.

Nietzsche, Friedrich. 1968. *Basic Writings of Nietzsche.* Translated by Walter Kaufmann. New York, NY. Modern Library.

Nietzsche, Friedrich. 1968. *The Will to Power.* Translated by Walter Kaufmann and R.J. Hollingdale. New York, NY. Vintage Books.

Nietzsche, Friedrich. 1982. *The Portable Nietzsche.* Translated by Walter Kaufmann. New York, NY. Penguin Books.

O'Neil, Cathy. 2016. *Weapons of Math Destruction: How Big Data Increases Inequality and Threatens Democracy.* New York, NY. Broadway Books.

Ormiston, Gayle L. and Schrift, Alan D.. 1990. *The Hermeneutic Tradition: From Ast to Ricoeur.* Albany, NY. State University of New York Press.

Pangilinan, Erin. 2019. *Creating Augmented and Virtual Realities: Theory and Practice for Next-Generation Spatial Computing.* Cambridge, UK: O'Reilly Media.

Parsons, Talcott. 1964. *The Social System.* New York, NY: The Free Press.

Parsons, Talcott and Shils, Edward A. 2001. *Toward a General Theory of Action: Theoretical Foundations for the Social Sciences.* New Brunswick, USA: Transaction Publishers.

Parsons, Talcott. 1968. *The Structure of Social Action.* New York, NY: The Free Press.

Pascal, Blaise. 1995. *Pensees.* Translated by A.J. Krailsheimer. New York, NY. Penguin Books.

Petzold, Charles. 2008. *The Annotated Turing: A Guided Tour through Alan Turing's Historic Paper on Computability and the Turing Machine.* Indianapolis, IN. Wiley Publishing, Inc.

Piaget, Jean. 2001. *The Psychology of Intelligence.* London, UK: Routledge.

Piketty, Thomas. 2014. *Capital in the Twenty-First Century.* Translated by Arthur Goldhammer. Cambridge, MA. The Belknap Press of the Harvard University Press.

Plato. 1980. *The Collected Dialogues of Plato.* Edited by Edith Hamilton and Huntington Cairns. Princeton, NJ. Princeton University Press.

Popper, Karl. 2002. *The Poverty of Historicism.* London, UK. Routledge.

Popper, Karl. 2002. *Conjectures and Refutations.* London, UK. Routledge.

Postman, Neil. 1986. *Amusing Ourselves to Death: Public Discourse in the Age of Show Business.* New York, NY. Penguin Books.

Putnam, Hilary. 2002. *The Collapse of the Fact/Value Dichotomy and Other Essays.* Cambridge, MA. Harvard University Press.

Putnam, Hilary. 1998. *Reason, Truth, and History.* Cambridge, UK. Cambridge University Press.

Putnam, Hilary. 1988. *Representation and Reality.* Cambridge, MA. The MIT Press.

Quine, Willard Van Orman. 1980. *From a Logical Point of View: Nine Logico-Philosophical Essays.* Cambridge, MA. Harvard University Press.

Rawls, John. 1971. *A Theory of Justice.* Cambridge, MA. Harvard University Press.

Rorty, Richard. 2009. *Contingency, Irony, and Solidarity.* Cambridge, UK. Cambridge University Press.

Roth, Michael. 1996. *The Poetics of Resistance: Heidegger's Line.* Evanston, IL. Northwestern University Press.

Roth, Michael. 2019. *Telemetry Phenomenology Commonwealth: Corporate Surveillance and the Colonization of Personality.* Kirkland, WA: Lensgrinder, Ltd.

Rousseau, Jean-Jacques. 1984. *The Social Contract.* Translated by Maurice Cranston. New York, NY. Penguin Books.

Rouvroy, Antoinette and Poullet, Yves. 2009. "The Right to Informational Self-Determination and the Value of Self-Development: Reassessing the Importance of Privacy for Democracy" from *Reinventing Data Protection?* Berlin, Germany. Springer.

Sartre, Jean-Paul. 1984. *Being and Nothingness.* Translated by Hazel Barnes. New York, NY. Washington Square Press.

Sartre, Jean-Paul. 1982. *Critique of Dialectical Reason, Volume I: Theory of Practical Ensembles.* Translated by Alan Sheridan-Smith. London, UK. Verso Books.

de Saussure, Ferdinand. 1966. *Course in General Linguistics.* Translated by Wade Baskin. New York, NY: McGraw Hill.

Scheler, Max. 1992. *On Feeling, Knowing, and Valuing: Selected Writings.* Chicago, IL: The University of Chicago Press.

Scheler, Max. 2012. *Problems of a Sociology of Knowledge.* Translated by Manfred S. Frings. London, UK: Routledge.

Scheler, Max. 1992. *Selected Philosophical Essays.* Translated by David R. Lachterman. Evanston, IL: Northwestern University Press.

Scheler, Max. 1973. *Formalism in Ethics and Non-Formal Ethics of Values: A New Attempt toward the Foundation of an Ethical Personalism.* Translated by Manfred S. Frings and Robert L. Funk. Evanston, IL: Northwestern University Press.

Scheler, Max. 1994. *Ressentiment.* Translated by Lewis B. Coser and William W. Holdheim. Milwaukee, WI: Marquette University Press.

Scheler, Max. 2008. *The Nature of Sympathy.* New Brunswick, NJ: Transaction Publishers.

Schmitt, Carl. 1985. *Political Theology: Four Chapters on the Concept of Sovereignty.* Translated by George Schwab. Chicago, IL: The University of Chicago Press.

Schneier, Bruce. 2015. *Data and Goliath: The Hidden Battles to*

Collect Your Data and Control Your World. New York, NY. WW Norton & Company.

Schoeman, Ferdinand (editor). 1984. *Philosophical Dimensions of Privacy: An Anthology.* Cambridge, UK. Cambridge University Press.

Schutz, Alfred. 1967. *Phenomenology of the Social World.* Translated by George Walsh. Evanston, IL: Northwestern University Press.

Sheehan, Thomas (ed). 1981. *Heidegger: The Man and the Thinker.* Chicago, IL. Precedent Publishing, Inc.

Silver, Nate. 2015. *The Signal and the Noise: Why So Many Predictions Fail - But Some Don't.* New York, NY. Penguin Books.

Simmel, Georg. 1972. *On Individuality and Social Forms.* Chicago, IL: University of Chicago Press.

Simmel, Georg. 1990. *The Philosophy of Money.* Translated by T.B. Bottomore and David Frisby. London, UK: Routledge.

Simondon, Gilbert. 2017. *On the Mode of Existence of Technical Objects.* Translated by Cecile Malaspina and John Rogove. Minneapolis, MN: Univocal.

Sloterdijk, Peter. 2017. *In the World Interior of Capital.* Translated by Wieland Hoban. Cambridge, UK. Polity Press.

Smart, J.J.C. 2009. *Philosophy and Scientific Realism.* London, UK. Routledge.

Smith, Adam. 1994. *The Wealth of Nations.* New York, NY. The Modern Library.

Solove, Daniel J. 2009. *Understanding Privacy.* Cambridge, MA. Harvard University Press.

Spinoza, Baruch. 1982. *The Ethics.* Translated by Samuel Shirley. Indianapolis, IN. Hackett Publishing Company.

Swift, Jonathan. 2003. *Gulliver's Travels.* New York, NY: Penguin Books.

Thompson, Evan. 2010. *Mind in Life: Biology, Phenomenology, and the Sciences of Mind.* Cambridge, MA: The Belknap Press.

Thucydides. 2013. *The War of the Peloponnesians and the Athenians.* Translated by Jeremy Mynott. Cambridge, UK: Cambridge University Press.

Tönnies, Ferdinand. 2001. *Community and Civil Society.* Translated by Jose Harris and Margaret Hollis. Cambridge, UK: Cambridge University Press.

Vanderplas, Jake. 2016. *Python Data Science Handbook: Tools and Techniques for Developers.* Cambridge, UK: O'Reilly Media.

Vaughan, William. 2018. Correspondence.

Vaughan, William. 2019. *Art in the Expanded Field: The 20th Century Aesthetic Kantgeist.* Unpublished Manuscript.

Von Mises, Ludwig. 2013. *The Theory of Money and Credit.* Translated by H.E. Batson. New York, NY: Skyhorse Publishing.

Wark, McKenzie. 2012. *Telesthesia: Communication, Culture and Class.* Cambridge, UK: Polity Press.

Warren, Samuel D. and Brandeis, Louis D. 1890. *The Right to Privacy.* Cambridge, MA. Harvard Law Review. Vol. 4, Num. 5.

Weber, Max. 2002. *The Protestant Ethic and the "Spirit" of Capitalism.* Translated by Peter Baehr and Gordon C. Wells. New York, NY. Penguin Classics.

Weber, Max. 1978. *Economy and Society.* Edited by Guenther Roth and Claus Wittich. Berkeley, CA. University of California Press.

Weber, Max. 2004. *The Vocation Lectures: Science as a Vocation / Politics as a Vocation.* Translated by Rodney Livingstone. Indianapolis, IN: Hackett Publishing Company.

Westin, Alan. *Privacy and Freedom.* 1967. New York, NY. IG Publishing.

Wiener, Norbert. 1954. *The Human Use of Human Beings: Cybernetics and Society.* New York, NY: Da Capo Press.

Wiener, Norbert. 2013. *Cybernetics: or, Control and Communication in the Animal and the Machine.* Mansfield Center, CT: Martino Publishing.

Wittgenstein, Ludwig. 2001. *Philosophical Investigations.* Translated by G.E.M. Anscombe. Malden, MA. Blackwell Publishing.

Wu, Tim. 2016. *The Attention Merchants: The Epic Scramble to Get Inside Our Heads.* New York, NY. Vintage Books.

Young-Bruehl, Elisabeth. 2004. *Hannah Arendt: For Love of the World.* New Haven: Yale University Press.

Zaharia, Matei. 2018. *Spark: The Definitive Guide.* Cambridge, UK: O'Reilly Media.

Zheng, Alice. 2018. *Feature Engineering for Machine Learning.* Cambridge, UK: O'Reilly Media.

Zizek, Slavoj. 2016. *Refugees, Terror and Other Trouble with the Neighbors: Against the Double Blackmail.* Brooklyn, NY. Melville House.

Zizek, Slavoj. 2007. "Why Heidegger Made the Right Step in 1933". Volume 1.4. International Journal of Zizek Studies.

Zizek, Slavoj. 1999. *The Ticklish Subject: The Absent Centre of Political Ontology.* London, UK. Verso.

Zuboff, Shoshana. 2019. *The Age of Surveillance Capitalism: The Fight for a Human Future at the New Frontier of Power.* London, UK: Profile Books.

Made in the USA
Middletown, DE
26 July 2023

35758861R00163